गोरखबानी

मूलपाठ एवं व्याख्या

(अंग्रेज़ी व हिन्दी)

गोरखबानी

मूलपाठ एवं व्याख्या

(अंग्रेज़ी व हिन्दी)

उदय प्रताप सिंह

वाणी प्रकाशन

वाणी प्रकाशन
4695, 21-ए, दरियागंज, नयी दिल्ली 110 002
फ़ोन : +91 11 23273167 फ़ैक्स : +91 11 23275710

शाखाएँ
अशोक राजपथ, पटना 800 004, बिहार
कॉफ़ी हाउस कैम्पस, महात्मा गांधी मार्ग, इलाहाबाद 211 001, उत्तर प्रदेश
महात्मा गांधी अन्तरराष्ट्रीय हिन्दी विश्वविद्यालय, वर्धा 442 001, महाराष्ट्र

www.vaniprakashan.com
marketing@vaniprakashan.in
sales@vaniprakashan.in

Gorakhbani : Moolpath Evam Vyakhya
by Uday Pratap Singh

ISBN : 978-93-5518-042-1
Religion/Culture

प्रथम संस्करणः 2022, प्रकाशित प्रतियाँः 600

मूल्य : ₹ 695

आर. टेक ऑफ़सेट प्रिंटर्स, दिल्ली-110032 में मुद्रित
वाणी प्रकाशन का लोगो मक़बूल फ़िदा हुसेन की कूची से

भूमिका

पहली बार महायोगी गोरखनाथ ने 'पतंजलि योग' को व्यावहारिक स्वरूप प्रदान किया था। अतः भारतीय धर्म साधना के इतिहास में उन्हें महत्त्वपूर्ण धर्माचार्य के रूप में स्मरण किया जाता है। वह नाथपन्थ के प्रवर्त्तक महायोगी थे। यद्यपि स्वयं को आदिनाथ-शिव के नाती और मत्स्येन्द्रनाथ के पुत्र रूप में स्वीकार करते हैं। उनके इस कथन का सीधा आशय है नाथपन्थ के आदि प्रवर्त्तक महायोगी शिव हैं। उनके सन्देश को विश्व में प्रचारित-प्रसारित योगी मत्स्येन्द्रनाथ ने किया। प्रतिभाशाली गोरखनाथ इन्हीं मत्स्येन्द्रनाथ के शिष्य थे।

महायोगी गोरखनाथ का समय नैतिकता के संक्रमण काल से गुज़र रहा था। बौद्धधर्म के पतन के अनन्तर कई स्वयंभू सम्प्रदाय मोक्ष प्रदान करने का आकर्षण उत्पन्न करने लगे थे। उसी क्रम में 'बज्रोली' जैसी जटिल योग-क्रिया को—सम्भोग से जोड़ दिया गया। मोक्ष प्रदान करने के साधनों में उसे प्रमुख घोषित किया गया। सहजता व स्वाभाविकता के नाम पर अनियन्त्रित जीवन दर्शन विकसित होने लगा। स्वयंभू सम्प्रदाय जीवन में पंचमकारों को सम्मिलित कर समाज को नैतिक एवं चारित्रिक दृष्टि से ह्रासोन्मुख करने लगे। ये लोग मोक्ष की परिभाषा इन्द्रियों के सुख में ढूँढ़ रहे थे और तथाकथित साधना (भोग) के केन्द्र में नारी को स्थापित करने लगे। इस तरह मनमाने ढंग से सम्प्रदायों का जन्म होने लगा। स्वच्छन्दता और स्वैराचार जीवन को ग्रसित कर चुके थे। उसके भयंकर परिणाम समाज में देखने को मिल रहे थे। यह आठवीं से दसवीं सदी का समय था। अतः विविध वेशधारी साधुसन्तों, सिद्ध-योगियों और फ़क़ीरों की करिश्माई हरकतों से जनमानस ऊबने लगा था। सत्यपक्ष और सहज-स्वाभाविक जीवन लुप्त हो गया था। आत्मा-परमात्मा, परमशक्ति, धर्म व अध्यात्म वाह्याडम्बर से ढँक चुके थे। चमत्कार और दैवी कृपा में पूरा समाज निमग्न होता जा रहा था। कर्मनिष्ठा और कार्यकुशलता को आलस्य, भोग विलास और निष्क्रियता ने श्रीहीन कर रखा था।

नैतिक ह्रास और चारित्रिक पतन के समय में गुरु गोरखनाथ का आना समाज के लिए वरदान सदृश था।

गोरखनाथ की दृष्टि में मन की शक्ति अपार होती है। मन ही योगी-भोगी, निरोगी बनाता है। वही शिव-शक्ति तथा पंचमहाभूतों से बना शरीर का प्राणतत्त्व होता है। मन की साधना समस्त वाह्याचारों को निरस्त करती हुई यथेच्छ को प्राप्त करने की शक्ति देती है। उनके मतानुसार मन को संसार से निर्लिप्त कर जीवन के लक्ष्य को प्राप्त किया जा सकता है। अतः तत्कालीन संक्रमण युक्त समाज में गोरखनाथ की वाणियों का महत्त्व बढ़ता जा रहा था। जनता उधर आकर्षित होने लगी थी। आडम्बरों में उलझा धर्म अब योग की शरण में आ गया था। योग के प्रयोग से जीवन आनन्दमय हो जाता है इस प्रकार का विश्वास समाज में पनपने लगा था। नैतिकता की महत्ता, मर्यादित जीवन और अध्यात्म के वास्तविक स्वरूप को व्यक्त करने में गोरखनाथ अद्वितीय महायोगी दिखायी पड़ते हैं। सुन्दर और मर्यादित समाज में आदर्श नागरिक का जन्म होता है। नैतिक व न्यायपूर्ण समाज से किसी देश की महत्ता का आकलन होता है। नवीं-दसवीं शती में गुरु गोरखनाथ का नाथ सम्प्रदाय इसी भाव की आधारशिला रखता है।

हिन्दी के हज़ार-बारह सौ वर्षीय इतिहास में गोरखनाथ का महत्त्व कई दृष्टियों से आँका जाता है। पहली बात तो यह है कि हिन्दी भाषा का प्राथमिक स्वरूप उनकी 'बानियों' में प्रस्फुटित हुआ है। भाषा की दृष्टि से वे हिन्दी के प्रथम कवि माने जाते हैं। उनके पूर्व या समानान्तर कुछ सहजयानी सिद्धों ने हिन्दी में अपनी बात कहनी शुरू की थी। वही हिन्दी का प्राथमिक स्वरूप है। 'सबद हमारा सरतर साँचा रहणि हमारी साँची' जैसे प्रयोग हिन्दी के आदि स्वरूप को प्रकट करते हैं। हिन्दी भाषा के विकास की दृष्टि से गोरखनाथ महत्त्वपूर्ण मोड़ पर खड़े दिखते हैं। साहित्य की दृष्टि से हिन्दी के आदिकालीन साहित्य में नाथपन्थी बानियों का विशिष्ट महत्त्व है। कालान्तर में उनकी भाव भंगिमा, कथन शैली, शब्दावली, कहने का साहस, और बेपरवाह व्यक्तित्व का अवतरण निर्गुण मार्गी सन्तों में दिखायी पड़ता है। भाषा के साथ भाव (साहित्य) की दृष्टि से गोरखनाथ का अपना महत्त्व है। भारत की प्राचीनतम विद्या-योग को आधुनिक जीवन में उपयोगी बना देना गोरखनाथ के वश की ही बात है।

'गोरखबानी : मूलपाठ एवं व्याख्या' की आवश्यकता वर्षों से महसूस की जाती रही है। उच्च कक्षाओं में उच्च शिक्षा प्राप्त प्राध्यापक भी गोरखबानी की व्याख्या करने में स्वयं को असहज और दूसरे शब्दों में कहें तो अक्षम मानते रहे हैं। कई प्रकार के आक्षेप मढ़ते हुए ऐसे प्राध्यापक कहते सुने गये हैं कि–

गोरखनाथ को पाठ्यक्रम में रखने की आवश्यकता ही क्या है? ये कहते हुए वे सम्भवतः भूल जाते हैं कि हिन्दी में 'गोरखबानी' का महत्त्व भाषा और साहित्य दोनों दृष्टियों से अद्वितीय है। इन्हें पाठ्यक्रम से विस्थापित कर देने पर इतिहास का एक महत्त्वपूर्ण अध्याय ही समाप्त हो जायेगा। इसके अभाव में जो इतिहास बनेगा वह अधूरा होगा, और धर्म-संस्कृति की सनातन परम्परा कहीं न कहीं खंडित दिखेगी।

वर्षों से 'गोरखबानी' के पठन-पाठन में तल्लीन रहने से नाथपन्थ की मेरी समझ निरन्तर विकसित होती रही है। छात्रों तथा प्राध्यापकों तक 'बानी' में निहित साहित्य का सन्देश पहुँचे इस दृष्टि से यह कार्य सम्पन्न किया गया है। पीताम्बरदत्त बडथ्वाल, हजारी प्रसाद द्विवेदी और 'गोरखबाणी'—गोरखनाथ मन्दिर से नियमित प्रकाशित होने वाली पत्रिका के आधार पर मूलपाठ का सम्पादन किया गया है। अतः पाठानुसन्धान की दृष्टि से भी यह महत्त्वपूर्ण कार्य है। कोशिश की गयी है कि सरल एवं सुबोध भाषा में इसकी व्याख्या प्रस्तुत की जाये। साथ ही जीवन की अद्यतन गतिविधियों से सम्पृक्त कर गोरखबानी की प्रासंगिकता को व्यक्त करने का प्रयास हुआ है। इधर कई विश्वविद्यालयों में 'गोरखबानी' पाठ्यक्रम में सम्मिलित की जाने लगी है। गुरु गोरखनाथ के व्यक्तित्व एवं कृतित्व से प्रभावित आज का युवा मानस जीवन को नैतिक व मर्यादित बनाने में सक्षम हो सकेगा। गोरखनाथ की बानियों के इधर कई सम्पादन आये हैं। पर सभी पिष्टपेषण जैसे लगते हैं। उनमें गतानुगतिक पद्धति की प्रधानता है। प्रयास किया गया है कि इन सबसे पृथक् गोरखबानी की एक ऐसी सरल व सुबोध व्याख्या युवाओं तक पहुँचे—जिसमें जीवन का राग हो, साहित्य का रंग हो और समाज को नयी दिशा देने की कूबत भी हो।

'वाणी प्रकाशन' देश का एक प्रतिष्ठित अधिष्ठान है। निश्चित ही वाणी के माध्यम से 'गोरखबानी' सर्व सुलभ हो सकेगी ऐसा विश्वास है। कम समय में सुन्दर प्रस्तुति वाणी प्रकाशन के स्वभाव का अनिवार्य अंग है। उसका लाभ इस पुस्तक को सहजतः मिल गया है।

उदय प्रताप सिंह
अध्यक्ष, हिन्दुस्तानी एकेडेमी, प्रयागराज

अनुक्रम

The Tenets of Guru Gorakhnath Gorakhbani – Original Text And Meaning

Great yogi Gorakhnath is known as the first poet of the Hindi language. The initial language used by him , with the passage of time, developed into what we know as the Hindi of today. It's universal pervasion in the form of various aspects of Hindi literature is available today. There is a long list of his writings. It exists both in Sanskrit and Hindi. But here, for our particular purpose, his Hindi writings are required. This is an ancient form of Hindi, therefore it has an important contribution in the growth and development of literature and language. In the primordial Hindi literature, 'Gorakhbani' has a special significance from the point of view of both language and literature.

The Gorakhnath temple, Gorakhpur (Uttar Pradesh) regularly publishes a journal called 'Yogvani'. The earlier editor late Sri Ramlal had published the vani (tenets) in a collection called 'Gorakhbani'. Much before late Sri Ramlal, the student of Acharya Ramchandra Shukla, Dr. Pitambar Dutt Badthawal had edited a book called 'Gorakhbani' the Nagari Pracharini Sabha, Kashi has published it about 70 years back. This book has also used Dr. Badthwal's book as a base. Apart from this, reference has been taken at times from the 'Gorakhbani' published in Yogvani by Gorakhnath temple. We are indebted to both the sources. We hope that these vanis (principles) will act as a bridge in the development of Hindi language and in the understanding of the ancient Hindi language.

SABADI

बसती न सुन्यं सुन्यं न बसती अगम अगोचर ऐसा।
गगन-सिषर महिं बालक बोलै ताका नाँव धरहुगे कैसा ॥1॥

Guru Gorakhnath defines the highest reality and says that it is impenetrable, inaccessible, it cannot be seen. There is no habitation where he resides, nor is there a vaccum. He is the universal spirit sitting on the highest peak of the mountain (an evolved state). He is like an unnamed child. It cannot be associated with a salutation, nor can it be addressed. He is the father of social harmony. It is impossible to name him. He is beyond name.

अदेषि देषिवा देषि बिचारिवा अदिसिटि राषिबा चीया।
पाताल की गंगा ब्रह्मंड चढ़ाइबा तहां बिमल बिमल जल पीया ॥2॥

To witness the formless one one has to reach the higher state of meditative,contemplative practice. After one witnesses it through yogic powers, one has to contemplate on its form , has to ruminate (chintan) on it subtly, those practitioners who through pranayama (deep breathing) are able to move the vital life energy or prana vayu from downwards to upward, he is the one who tastes the sweet water (of experience).

इहां ही आछै इहां ही अलोप। इहां ही रचिलै तीनि त्रिलोक।
आछै संगै रहै जू वा। ता कारिण अनंत सिधा जोगेस्वर हूवा ॥3॥

The undestroyable (akshay) supreme reality is situated here in the body in the Brahmrandhra or the Sahasrara chakra–the energy centre situated at the crown of the head, symbolized by the thousand petalled lotus.. this is that secret place (alope). All the three worlds were created here. The expressed form of the supreme reality-‘ brahm’–is this internal universe–‘brahmand’. From this centre–the brahmarandhra–it has manifested itself the most. This indestructible supreme reality which is with us always, because of it, to obtain which many perfected beings enter the path of yoga to become the lord of yoga.

वेद कतेब न षांणीं बांणीं। सब ढंकी तलि आंणीं।
गगनि सिषर महि सबद प्रकास्या। तहं बूझै अलष विनांणीं ॥4॥

The supreme reality or God has not been defined clearly by

either the Vedas or other holy books of religion. All these infact, just cover it with a layer. Instead of expressing the truth, they cover it up. If there is a desire to know the real meaning of the form of supreme reality then in the crown of the head, the effulgent sound that comes through profound meditation, in that discerning knowledge of the unaimed (alakshya) is obtained.

अलष बिनांणीं दोइ दीपक रचिलै तीन भवन इक जोती।
तास बिचारत त्रिभवन सूझै चुणिल्यौ मांणिक मोती ॥5॥

The supreme consciousness in the form of discerning knowledge created two lamps–the expressed reality and the unexpressed reality, the one with form and with an alternative Samadhi (profound meditation) and the one without alternative–the highest form of Samadhi where all distinctions cease–even self –consciousness. These two lamps have the light of the invisible. All three worlds emanate from the light. Contemplation on that light leads to a vision of the three worlds. The individual self in the form of a swan–the atman–picks up the pearls of wisdom and goes on to experience the ruby like state of eternal emancipation.

वेदे ने सास्त्रे कतेबे न कुरांणे पुस्तके न बंच्या जाई।
ते पद जांनां बिरला जोगी और दुनी सब धंधै लाई ॥6॥

That Supreme Being cannot be known either by the Vedas, the Shastras, the Quran or any other religious scripture, nor can it be expressed through the chanting of any traditional book of knowledge. It can only be attained by a yogi. That too, not the one with any outward show or ostentation, but the rare one who has mastered pranayama or deep breathing can do this. Apart from the yogi, other people term it as just another skill in life.

हसिबा षेलिबा रहिबा रंग। काम क्रोध न करिबा संग ॥
हसिबा षेलिबा गाइबा गीत। दिढ़ करि राषि आपनां चीत ॥7॥

Regarding the control of the chitta (a composite word for mind, intellect and ego) or consciousness the great Yogi Gorakhnath says that a person should practice leading a life of simplicity, keep the spirit of utmost happiness, jump and play, stay in a state of joy–these should be the activities of the yoga practitioner. He should sing songs steeped in spirituality. A yoga practitioner should stay away from lust and anger. Apart from this, it is the supreme duty of the yoga practitioner to practice the firmness of the mind.

हसिबा षेलिबा धरिबा ध्यान। अहनिसि कथिबा ब्रह्म गियान ॥
हसै षेलै न करै मन भंग। ते निहचल सदा नाथ के संग ॥8॥

The practitioner who laughs, plays, stays joyous and carefree and stays immersed day and night in the contemplation of God. The one who laughs and prays but at the same time has control over his mind consciousness, he is the one who is forever doing spiritual practice with Gorakhnath.

महंमद महंमद न करि काजी महंमद का विषम बिचारं।
महंमद हाथि करद जे होती लोहै घड़ी न सारं ॥9॥

Addressing the Qazi or head priest belonging to the Muslim religion Gorakhnath says that by merely saying Muhammad Muhammad one does not acquire faith in religion. His (Muhammad's) views were capable of reintegrating and reorganizing many inconsistencies.

सबदै मारी सबदैं जिलाई ऐसा महंमद पीरं।
ताकै भरमि न भूलै काजी सो बल नहीं सरीरं ॥10॥

Muhammad sahab's pain towards the suffering masses can be allayed through the knowledge of the supreme reality or shabd (word). It is the word (knowledge of the supreme) that can extinguish all kinds of discrepancies. Therefore do not become a blind follower of Muhammad sahab. Instead, develop the power to recognize the highest principle propounded by him.

नाथ कहंतां सब जग नाथ्या गोरष कहतां गोई।
कलमा कागुर महंमद होता पहलैं मूबा सोई ॥11॥

Yogi Gorakhnath points out the founder of Islam-Muhammad's deficiencies related to contemplation and says in a mysterious manner that the moment Nath Panth occurred, the entire universe got assimilated in it. The practice of kalma etc leads to the breath being stuck in the middle. Only through the yogic practices can immortality be achieved. Only by chanting the name of Allah, supreme truth cannot be achieved.

सारमसारं गहन गंभीरं गगन उछलिया नादं।
मानिक माया फेरि लुंकाया झूठा बाद-बिबादं ॥12॥

The purpose (real purpose) reality of life is in producing the Nada or the divine sound. That sound (it is the unstruck sound, that which is heard effortlessly) is achieved by the yoga practitioner who perfects his deep breathing and thereby acquires the true bliss in life. The being entangled in illusion is forever lost in the dazzle of material things like precious stones –ruby etc. He thinks that the way to obtain supreme principle is through arguments, discussions and counter discussion and intellectual discourse but eventually, he is disappointed.

कोई बादी कोई बिबादी जोगी कौं बाद न करनां।
अठसठि तीरथ समंदि समावैं यूँ जोगी कौं गुरुमुषि जरनां ॥13॥

The life of a yogi is without controversies. The one who engages in a lot of arguments wastes both his time and life. Therefore instead of being argumentative, he should focus on the contemplation of the supreme reality. The one who stays unaffected by outer attractions discovers the 68 pilgrimages in his body itself, he is the true disciple of the master, and he is indeed a real, actual seeker.

उतपति हिन्दू जरणां जोगी अकलि पीर मुसलमानी।
ते राह चीन्हों हो काजी मुलां ब्रह्मा बिस्न महादेव मांनीं ॥14॥

All are Hindus by birth and yogis by old age. Other subliminal impressions are formed when one enters society. Similarly the significance of an experience rich yogi and the Islamic pir is greater. Therefore, O Qazi ! try to understand the root principle. Brahma, Vishnu and Mahesh are the primordial powers, energies.

मांन्यां सबद चुकाया दंद। निहचै राजा भरथरी परचै गोपीचंद।
निहचै नरवै भए निरदंद। परचै जोगी परमानंद ॥15॥

The one who followed the words of the master, his doubts were destroyed. This decision made King Bhatrihari, gave him spiritual accomplishments, and introduced King Gopichand to the supreme reality. This firm decision made him above pleasure and pain with which he was able to witness his own reality and thus achieving ultimate bliss became a yogi.

अहनिसि मन लै उनमन रहै, गम की छांड़ि अगम की कहै।
छाड़ै आसा रहै निरास, कहै ब्रह्मा हूँ ताका दास ॥16॥

The sign of the one contemplating on the Absolute Principle is that he will always be in a state of detachment. Meaning detachment from the world and staying close to the supreme principle. The sign of a seeker is that he does not talk about this world but of the world of the supreme reality. He does not desire any object. The one leading life in this manner is the master of even Brahma (the creator) meaning he is full of supreme consciousness.

अरधै जाता उरधै धरै, कांम दगध जे जोगी करै।
तजै अल्यंगन काटै माया, ताका बिसनु पषालै पाया ॥17॥

The one who is able to direct the downward flowing semen upwards , and in this upward movement consequently kills the desire for physical union, the one who stops embracing woman and cuts the cord of illusion. The holy river Ganges washes the feet of Vishnu and he himself washes the feet of such a yogi.

अजपा जपै सुंनि मन धरै, पांचौं इंद्री निग्रह करै।
ब्रह्म अगनि मैं होमै काया, तास महादेव बंदै पाया ॥18॥

The seeker who constantly practices the ajapa japa – a conscious awareness of a mantra- the yogi does not have to say the mantra as he both understands and realizes the meaning of the mantra. It can be attained by anyone who engages in the practice of chanting mantras, through a progressive practise of learning till words are no longer merely spoken but deeply realized. So the yogi is in a state of ajapa japa and keeps his mind in the state of nothingness and keeps his five sense organs under control. He continuously contemplates on the supreme knowledge – in this manner the seeker becomes worthy of assuming the title of Mahadev.

धन जोवन की करै न आस, चित्त न राखै कांमनि पास।
नाद बिंद जाके घटि जरै, ताकी सेवा पारबती करै ॥19॥

The one who does not harbour a false ego about majesty, authority and youth. The one who does not look at a woman with lust. The one who safely protects the word given by the master (Guru) and the bindu (semen) given by God, even the primordial energy Parvati bows in service to him, implying that the one who has won over the urges of his sense–organs is the most exalted sage and seeker.

बालै जोबनि जे नर जती, काल दुकालां ते पर सती।
फुरतै भोजन अलप अहारी, नाथ कहै सो काया हमारी ॥20॥

Those ones who in childhood and in youth through restraint control their sense organs they can , in all circumstances, be stable in their truth. The ones who eat less in a less time. Gorakhnath says they are our very body. There is no difference between them and me.

सबदहिं ताला सबदहिं कूँची, सबदहि सबद जगाया।
सबदहिं सबद सूं परचा हूआ सबदहिं सबद समाया ॥21॥

Guru Gorakhnath talks about the philosophy of advait or monotheism and says that it is the word which is the supreme knowledge sitting inside the lock and it is word that wakes up the soul meaning it introduces one to the universal soul. When the individual soul meets the universal soul then all distinctions vanish by themselves.

पंथ बिन चलिबा अगनि बिनि जलिबा, अनिल तृषा जहटिया।
ससंवेद श्री (गुर) गोरष (नाथ) कहिया बूझिल्यौ पंडित पढ़िया ॥22॥

Walking without a path, burning without fire, quenching of thirst by air–all these things can only be known by experience. This is his knowledge gained by experience which Guru Gorakhnath has said–all the learned pandits need to understand this.

गगन मँडल मैं औधा कूवॉ तहाँ अमृत का बासा।
सगुरा होइ सु भरि-भरि पीवै, निगुरा जाइ पियासा ॥23॥

Towards the crown of the head there is a well of ambrosia. Life gains immortality from there. The one whose Guru has told him the path to seek that state, he joyously partakes of the nectar or ambrosia there whereas the seeker devoid of a Guru continuously suffers in thirst. All these practices can only be perfected by walking on the difficult path of yoga.

गगने न गोपंत तेजे न सोषंत पवने न पेलंत बाई।
यही भारे न भाजंत नडूवन्त कही तो को पतिआई ॥24॥

After acquiring the principle of self knowledge or the soul it is clear that of five elements of nature, neither can ether hide it nor can fire dry it, air cannot blow it away, the earth cannot break it by it 's weight. But if I say this who will believe me?. Because the qualities and activities associated with these elements that people at large see commonly, they will certainly find opposition in my utterance.

बास सहेती सब जग बास्या, स्वाद सहेता मीठा।
साच कहूँ तौ सतगुर मांनैं रूप सहेता दीठा ॥17॥

The entire world is suffused with the fragrance of the supreme principle of the universe from the essence of which all emanates and into which all returns. It is spread in the world like fragrance. It's taste makes the entire world sweet. The one who has tasted the bliss of the fundamental cosmic self , for him the bitterness of the world vanishes and the entire world apperars blissful. Because he sees the supreme principle in every form. The world appears beautiful because of that form. The faith in this truth can only be aroused by a realized master. The one who has not experienced supreme consciousness, how can he believe this ?

मरौ वे जोगी मरो, मरण है मीठा।
तिस मरणीं मरौ, जिस मरणीं गोरष मरि दीठा ॥26॥

O yogi ! die ! dying is a sweet experience ! how should that death be, Gorakhnath has shown that by dying. Implies you put yourself in a living-dead state. While being alive, go beyond your desires. Do not expect anything from anybody. It is then that you will witness that perfect state.

हबकि न बोलिबा, ठबकि न चालिबा, धीरैं धारिबा पावं।
गरब न करिबा सहजैं रहिबा, भणत गोरष रावं ॥27॥

Guru Gorakhnath says that speaking suddenly is a flaw. Making a sound while walking is erroneous. Keeping one's feet firmly and slowly while walking should be the nature of those desirous of decorum. One should not not have an attitude of arrogance towards any worldly object. One should try to lead a simple life. A person who practices such a way of life comes closer to becoming a yogi and is also called a dignified and honourable citizen.

भर्या ते थीरं झलझलंति आधा।
सिधें सिध मिल्या रे अवधू बोल्या अरु लाधा ॥28॥

Those who are full, complete with knowledge, they are stable and full of gravity., they do not go about exhibiting their knowledge. Those who have half-baked knowledge, they keep spilling out, because of their restlessness they keep on brandishing their knowledge here and there. They do not speak to perfected beings ! O realized seer ! when one realized being meets the other, then a conversation is possible. They also get benefitted by each other. A vessel that is full does not spill, only a half-full vessel keeps spilling out.

नाथ कहै तुम सुनहु रे अवधू दिढ करि राषहु चीया।
काम क्रोध अंहकार निबारौ तौ सबै दिसंतर कीया ॥29॥

The yogis have no home of their own,. The entire world is their home. That is why they keep on roaming everywhere. This is indicative of their renunciation but some get used to visiting places on a regular basis. That is why the message Gorakhnath has for the realized beings is that it is not neccesary to move about from place to place. If the chitta or consciousness is stable and lust and anger have been controlled, then consider all places have been visited. Because visiting holy places is done with the objective of abstention from worldly concerns and engagements, which is manifested by the stability of the chitta or consciousness.

स्वामी बन षंडि जाउं तो षुध्या व्यापै नग्री जाउं ता माया।
भरि भरि षाउं त विंद बियापै क्यों सीझति जब ब्यंद की काया ॥30॥

O master, when I go to the deep forests, I feel thirsty , hunger bothers me, when I go to the town,illusion, material things attract me and I eat and eat a lot and that increases my semen and I start desiring physical pleasures. This body is made up of water-drops (semen) how to make it perfect?

धाये न षाइबा भूषे न मरिबा अहनिसि लेबा ब्रह्म अगनि का भेवं।
हठ न करिबाा पड्या न रहिबा यूँ बोल्या गोरष देवं ॥31॥

One should not attack food with fervour. One should not overeat, nor should one die of starvation. One should receive the fire of divine knowledge day and night. One should not overwork the body nor should one lie idle.

थोड़ा बोलै थोड़ा षाइ तिस घटि पवनां रहै समाइ।
गगन मंडल मैं अनहद बाजै प्यंड पड़ै तो सतगुर लाजै ॥32॥

For leading a normal and happy life one should consume less food. One should spend less time in sleeping and should use it in contemplation of the supreme spirit. One should converse to a minimum. The one leading life in this manner has a constant flow of life giving breath energy. Such a seeker always hears the mystic sounds in the crown of his head–no other sound is heard.

अवधू अहार तोड़ौ निद्रा मोड़ौ कबहुँ न होइगा रोगी।
छठै छमासै काया पलटिया ज्यूँ को को बिरला बिजोगी ॥33॥

Gorakhnath addresses the avdhoots or perfected beings and says that food should be had in very small quantities and one should turn sleep towards the contemplation of the divine. After yogic practices in about six months to a year the body is purified and the practitioner will never fall prey to physical diseases. Such a person is counted as rarest of the rare.

देव कला ते संजम रहिबा, भूल कला अहारं।
मन पवना लै उनमनि धरिबा ते जोगी तत सारं ॥34॥

One should consume only that much food which is required to protect the body made of five elements and one should live in restraint to protect one's divine self. The yogis who combine the life breath to merge it with a state of nothingness those are the ones who reach the epitome of the elemental knowledge.

अवधू निद्रा कै घरि काल जंजालं अहार कै घरि चोरं।
मैथुन कै घरि जुरा गराजै अरध-उरध लै जोरं ॥35॥

The great yogi Gorakhnath addresses the practitioner walking on the path of yoga and says that the body experiencing excessive sleep is like a house of death which grips one untimely in it 's vicious hands and the ones eating excessively–their health is stolen by the thieves called disease. The ones engaging in excessive physical intercourse with women become arrested by old age very soon.

अति अहार यंद्री बल करै नासै ग्यांन मैथुन चित धरै।
ब्यापै न्यंद्रा झंपै काल ताकै हिरदै सदा जंजाल ॥36॥

The one who eat excessively become slaves to their sense organs. Their wisdom is destroyed and they daily think about intercourse with women. The one who is extremely fond of a deep sleep is often seen to be unhappy with the world.

घटि घटि गोरख बाहीं क्यारी। जो निपजै सो होइ हमारी।
घटि घटि गोरष कहै कहांणीं। काचै भांडै रहे न पांणीं ॥37॥

Gorakhnath says that each individual's body is like a flower bed where the work of tillage and sowing goes on–symbolically meaning that God is present in the form of a seed in our heart but it is the flower-bed that belongs to Gorakh or supreme consciousness where something can grow. It means only he can merge in supreme consciousness whose heart has experienced the supreme reality. Gorakhnath is giving his discourse in every body, the unstruck sound is being heard but only those can benefit from it who have perfected their physical body. Can water stay in an unbaked vessel (those who have not perfected their bodies through practice cannot take advantage of it).

घटि घटि गोरष फिरै निरूता। को घट जागे की घट सूता।
घटि घटि गोरष घटि घटि मींन। आपा परचै गुर मुषि चींन्ह ॥38॥

Gorakh moves about without sound in every physical form, the supreme consciousness is present in every form. In some he is awakened, in some it is sleeping. In every form Gorakh is present. In every form Matsyendra is present. There is no distinction between the master and the disciple. Guru or the master is certainly like the Supreme Being and the disciple as well by following the path shown by him can reach the stage of being one with the super-consciousness. Gorakh has reached kailvaya pada-total emancipation by the influence of his Guru Matsyendranath. One should acquire self-knowledge by the teachings of the Guru.

पावड़ियां पग फिलसै अवधू लोहै छीजंत काया।
नागा मूनी दूधाधारी एता जोग न पाया ॥39॥

O realized seeker ! yoga is not perfected by trying various external means to control the body. The ones wearing paavadi slip often. The ones who entangle their body in iron chains end up harming it. The Naga sadhus and the Maunis–the silent ones and the ones subsisting only on milk–all these do not get the benefits of yoga.

दूधाधारी पर धरि चित। नागा लकड़ी चाहे नित।
मोनीं करै म्यंत्र की आस। बिन गुर गुदड़ी नहीं बेसास ॥40॥

The one who only subsists on milk, his mind resides in the homes of others for he often thinks that if a person sends over some milk it would be good. Naga wants to keep his body warm and is forever looking for some wood. The silent one or the Mauni always requires another person with him who can speak instead of him and show the path.

दषिणी जोगी रंगा चंगा, पूरबी जोगी बादी।
पछमी जोगी बाला भोला, सिध जोगी उतराधी ॥41॥

For the perfection of yogic practices the importance of Uttarakhand has been mentioned in other tenets (sabdis). Gorakhnath himself practiced yoga in the mountains of the Himalayas. We can deduce it from his statements.

अवधू पूरब दिंसि ब्याधि का रोग, पछिम दिसि मिर्तु का सोग।
दछिण दिसि माया का भोग, उत्तर दिसि सिधका जोग ॥42॥

O realized being ! listen the world of illusion is in the south (the lower portion of the body), the East has an expansion of diseases, the West is the door to death and the North (the crown of the head) is the land of meditation for the realized beings.

धूतारा ते जे धूतै आप। भिष्या भोजन नहीं संताप।
अहूठ पटण मैं भिष्या करै। ते अवधू सिव पुरी संचरै ॥43॥

The yogi is not cunning. If he is cunning then so much so that he cheats his own ego. He begs for food. He does not have any sorrows. The body is the town where he goes about begging for alms. O realized avdhoot ! such conniving people reside in the abode of Shiva i.e. in the sahasrara chakra in the crown of the head.

घरबारी तो घर की जाणै। बाहरि जाता भीतरि आणै।
सरब निरंतरि काटै माया। सो घरबारी कहिए निरञ्जन की काया ॥44॥

The yogi is not a householder. If he is one, then he is the kind who has full knowledge of his house. whatever is going out of the body (the breath and the semen) he takes it inside and saves it. He does not distinguish between anybody and stays unaffected by everything and demolishes all notions of an illusion. Such a householder, whose home (body) is pure and inhabited by the universal cosmic self, one should consider him equal to the cosmic self.

गिरही सो जो गिरहै काया। अभि अंतरि की त्यागै माया।
सहज सील का धरै सरीर। सो गिरही गंगा का नीर ॥45॥

Gorakhnath provides the definition of a householder and says that the one who takes care of his body with firmness and is free from the external and internal illusions. The one who is a representation of naturalness and simplicity–such a householder is pure and transparent like the water from river Ganga.

अमरा निरमल पाप न पुंनि। सत रज बिबरजित सुंनि।
सोहं हंसा सुमिरै सबद। तिहिं परमारथ अनंत सिध ॥46॥

The saint who is beyond the three qualities of nature–sattva, rajas and tamas, is bereft of good deeds and sins, has a clear conscience, and remembers the word sohum–sohum is a universal and natural mantra because it is produced in everybody as breath. As such, sohum is chanted by everybody just by concentrating on the breath because the breath chants it naturally, a sound of so is produced during inhalation and hum is produced during exhalation, this way he chants the unchanted, he perfects the endless supreme state.

पाषंडी सो काया पषालै। उलटि पवन अगनि प्रजालै।
ब्यंद न देई सुपनैं जाण। सो पाषंडी कहिए तत्त समान ॥47॥

So the one who is cunning , is the one who outwardly keeps his body very clean…but when he makes his breath rise upwards, upturns its movement. As a result his semen is not destroyed to the level of the dot, who is alert towards its dissipation even in his dream. Such kind of a conniving person is complete with the supreme principle.

मनवां जोगी गाया मढी। पंच तत्त ले कंथा गढी।
षिमा षड़ासण ग्यान अधारी। सुमति पावड़ी डंड बिचारी ॥48॥

In the hut called body the yogi called mind resides who had made a story of the five elements (principles) around him. He has the khadasan of forgiveness, khadasan is an implement by which one gets the benefit of sitting while still standing. He uses the adhari of knowledge, the wooden staff used by the seers and a contraption in it is called adhari, he used the khadau or wooden sandals of intellect and the staff of thoughts. Not of the body, but yoga of the mind is the ultimate yoga. Leaving aside outer world one should accept the inner world.

चालत चंदवा षिसि षिसि पड़ै। बैठा ब्रह्म अगनि परजलै।
आडै आसणि गोटिका बंध। जावत प्रथिमी तावत कंध ॥49॥

Restlessness makes the ambrosia flow away. By stability the fire of the universal cosmic self is lit. Slanted (meaning between the active and the passive there is a state where through practice a yogi can vanish at will). It is said that the perfected yogis keep a mantra charged tablet in the mouth and vanish and reaches immortality. The Yogi's body remains as long as this earth remains.

यहु मन सकती यहु मन सीव। यहु मन पांच तत्त का जीव।
यहु मन ले जै उनमन रहै। तौ तीनि लोक की बातां कहै ॥50॥

Yogi Gorakhnath describes the strength of the mind and says that the powers of the mind are limitless, this mind is Shiv–the highest principle, this mind is Shakti–the primordial energy. This mind is made up of the five elements. In spiritual practice the one who constantly raises it upwards he acquires the quality of knowing the present, past and future. Therefore practice of the consciousness (mind) is said to be the highest practice.

अवधू नव घाटी रोकि लै बाट। बाई बणिजै चौसठि हाट।
काया पलटै अबिचल बिध। छाया बिबरजित निपजै सिध ॥51॥

O realized being! (avdhoot) close the nine doors of the body and stop the path of the coming and going of air. Through this the sixty four joints will start having the movement of air. And this will definitely lead to a complete transformation of the body. This will also make the seeker perfect and will turn him into one who does not cast a shadow.

अवधू दंम कौं गहिबा उनमनि रहिबा, ज्यूं बाजबा अनहद तूरं।
गगन मंडल में तेज चमंकै, चंद नहीं तहां सूरं ॥52॥

O realized seeker one should catch the life giving prana energy, one should control the breath through pranayama. Doing this will perfect the state of renunciation, unmani, vairagya. when the anhad nada rises up then in the crown of the head there will be effulgence without the presence of any sun and the moon.

सास उसास बाइ कौं भषिवा, रोकि लेहु नव द्वारं।
छठै छमासि काया पलटिया, तब उनमँनी जोग अपारं ॥53॥

Yogi Gorakhnath says that one should control the movement of the breath, this opens the mouth of the nine doors. After achieving the meditative state the seeker should focus on yogic practices for six months to purify his body. A mind detached from the world is this state of being. It has immense power.

अवधू सहंस्र नाड़ी पवन चलैगा, कोटि झमंकै नादं।
बहतरि चंदा बाई सोष्या किरणि प्रकटी जब आदं ॥54॥

Guru Gorakhnath is specifying that through the practice of pranayama and by the movements of thousands of nerve currents, by the vibration of crores of sounds and the activation of 72,000 nerves (the sun and the moon) the light that emanates after that is the perfected state of practice of Nath Panth.

अमावस के घरि झिलिमिलि चंदा, पूनिंम कै घरि सूरं।
नादकै घरि ब्यंद गरजै, बाजंत अनहद तूरं ॥55॥

In the deep night of the no moon when the seventy two moon nerves are activated with the prana vayu or vital life breath and moving without any obstruction and in the sequence of practice in the full moon the effect of the sun nerves is clearly visible. In the the anahad nada when one has practiced to control the semen and it has reached it's zenith then it should be considered the highest state of practice.

उलटंत नादं पलटंत ब्यंद, बाई कै धरि चीन्हसि ज्यंद।
सुंनि मंडल तहाँ नीझर झरिया, चंद सुरजि ले उनमनि धरिया ॥56॥

When the moon and the sun, the ida and the pingala nerves meet, a state beyond the mind is achieved and then ambrosia or amrit – the nectar of immortality flows down. The essence of all sound or nada turns upside down. Nada is the active form of the subtle word principle which gradually transforms into a gross form. The shukra or semen meets it and leads to the creation of the universe. Its gross form that is instrumental in creating the universe moves towards its original source and the semen that moves down turns upwards. In the air element, which sees the effect of death the most, is recognized as the immortal principle, it is alive.

अवधू प्रथम नाड़ी नाद झमंकै, तेजंग नाड़ी पवनं।
सीतंग नाड़ी ब्यंद का बासा, कोई जोगी जानत गवनं ॥57॥

O mystic ! the very subtle Sushumna nadi which controls the central nervous system has the beat of the essence of all sound, the sun or the Pingala nerve, the hot one is charged with air, the cool one that is Ida one or the moon nerve has the semen residing in it, rare is the yogi who knows their working.

उठंत पवनां रवी तपंगा बैठंत पवनां चंद।
दहूँ निरंतरि जोगी बिलंबै, बिंद बसै तहाँ ज्यंदं ॥58॥

The air current flowing in the sun nerve does so with a great speed. When it moves in the moon nerve or ida then it becomes static. When the breath comes out, that is, during exhalation, the Pingala, the sun nerve is active and when the air enters the body, during inhalation, the moon nerve is active. Yogi takes refuge, not in any of them but in the Sushumna nerve. Because where the bindu resides, immortality resides.

केता आवै केता जाई, केता मांगै केता खाई,
केता रूप विरष तलि रहै, गोरष अनभै कासौं कहै ॥59॥

Many seekers think of external physical activity as yoga. So many of them keep coming and going. So many think asking for alms and eating it is yoga. So many think living away from habitation, under a tree is yoga. Therefore all of them are caught up with the external aspects. To whom should Gorakh talk about the real knowledge (abhay gyan).

पढ़ि देखि पंडिता रहि देषि सारं अपणी करणी उतरिवा पारं।
बंदत गोरखनाथ कहि धू साषी, घटि घटि दीपक षणि पसू न आंषी ॥60॥

Yogi Gorakhnath says that the intellectuals have deeply studied the scriptures, but what is the principle of the master of the universe, that they do not know. Duty is primary. That only will help one traverse this world into the next, not by merely quoting the scriptures.

सुसबदे हीरा बेधिले अवधू जिम्पा करि टकसालं।
औगुंन मध्ये गुंन करिले, तौ चेला सकल संसारं ॥61॥

O realized one ! The meaning of the word that is spoken contains a diamond. Diamond refers to the best, most exalted thoughts. It is necessary to take those to heart. One should control the tongue like a mint. Turn your vices into virtues and the entire world will become your disciple.

अभरा था ते सूभर भरिया नीझर झरता रहिया।
षांडै थैं षुरसाण दुहेला, यूं सतगुरि मारग कहिया ॥62॥

One that was devoid of the experience of the divine and therefore was half-filled. By practicing yoga, that got completely filled. It means that the knowledge was complete, he experienced supreme consciousness. For him the nectar of immortality started flowing. But the path from which it is made possible is the path shown by the Guru and this path is more sharp and difficult than a sword. This is a sharp knife stuck in a grindstone.

प्यंडै होइ तो पद की आसा, बंनि निपजै चौतारं।
दूध होई तो घृत की आसा, करणीं करतब सारं ॥63॥

The universe resides in the body in a subtle form like ghee (clarified butter) is present in milk. It can be experienced by yogic practices. Effort is the basis of all success.

मन मैं रहिणां भेद न कहिणां, बोलिबा अंमृत बांणी।
आगिला अगनी होइबा अवधू, तौ आपण होइबा पांणी ॥64॥

O follower of the path of yoga a display of one's practice, knowledge and achievements is not right. The perfection achieved by practices are kept safely by the seeker and are a proof of his gravity. He should stay true to his real self and should always speak sweetly. Even if there is a person infront of him who is engulfed in fire like anger, still the yogi should be cool like water to give evidence of his patience.

उनमनि रहिबा भेद न कहिबा, न पीयबा नींझर पांणी।
लंका छाड़ि पलंका जाइबा, तब गुरमुष लेबा बांणी ॥65॥

The seeker should always practice to stay in a state beyond the mind. It means that he should move opposite to the world. He should not exhibit the secret to meditative practice, to describe the process of having the immortal nectar is forbidden. Lanka, refers to this illusory material world and the one who has renunciated it and inhabits the world of meditative practice becomes capable of partaking the ambrosia like talk that comes out of the master's mouth.

नग्री सोभंत बहु जल मूल बिरषा, सभा सोभंत पंडिता पुरषा।
राजा सोभंत दल प्रवांणी, यू् सिधा सोभंत सुधि बुधि की वांणीं ॥66॥

A city is beautified by the presence of gardens and ponds. A gathering finds its glory by the presence of learned people. The glory of a king lies in his trusted army. Similarly the glory of a realized being lies in his soft, voice which is full of pure intelligence and spiritual grace.

बिरला जाणंति भेदांनिभेद बिरला जाणंति दोह पष छेद।
बिरला जाणंति अकथ कहांणीं, बिरला जाणंति सुधिबुधि की बांणीं ॥67॥

Rare is the soul who knows the distinction of the indistinguished or the secret of monism, very few know the elimination of the side (paksha) of dualism, still very few know the unspoken tale of the supreme consciousness. Rare are the ones who know the voice of a refined intellect.

उत्तरखंड जाइबा सुंनिफल खाइबा, ब्रह्म अगनि पहरिबा चीरं।
नीझर झरणै अंमृत पीया यूं मन हूवा थीरं ॥68॥

A lot of ascetics who have achieved a lot, in the hope of the ultimate yogic accomplishment wear saffron robes and go to the region of Uttarakhand (Badrinath etc) and subsist there on the water from the springs and the fruits and berries from the jungle. But Gorakhnath tells them about the Uttarakhand which is the crown of the head, wearing the clothes of the fire of divine consciousness, drinking the nectar from the ambrosia that falls in a stream there and eat the fruit of realization of the supreme consciousness that is available there. This is how Gorakh calmed down his restless mind.

हिन्दू ध्यावै देहुरा मुसलमान मसीत।
जोगी ध्यावै परम पद जहा देहुरा न मसीत ॥69॥

The Hindu goes to the temple to pray and meditate. The Muslim goes to the mosque. Yogi is different from both of them. Where there is no need for a temple,no need for a request for reaching the highest state of meditation nor is there a need for a mosque. The yogi completes his spiritual practice in his world of the supreme -consciousness.

हिन्दू आषैं अलष कौं, तहाँ राम अछै न षुदाइ।
प्यंडे होइ तो मरै न कोई, ब्रह्मांड देखै सब लोई ॥70॥

The Hindus say that their God is Ram, the Muslims say he is Khuda. But the inexplicable supreme consciousness that the yogi talks about,is neither Ram nor Khuda. The inexplicable supreme consciousness is beyond Ram and Khuda.

प्यंडे होइ तो मरै न कोई, ब्रह्मांड देषै सब लोई।
प्यंड ब्रह्मंड निरंतर बास, भणंत गोरष मछ्यंद्र का दास ॥71॥

If the Supreme Being resided in the body nobody would ever die. If he was in the universe he could have been seen by all. The disciple of Matsyendra, Gorakh says that he is beyond the individual and the universe.

बैठा अवधू लोह की षूंटी, चलता अवधू पवन की मूंठी।
सोवता अवधू जीवता मूवा, बोलता अवधू प्यंजरै सूवां ॥72॥

The seekers (avdhoot) who are stable at one place and make it their home are unwavering like an iron hook. The yogi who is constantly moving is like the air. The yogi who is constantly sleeping is like the dead though he is alive and the yogi who is constantly giving lectures is like a parrot who has been taught to repeat the same lines over and over again.

गोरष कहै सुणह रे अवधू जग मैं ऐसैं रहणां।
आंषै देषिवा कांनै सुणिबा मुष थैं कछू न कहणां ॥73॥

Guru Gorakhnath alerts the seekers of his path to the many desirable and undesirable things that are seen in this world. To see them and yet not utter a word are the signs of a saint. Hearing something which is proper or improper and yet not reacting to it is the quality of an avdhoot.

नाथ कहै तुम आपा राषौ, हठ करि बाद न करणां।
यह जुग है कांटे की बाड़ी, देषि देषि पग धरणां ॥74॥

Guru Gorakhnath says that have control over your own self. Getting into arguments and counter-arguments will lead to the diminishing of spiritual practices. This world is full of thorns. Therefore one should make an effort to tread very carefully here. Any obstacle can come in the way.

गोरष कहै सुणौ रे अवधू सुसूपाल थैं डरिये।
ले मुदिगर की सिर मैं मेलै, तौ बिनही षूटी मरिये ॥75॥

Gorakhnath says O realized one! One should be scared of death in the form of Shishupal, if he hits his weapon on the head, one can meet an untimely death.

Calling Shishupal as death seems a bit out of sync. But there is no doubt that since he was a sworn enemy of Krishna such an epithet can then be ascribed to him.

दृष्टि अग्रे दृष्टि लुकाइबा सुरति लुकाइबा कांन।
नासिका अग्रे पवन लुकाइबा, तब रहि गया पद निरबांन ॥76॥

One should try to remove the sense organs from sensory pleasures, save the eyes from sighting, the ears from listening, the nose from the air around. Doing this will lead us to the state of nirvana. Here the withdrawal of the senses into the mind is needed.

अवधू मनसा हमारी गींद बोलिये, सुरति बोलिये चौंगानं।
अनहद ले षेलिबा लागा, तब गगन भया मैदानं ॥77॥

O realized being! The mind is a ball and the inverse walk of the mind–that is–realization of the self–is the playground. Making the essence of all sound as my horse I start playing. This way the crown of the head, the seat of the thousand petalled lotus became my playground.

पंच तत्त सिधां मुडाया तब भेटिलै निरंजन निराकारं।
मन मस्त हस्ती मिलाइ अवधू, तब लूटिलै अषै भंडारं ॥78॥

When the perfected beings took the five elements into their control, then they met the pure one without form. O realized one when one meets the mind in the form of a mad elephant and owns it it is then that the never ending stores (the world of the supreme consciousness) is laid open for one to loot.

अरध-उरध बिचि धरी उठाई, मधि सुनिं मैं बैठा जाई।
मतवाला की संगति आई, कथंत गोरषना परमगति पाई ॥79॥

Non-deliberate retention of breath, 'kevala kumbhak' is described here by which he reached the crown of the head. There the divine principle of Shiva found company. This way Gorakhnath says he reached the absolute state.

डंडी सो जे आप डंडै, आवत जाती मनसा षंडै।
पंचौ इंद्री का मरदै मांन, सो डंडी कहिये तत्त समांन ॥80॥

He can be called a dandi or staff bearer who demolishes his pride (ego) and the constantly changing desires. He wins over the five sense organs. Such a seer merges with the supreme principle.

पाया लो भल पाया लो सबद थांन सहेली थीति।
रूप संहेता दीसण लागा, तब सर्व भई परतीति ॥81॥

I received. Received well, through the word reached the place which is the seat of supreme consciousness. Then I started to witness the supreme reality in its form and then I was convinced beyond doubt , there was no doubt about liberation now.

अरधंत कवल उरधंत मध्ये प्रांण पुरिस का बासा।
द्वादस हंसा उलटि चलैगा, तब हीं जोति प्रकासा ॥82॥

When the lotus which is lower, from that to the higher lotus witness the supreme being in the form of breath, then the life breath instead of going outward starts moving inward and then one will be able to witness the divine light.

आसण बैसिबा पवननिरोधिबा, थांन-मांन सब धंधा।
बदंत गोरखनाथ आतमां विचारंत, ज्यू जल दीसै चंदा ॥83॥

Sitting in an asana, controlling breath through pranayama are all activities related to place or status. Otherwise the importance of place is that sitting here one can perfect yoga through practice, all else unnecessary. These do not hold importance. They are mere outer resources. The things that lead to an inside out knowledge they are everything in the path of yoga. Gorakhnath says that while contemplating on the soul the world seems like a reflection of the universal spirit just like the moon is reflected in water.

गोरष बोलै सुणि रे अवधू पंचौं पसर निबारी।
अपणी आतमां आप बिचारी, तब सोवौ पान पसारी ॥84॥

Gorakhnath says O seer control the five sense organs, it is expected to undertake the journey of one's soul in a thoughtful manner. The seeker who understands the echo of his soul, his path of practice will become easy.

अहार न्यंद्रा बैरी काल, कैसे कर रखिबा गुरू का भंडार।
अहार तोड़ो, निंद्रा मोड़ौ, सिब सकती लै करि जोड़ौं ॥85॥

For the yoga practitioner excess food and excessive sleep are like death. The practitioner who is seeped in these two pleasures cannot understand the teachings of his Guru. The practitioner who gradually reduces his food intake to a minimum and the one who stays away from slumber and procrastination can only help fructify the prayers to 'Shiva' and 'Shakti' successfully.

तब जांनिबा अनाहद का बंध, ना पड़ै त्रिभुवन नहीं पड़ै कंध।
रकत की रेत अंग थे न छूटै, जोगी महतां हीरा न फूटै ॥86॥

One is understood to have achieved the Anahat, tied it, when there is no obstacle left in the three worlds for the yogi, his body does not degenerate, the essence of the blood, the sperm does not fall out of the body, and the yogi says that the diamond (referring to the pristine white light of divine experience) is not destroyed implying the experience of the super consciousness takes place infront of oneself.

सबद एक पूछिबा कहौ गुरु दयालं, बिरिधि थै क्यूं करि होइबा बालं।
फूल्या फूल कली क्यूं होई, पूछें कहै तो गोरष सोई ॥87॥

We ask you a question, O kind master, please reply to it. How can one turn into a child from an old man, the flower that has blossomed, how can it turn into a bud again. By watering the source of the fire of cosmic consciousness the flower that has blossomed can turn into a bud again.

उलट्या पवनां गगन समोइ तब बाल रूप परतषि होई।
उदै ग्रहि अस्त हेम ग्रहि पवन मेला, बंधिलै हस्तिय निज साल भेला ॥89॥

One should upturn the breath (air) and merge it in the crown of the head. Then the child becomes manifest. The house of it's rise is brought to an end-meaning the sun placed in the root chakra or the muladhar chakra is brought to a sunset and the moon that is the house of snow –the crown of the head –where the air is collected and therefore the elephant signifying the mind is tied there for yoga to be perfected meaning it comes under the soul.

बारा कला सौषै सोला कला पोषै, चारि कला साधै अनंत कला जीवै।
ऊरम धूरम जोती ज्वाला सीधि साधंत चारि कला पीवै ॥90॥

The twelve aspects make a practitioner lose sheen and the sixteen aspects nourish him, but the one who masters the four aspects he stays alive till the end of time. The practitioner who is an expert in the yoga practices involving the upper and the lower parts integrates the four aspects within himself.

असाध साधंत गगन गाजंत, उनमनी लागंत ताली।
उलटंत पवनं पलटंत बांणीं, अपीव पीवत जे ब्रह्मग्यांनीं ॥91॥

The seeker who perfects the impossible, through yoga he roars continuously in the cave of the sky, i.e. the crown of the head, he practices the unmani mudra or the beyond the mind mudra. It points to a state which is beyond thought and all worldly and materialistic attachments are released, the yogi attains a state which is free of thoughts, ignorance and duality cease here. It is a state beyond thought and the yogi dissolves in time, he makes the breath(air) go turn upwards from downwards and fills his voice with harmony– such a realized seer partakes of the nectar of immortality and is known as one who has experienced the realization of the supreme.

अलेष लेषंत अदेष देषंत, अरस परस ते दरस जांणीं।
सुंनि गरजंत बाजंत नाद अलेष लेषंत ते निज प्रवांणीं ॥92॥

That which cannot be written, he describes that writing, that which cannot be seen, he is a witness to that, the one who touches supreme consciousness meaning the one who has directly experienced it, filling the crown of the head with the roar of the sound of the unstruck sound by his own personal experience knows the supreme consciousness.

निहचल घरि बैसिबा पवन निरोधिबा कदै न होइगा रोगी।
बरस दिन मैं तीनि बार काया पलटिबा, नाग बंग बनासपती जोगी ॥93॥

That practitioner which never fall prey to diseases who sits in a posture (asana) without fear and by retention of breath (kumbhaka) hold it for long. The one who undergoes a complete transformation (kayakalpa) of his body thrice a year becomes the absolute realized being.

षोड़स नाड़ी चंद्र प्रकास्या द्वादस नाड़ी भांनं।
सहंस्र नाड़ी प्रांण का मेला, जहां असंष कला सिव थांनं ॥94॥

The place where sixteen channels through which energy flows in the subtle body in the form of moon…that is Ida and the twelve channels in the form of the sun, that is, Pingala–are effulgent and the thousands of nerves where the vital life force meet that is the place with innumerable aspects–the abode of Shiva.

अवधू ईडा मारग चंद्र भणीजै, प्यंगुला मराग भानं।
सुषमनां मारग बांणीं बोलिये त्रिय मूल अस्थांनं ॥95॥

Describing the various energy channels Gorakhnath says that the Ida nadi is representative of the moon and the Pingala nadi is representative of the sun. Sushumna energy channel is representative of voice. In this manner it is extremely important for the yogi to know about these energy channels.

अबधू काया हमारी नालि बोलिये दारू बोलिये पवनं।
अगनि पलीता अनहद गरजै ब्यंद गोला उड़ि गगनं ॥96॥

O realized seer, this body is like a shotgun and the breath is like dynamite. The unstruck sound is lit up with fire and an explosion takes place and the bullet of the sperm is discharged and goes to the crown of the head, that is the seeker becomes one who converts semen into ojas and lives in perpetual celibacy. He has , through austere devotion, obtained command over seminal discharge.

काजी मुलां कुरांण लगाया, ब्रह्म लगाया वेदं।
कापड़ी संन्यासी तीरथ भ्रमाया न पाया नृबांण पद का भेवं ॥97॥

The religious heads of the Muslims, the Qazis and the mullas kept on explaining the Quran. The Brahmins got tired discussing the Vedas,. The saints and sages kept on visiting various holy pilgrimages but still could not achieve the highest spiritual state. They could not acquire the knowledge that breath control is important for achieving the highest spiritual state.

देवल जात्रा सुंनि जात्रा, तीरथ जात्रा पांणीं।
अतीत जात्रा सुफल जात्रा बोलै अंमृत बांणीं ॥98॥

The visit to the temple yields zero results, one does not get any benefit from it. Going to pilgrimages is as fruitless , it is only a journey in water after all. The successful journey is that of the past, it is one where one meets the realized saints and hermits and hears their valuable words. Their company and discourses bestow one with such benefits and blessings that are not possible with any other thing.

अधरा धरे बिचारिया, धर या ही मैं सोई।
धर अधर परचा हूवा, तब उती नाहीं कोई ॥99॥

We contemplated on the supreme principle in the crown of the head that is without the earth or base. The supreme consciousness is there in that high place without the earth, but he is also present on the earth. This means in the body the supreme principle is spread from the root chakra to the crown chakra. It is present in a gross form at one place whereas in some other place it is present in a subtle form. When the sky and the earth meet, the Kundalini energy present in the root chakra is acquainted with Shiva present in the crown chakra then nothing apart from experiential knowledge remains for the seeker.

ऊभा मारूं बैठा मारूं, मारूं जागत सूता।
तीनि लोक भग जाल पसार्‍या, कहां जाइगौ पूता ॥100॥

It is the cry of the lord of death that you cannot escape him. Standing, sitting, awake, asleep whichever situation one is in, he can kill one in that state. To catch you I have spread the reproductive organ like a web in all the three worlds. How will you escape that?

ऊभा षंडौं बैठा षंडौं षंडौं जागत सूता।
तिहूं लोक तैं रहूँ निरंतरि तौ गोरख अवधूता ॥101॥

The yogi should constantly practice to control his desires. The seeker who is diligently trying to control his sense-organs while sitting-standing, asleep-awake conditions, he is that unique one in the three worlds who can be exalted to the position of Yogi Gorakhnath.

न्यंद्रा कहै मैं अलिया बलिया, ब्रह्मां विष्न महादेव छलिया।
न्यंद्रा कहै हूं षरी बिगूती, जागै गोरष हूँ पड़ि सूती ॥102॥

Sleep says that I am the one with a web, I cause delusion and am very strong, I have even tricked the holy trinity of Brahma, Vishnu and Mahesh. But Gorakhnath has really treated me badly. He knows and here I am lying down and sleeping.

जोगी सो जे मन जोगवै, बिन बिलाइत राज भोगवै।
कनक कांमनी त्यागें दोइ, सो जोगेस्वर निरभै होइ ॥103॥

He is a yogi who protects his mind and experiences, in the in the divine nothingness or the crown of the head, kingdom of the supreme consciousness without a real physical country. That king of yogis who sacrifices (gives up the lure of gold and women), he becomes fearless.

संन्यासी सोई करै सर्बनास, गगन मंडल महिमांडै आस।
अनहद सुमन उनमन रहै, सो संन्यासी अगम की कहै ॥104॥

He is a mendicant, a saint, who demolishes all his physical desires and continuously through yoga mudra places the air in the sky that is the crown of the head and becomes desirous of partaking the nectar of supreme consciousness. Such a saint is forever listening to the unstruck sound and ventures into the state beyond thought with a healthy mind. In this way a saint always talks about the unreachable spiritual world.

लाल बोलंती अम्है परि, उतरिया मूढ़ रहै उर वारं।
थिति विहूणा झूठा योगी, ना तस वार न पारं ॥105॥

Such a yogi is not a true one who walks along with illusion and foolishness. He is not still but continuously restless and he cannot be trusted.

उलटिया पवन षट्चक्रबेधिया तातै लोहै सोषिया पाँणी।
चंद सूर दोऊ निज करि राख्या ऐसा अलष बिनांणी ॥106॥

That yoga practitioner who through his practice of deep breathing has struck the six petalled lotus he can even dry up water made of iron, the one who has the Ida and Pingala energy channels in his control. Such a seeker, the one who has seen the absolute reality, is very rare.

नाद हमारै बावै कवन, नाद बजावै टूटै पवन।
अनहद सबद बाजता रहै, सिद्ध संकेत श्री गोरख कहै ॥107॥

The yogi who continuously experiences nada or the sound within his innermost realm he does not need to play any external musical instrument. With the playing of the sound there is an obstacle in the flow of air. He is a yogi in whose heart the Anahat nada is always playing, says Yogi Gorakhnath. Anahat nada is the mystic sound heard by a yogi during meditation. It is a sign of the purification of nadis.

सुणि गुणवंता सुणि बुधिवंता, अनंत सिधां की बांणी।
सीस नवावत सतगुर मिलिया, जागत रैंणि बिहांणी ॥108॥

O saint full of sublime qualities listen, the eternally realized one Gorakhnath says that only with humility and politeness one is able to meet a Guru. The Guru who makes us aware of the path of truth, the seeker wakes up night and day to acquire that. It implies that constant practice is necessary to reach the goal.

भिष्या हमारी कामधेनि, बोलिए संसार हमारी बाड़ी।
गुरु परसादै भिष्या पाइबो, अंत कामि न होइगी भारी ॥109॥

For a saint and a yogi alms is the divine wish-fulfilling cow 'kamdhenu 'and the entire world is a shelter. After the Guru is pleased with the disciple can he get the alms like kamdhenu. Towards the end of his life such a seeker faces no problem.

बड़े बड़े कूले मोटे मोटे पेट, नहीं रै पूता गुरू सौं भेट।
षड़ षड़ काया निरमल नेत, भई रे पूता गूरू सौं भेट ॥110॥

The ones with big, huge bodies, with pot-bellies acquired after eating endlessly have never met a Guru. These people got entangled in the world. After having the grace of the Guru, one develops a slim body and a pure mind.

निरति न सुरति जोगं न भोगं, जुरा मरण नहीं तहाँ रोगं।
गोरष बोलैं एकंकार, नहि तहँ बाचा ओअंकार ॥111॥

In that ultimate abode-in the spiritual world–the various stages of meditative practices like nirati-surati, various activities like yoga and partaking of physical pleasures,old age and disease free body and the chanting of Om are all next to nothing. There the seeker and the sought are one, the individual soul and the universal soul are one, there nothing of the physical delusion is seen. The world where there the empire of harmony is spread.

उदै न अस्त राति न दिन, सरबे सचराचर भाव न भिन।
सोई निरंजन डाल न मूल, सब ब्यापीक सुषम न अस्थूल ॥112॥

That pure, supreme consciousness resides in a place where there is no night, no day, no sunrises or sets, it is different from all living and non-living aspects. That formless supreme consciousness is different from flowers and fruit. There is no expansion or contraction there, there is no gross or subtle form.

ब्रह्मांड फूटिबा नगर सब लूटिबा, कोई न जांणवा भेवं।
बदंत गोरषनाथ प्यंड दर जब घेरिबा, तब पकड़िबा पंच देवं ॥113॥

When the Kundalini energy enters the cosmic or crown of the head and there is an internal explosion and that city of nothingness should be looted, nobody knows that secret.. Gorakhnath says that when the house in the form of the body is surrounded only then can the master of the five sense organs–the mind consciousness–can be controlled.

अहंकार तूटिबा निराकार फूटिबा, सोषीला गंग जमन का पानीं।
चंद सूरज दोऊ सनमुषि राषिला, कहो हो अवतू तहां की सहिनांणी ॥114॥

One should break one's pride, one should manifest the formless soul, just like the seed sprouts up from the earth similarly when the ego is broken the soul becomes manifest. Where the Ida- Yamuna and Pingala-Ganga's water has been dried up that is there effect has been neutralized to merge them in the Sushumna, there opposing natures–the sun-pingala and the moon-ida has been finished and brought into the sushuma–the nadi that controls the central nervous system. O realized one tell me it 's outer signs and symbols.

चेता रे चेतिबा आपा न रेतिबा, पंच की मेटिबा आसा।
बंदत गोरष सति ते सूरिवां उनमनि मन मैं बासा ॥115॥

Individual full of consciousness, one should always be alert. One should not trouble one's soul. One should end the hope of deriving false pleasures from the five sense organs. Gorakhnath says those are the real brave ones who go into a state beyond thoughts and reside there.

सिध के संकेत बूझिलै सूरा, गगन अस्थांनि बाइलै तूरा।
मोंमा के मारग रोपीलै भांणं, उलट्या फूल कली मैं आंणं ॥116॥

O brave seeker ! try to understand the gesture of the perfected seer. In a desolate place try to hear the anahat nada. Try to put the opponent of the moon, that is, the sun, on to the path of the fish, meaning by the use of yogic powers bring the moon forth so that the nectar of immortality can be tasted. The fish is forever swimming against the current of the river, but which path has it undertaken nobody knows below the water. Therefore it is known as the path of the fish. It is from this that the flower will burst and turn into a bud, the old will turn into a child.

बास बासंत तहां प्रगट्या षेलं। द्वादस अंगुल गगन घरि मेलं।
बदंत गोरख पूतां होइबा चिराई। न पडंत काया न जंम घरि जाई ॥117॥

Where there is the fragrance of the supreme consciousness meaning the one who has experienced the expanse of the supreme consciousness, there the play of light starts happening by itself. The yogis of the prana vayu or the vital life force state that the vital life forces resides outside the nose up to a distance of twelve fingers. So by dwadash angul what is implied is life breath. By entering the prana vayu into nothingness or shunya one obtains a very long life, the body does not decay. Here the lord of death, Yama, does not enter, meaning immortality is here.

अंन का मांस अनिल का हाड़ तल का बंद भषिवा बाई।
बंदत गोरषनाथ पूता होइबा चिंराई न पड़ै घट न जंम घरि जाई ॥118॥

Gorakhnath talks about the supreme principle and says the world where the air is the bone and there is a mound of grain. The gist of what he is saying is that the one who is used to that world – he became one with that–he loses the fear of death.

ऊं लोहा पीर। तांबा तकबीर। रूपा महंमद सोना षुदाई।
दुहु बिचि दुनिया गोता षाई। हमतो निरालंभ बैठे देखते रहैं,
ऐसा एक सुषन बाबा रतन हाजी कहै ॥119॥

Gorakhnath ji remembers Baba Ratna Haji and says that the pir is like iron, Mohammmad's being is unique and 'khuda' or 'Ishwar' is like gold. Between these delusions the world is led astray. But the yogi is stable without any support. He is worry free.

कहणि सुहेली रहणि दुहेली कहणि रहणि बिन थोथी।
पढ्या गुंण्या सूवा बिलाई षाया पंडित के हाथि रह गई पोथी ॥120॥

It is easy to talk about the God principle but the practice to reach him is very difficult. Verbal utterances are simple but to walk on the path of duty is extremely difficult. An utterance without duty is meaningless. The voice without duty rings hollow. The pandit had made his parrot learn some sentences by rote but he was devoid of any duty, did not do any work hence it was easy for the cat to prey on him. The book of knowledge stayed in the pandit's hand while his parrot fell prey to the cat.

कहणि सुहेली रहणि दुहेली बिन षायां गुड़ मींठा।
खाई हींग कसूर बषांणै गोरष कहै सब झूठा ॥121॥

It is easy to say but difficult to live your words, without eating jaggery the mere mention of the word sweet does not make one experience sweetness. The person without experience remains in delusion. He cannot distinctly see reality. He eats asafoetida and calls it camphor. Gorakh says all this is a false experience.

मूरिष सभा न बैसिबा अवधू पंडित सौं न करिबा बादं।
राजा संग्रामे झूझ न करबा हेलै न षोइबा नादं ॥122॥

Mystic ! one should not sit in the assembly of fools, one should not argue about the scriptures from a learned Brahmin. Doing that is totally useless, a waste of time. One should not fight with the king. The King is not brave in the area the seeker is brave. The King has physical power while the seeker has the power of the soul. Therefore there cannot be a feeling of competition between the two. One should not lose the anahat nada–the unstruck sound carelessly.

हिरदा का भाव हाथ मैं जाणिये यहु कलि आई षोटी।
बदंत गोरष सुणौं रे अवधू करवै होई सु निकसै टोटी ॥123॥

This is the age of Kali (Kali yug). It is full of evil deeds. The kind of feelings that are there in the heart, the hand undertakes those very activities. Gorakhnath says whatever is filled in the pot will come out by it 's spout.

जल कै संजमि अटल अकास अन कै संजमि जोति प्रकास।
पवनां संजमि लागै बंद ब्यंद कै संजमि थिरह्वै कंद ॥124॥

By the discipline of the water the sky becomes stable (unmovable), one's inner eyesight becomes firm on the crown of the head. By the control of the grains the light becomes evident, by the control of the air, all the nine entry points are locked and by the control of the semen the body becomes stable.

सबद मिंदौ रे अवधू सबद बिंदौ थांन मांन सब धंधा।
आतमां मधे प्रमातमां दीसै ज्यौं जल मधे चंदा ॥125॥

O mystic, acquire the word, acquire the word. Place, position and pilgrimage are mere rituals. They are worldly ways. By knowing the word you would know that God appears just like the moon appears in its shadow in water.

आसण दिढ़ अहार दिढ़ जे न्यंद्रा दिढ़ होई।
गोरष कहै सुणौं रे पूता मरै न बूढ़ा होई ॥126॥

Guru Gorakhnath says that the one who is able to sit calmly in the lotus pose–the padmasana, and the one who eats sparingly and has control over his sleep cannot ever die though he might attain old age.

कोई न्यंदै कोई ब्यंदै कोई करै हमारी आसा।
गोरष कहे सुणौं रे अवधू यहु पंथ परा उदासा ॥127॥

Guru Gorakhnath says that some criticize the path of yoga that has been developed in the search for the supreme principle, some others worship that path, some other are hung in the duality between hope and despair, but this path is different from all, without bias to any and is devoid of any kind of desire.

इक लष सींगणि नव लष बांन। बेध्या मींन गगन अस्थांन।
बेध्या मींन गगन कै साथ। सति सति भाषंत श्रीगोरखनाथ ॥128॥

The practice of yoga is like rolling threads over one lakh bows and arrows meaning it has the capacity to kill nine lakhs. By it the fish situated in the crown of the head got targeted (hit). Gorakhnath says this to be the very truth that by the knowing the ultimate truth even the crown of the head can be pierced or hit. meaning that for a little while not only has knowledge been acquired but it has acquired stability also.

तूटी डोरी रस कस बहै। उनमनि लागा अस्थिर रहै।
उनमनि लागा होइ अनंद। तूटी डोरीं बिनसै कंद ॥129॥

For the seeker the moment the thread of concentration is broken the sweet fluid of spiritual knowledge flows away, the mind that has been away from the world becomes feeble. In that state of beyond thought the mind was full of bliss but after it broke the entire spiritual practice melted.

सबद बिन्दौ अवधू सबद बिन्दौ सबदे सीझंत काया।
निनांणवै कोडि राजा मस्तक मुडाइले परजा का अंत न पाया ॥130॥

O mystic, reach the supreme principle, acquire the word or the supreme principle. The body is perfected through word. To acquire this word 99 crores kings became disciples and how many amongst the subjects became so, there is no count of that.

षरतर पवनां रहै निरंतरि। महारस सीझै काया अभिअंतरि।
गोरख कहै अम्हे चंचल ग्रहिया। सिव सक्ती ले निज धरि रहिया ॥131॥

The sharp wind blows continuously. After restlessness ceases, the body perfects the maharaas, Gorakh says that he has controlled the mind and by the union of Shiva and Shakti started living in our own house that is–acquired realization of the self.

पेट कि अगनि बिबरजित दिष्टि की अगनि षाया।
यांन गुरू का आगैं ही होता पणि बिरलै अवधू पाया ॥132॥

I did not eat from the digestive fire of my stomach but I ate from the fire of my eyes (implying that through true knowledge I could eat up illusion) this knowledge from the Guru was available earlier also but only the rare mystic knows it.

अगम अगोचर रहे निहकांम। भंवर गुफा नांहीं बिसराम।
जुगति न जांणै जागैं राति। मन काहू कै न आवैं हाथि ॥133॥

The supreme principle is beyond reach, invisible and desireless. To know that supreme principle one has to undergo many processes. The practitioner who does not have any solution to achieve that, even if he stays awake the whole night, he cannot achieve it.

नव नाड़ी बहोतरी कोठां। ए अष्टांग सब झूठा।
कूंची ताली सुषमन करै उलटि जिभ्या ले तालू धरै ॥134॥

The nine energy channels their seventy two thousand beats and all aspects of the eight fold path of yoga all fail when the yogi controls the Sushumna in the opposite direction and also upturns his tongue to touch it to the upper inside part of the mouth.

पंडित ग्यांन मरौ क्या झूझि। औरै लेहु परमपद बूझि।
आसण पवन उपद्रह करैं। निसिदिन आरम्भ पचि-पचि मरैं ॥135॥

O knowledgable beings ! why do you die fighting a battle with external things. No benefit will accrue from this. You should move towards the real knowledge, knowledge of the supreme state. That supreme state is different from these. Without this subtle knowledge the asana–yogic postures and pranayama–breath control creates disturbance. Dying day and night i.e. doing yogic activity will still yield only initial success.

उनमन जोगी दसवैं द्वार। नाद ब्यंद ले धूंधूंकार।
दसवे द्वारे देइ कपाट। गोरख षोजी औरै बाट ॥136॥

The yogi is engaged in profound meditation in the tenth door the crown of the head and he hears the great sound emanating from the nada and the bindu, he hears the unstruck sound but Gorakhnath has closed the tenth door as well and has found the supreme consciousness through the path itself.

आरम्भ जोगी कथीला एकसार षिण षिण जोगी करै सरीर विचार।
तलबल ब्यंद धरिबा एकतोल। तब जांणिबा जोगी आरंभ का बोल ॥137॥

The first step of a yogi is one where he is one with his essence, he is pure and every moment keeps contemplating on his body and protects the semen in a balanced manner in his entire body. Then one should understand that the yogi is experiencing the signs of the state of ghat. Ghat refers to an earthern vessel and also to the human body.

घट हीं रहिबा मन नजाई दूर। अब निस पीवै जोगी बारुणीं सूर।
स्वाद बिस्वाद बाई काल छींन। तब जांनिबा जोगी घट का लछीन ॥138॥

When the yogi resides in his body, his mind does not wander far, then he partakes of the immortal nectar. Pleasure, pain and death have become weak by the practice of kevali kumbhak, then one should understand that the body has started to experience the signs of the state of ghat.

परचय जोगी उनमन षेला। अहनिसि इंछ्या करै देवता स्यूं मेला।
षिन षिन जोगी नांना रूप। तब जांनिबा जोगी परचय सरूप ॥139॥

One who has merged in the state of profound thoughtless Samadhi is called a yogi. Night and day he meets the supreme consciousness at will and can change into various kinds of forms in a split second , then one should understand that the yogi has been introduced to his real self.

निसपती जोगी जानिबा कैसा। अगनी पांणीं लोहा मांनैं जैसा।
राजा परजा संमि कर देष। तब जांनिबा जोगी निसपतिका भेष ॥140॥

The attainment of the nishpatti state–that is, state of becoming one with body, mind and self–is the sign of a yogi. Just like iron is purified through water and air similarly through various difficult practices the yogi becomes pure (for purifying iron it is heated on fire and the fire is doused by putting it in water) and when the yogi starts seeing everybody-be it the king or his subjects with an equal eye, then one should understand that he has achieved the nishpatti state.

अवधू षारै षिरै षाटै झरै मीठै उपजै रोंग।
गोरष कहै सुणौ रे अवधू अंनै पांणीं जोंग ॥141॥

By consuming a lot of salt the semen is destroyed, it falls due to sour taste. By eating a lot of sweet food diseases are created in the body. That is why Gorakh says O mystic! Listen, yoga can only be perfected by grain and water (one should not hanker after the sour sweet tastes).

बजरी करंतां अमरी राषै अमरि करंतां बाई।
भोग करंतां जे ब्यंद राषे ते गोरष का गुरभाई ॥142॥

The one who practices Vajroli kriya and while doing that protects amroli, and while doing amroli protects the air, and while engaging in intercourse protects the semen, he is the brother of Gorakh, that is, he has achieved perfection equal to Gorakh.

भग मुषि ब्यंद अगनि मुषि पारा। जो राषै सो गुरू हमारा ॥143॥

The practice of celibacy and keeping the mind away from the sensory pleasures is a very difficult path. This journey is not possible with the actions of the body. For this the consciousness has to enter the thoughtless state. In this context Guru Gorakhnath says that the one who while having intercourse with a woman is still able to protect his semen from falling and saves mercury from fire implying of sensory pleasures – he is the master the rest are all pupils. O mystic, the one who does such a difficult penance is the master of even god this is uttered by Gorakhnath who is the grandson of Shiva and the disciple of Matsyendranath

जिभ्या स्वांद् तत तन षोजै हेला करै गुरू बाचा।
अगनि बिहूँणां बंध न लागै। ढलकि जाइ रस काचा ॥144॥

The one who tries to find the ultimate reality in the taste of the tongue and in this manner flouts the teachings of the Guru, the rasa- taste or chyle–one of the seven constituents of the body–is not baked by the fire of yoga and because it is unbaked it just scatters away.

अवधू ईस्वर हमारैं चेला भणींजै मछींद्र बोलिये नाती।
निगुरी पिरथी परलै जाती ताथैं हम उल्टी थापना थापी ॥145॥

This earth is full of people who have no good qualities. That is why I Gorakhnath have established the opposite practice. The one who spends a lot of time in eating and partakes food with desires–his body disintegrates as quickly. He becomes incapable of doing yoga and on top of it becomes entangled in various worldly problems as well.

भरि भरि षाइ ढरि ढरि जाइ। जोग नहीं पूता बड़ी बलाइ।
संजंम होइ बाइ संग्रहौ। इस बिधि अकल पुरिस कौ गहौ ॥146॥

The body that partakes of delicious food becomes ill very soon. The one who through discipline reaches the kumbhak state (retention of breath) he is the one who can see the divine. The practice of deep breathing is the ultimate practice of eating in yoga and through its perfection one achieves a disease free state. All the diseases are decimated because of it.

षांये भीं मरिये अणषांये भी मरिये। गोरष कहै पूता संजंमि हीं तरिये।
मधि निरंतर कीजै बास। निहचल मनुवा थिर होइ सास ॥147॥

The one who eats a stomach full meets death as does the one who eats very less. Gorakh says O disciple! a balance between these two can only lead to liberation. That is why one should adopt a life of the middle path by which the mind becomes peaceful and the breath becomes stable.

पवन हीं जोग पवन हीं भोग। पवन हीं हरै छतीसौं रोग।
या पवन कोई जांणै भेव। सो आपैं करता आपैं देव ॥148॥

The breath is yoga, the breath is sensory pleasures, the breath dissolves all kinds of diseases. Rare is the one who knows the secret of this breath. The one who knows is like the creator.

ब्यंद हीं जोग व्यंद हीं भोग। व्यंद ही हरै चौसठि रोग।
या बिंद का कोई जांणै भेव। सो आपैं करता आपैं देव ॥149॥

Bindu is yoga, bindu is sensory pleasures, the bindu dissolves all kinds of diseases, rare is the one knows the secret of this. The one who knows this is like the creator, he is supreme consciousness.

साच का सबद सोना का रेख निगुरां कौं चाणक सगुरा कौं उपदेश।
गुर का मुंड्या गुंण मैं रहै। निगुरा भ्रमै औगुण गहै ॥150॥

The word of truth is like a line of gold, which passes the test of every touchstone, but the discourse about truth is given only to those who have a capable yogi as their master. The one without masters knows deceit and cunning because without the Guru he cannot learn anything , the one whom the Guru has made his disciple with the initiation into the mantra he is the one who inculcates qualities. The one who has not sought shelter in the Guru is forever in delusion and falls prey to various vices.

अवधू बूझना ते भूलना नहीं अनबूझ मग हारै।
सूंने जंगल भटकत फिरहीं, मारि लिहीं बटमारै ॥151॥

O mystic the one who has understood the highest principle he does not forget it. But for those who do not understand it, they lose their path and wander in desolate jungles where robbers loot them of all their valuables.

गुरु की बाचा षोजैं नाहीं, अहंकारी अहंकार करै।
षोजी जीवैं षोजि गुरू कौं, अहंकारी का प्यंड परै ॥152॥

Guru Gorakhnath states that the display of pride or ego in the name of practice and accomplishments is untruth. Such a person can neither follow the principles laid down by a Guru nor can he make an effort to find one. The seeker who is in search of a Guru is the one who is capable of reaching perfection. The arrogant one merely limits himself to the outer display

यंद्री का लड़बड़ा जिभ्या का फूहड़ा। गोरख कहै ते पर्तषि चूहड़ा।
काछ का जती मुष का सती। सो सतपुरुष उतमो कथी ॥153॥

Gorakhnath ji says that for the saint to achieve perfection he has to control his sense organs. The one who uses undesirable language, cannot control his sense organs that person is called ill - mannered and uncontrolled. In this sequence Gorakhnath says that the one who practices celibacy and speaks in a measured language can indeed be called a person full of goodness

अवधू मन चंगा तो कठौती ही गंगा। बांध्या मेल्ह्या तो जगत्र चेला।
बदंत गोरष सति सरूप। तत बिचारैं ते रेष न रूप ॥154॥

O seeker listen! the purity of the mind is the biggest treasure. Therefore the one whose mind is pure for him the water in a wooden vessel is equal to the pure water of the holy Ganges. He who has control over the senses organs is the master of the world. Gorakhnath says that the indestructible ultimate reality in the form of truth is beyond any form or line and it is the ultimate principle whose expanse can be seen in the universe.

सीषि साषि बिसाह्या बुरा। सुपिनैं मैं धन पाया पड़ा।
परषि परषि ले आगैं धरा। नाथ कहै पूता षोटा न षरा ॥155॥

Mere learning does not lead to anything. The one who learnt this and that and acquired vices and saw dreams and inspected everything and gathered wealth but Nath says O son actually that wealth is neither pure nor impure. Because that is not wealth at all.

आओ देबी बैसो। द्वादिस अंगुल पैसो।
पैसत पैसत होइ सुष। तब जनम मरन का जाइ दुष ॥156॥

O Devi Kundalini power come sit, the twelve finger long life breath meaning the one in which it flows, that is, the Sushumna energy channel please enter that. Once it enters one will receive happiness and the fear of life and death will vanish.

स्वांमी काची बाई काचा जिंद। काची काया काचा बिंद।
क्यंकरि पाकै क्यूंकरि सीझै। काची अगनीं नीर न षीजै ॥157॥

Master all the natural things become ripe only through practice. The breath is raw, life is raw, body is raw and semen is also raw. How can they become ripe, how can they be perfected. Without the fire of yoga, with raw fire even water cannot be perfected.

तौ देवी पाकी बाई पाका जिंद। पाकी काया पाका बिंद।
ब्रह्म अगनि अषंडित बलै। पाका अगनीं नीर परजलै ॥158॥

Divine lady- the life breath, life, body and semen become ripe when the fire of cosmic consciousness lights up in an indivisible manner. In this way by being perfected by the fire of cosmic consciousness or the fire of yoga the water filled nature awakens.

सोवत आडां ऊभां ठाढां अगनीं ब्यंद न बाई।
निश्चल आसन पवनां ध्यानं अगनीं ब्यंद न जाई ॥159॥

The one who sleeps in a slanting way, or keeps standing in normal circumstances , cannot protect fire, semen and air, but when through breath/air and meditation these three things become pure then fire and semen are not destroyed.

उगवंत सूर पत्र पूर काल-कंटक जाइ दूर।
नाथ का भंडार भर पूर रिजक रोजी सदा हजूर ॥160॥

After the sunrise, that is, after witnessing the ultimate reality the thorn of death is removed away. Meaning that the seeker ceases to be worried about himself. The stores of the Nath are full. Everyday he brings forth food for everyone.

थांन मांन गुर ग्यांन। बेधां बोध सिधां परग्रांम।
चेतनि बाला भ्रम न बहै। नाथ की कृपा अषंडित रहै ॥161॥

The one who obtains respect through place – condition, stability, firmness, and absorbs the knowledge imparted by the Guru, through the piercing of the Kundalini he achieves knowledge and lives on earth as if it is not his ultimate abode, lives without being entangled, that seeker who is a disciple of the Guru who is consciousness does not flow away in dissipation. It means that the Guru's grace is forever with him

अधिक तत्त ते गुरू बोलिये हींण तत ते चेला।
मन मांनैं तौ संगि रमौ नहीं तौ रमौ अकेला ॥162॥

The Guru is the reservoir of various kinds of knowledge. That is why he is called a Guru. The student or the disciple is less than him in knowledge and concentration. In this situation also the saint should keep the company of the Guru according to his mind's desire. If the mind is not drawn to such a Guru then wandering alone will be a better option.

चलंत पंथा तूटंत कंथा उडंत पेहा बिचलंत देहा।
छूटंत ताली हरि सूंनेहा ॥163॥

By walking on any path of righteousness many different paths are made and most of the accepted norms scatter and fall apart. In such a situation the attachment to the physical body vanishes. In the sequence of practice when true love develops for Hari, that is, for God, then meditation and other practices simply disappear.

पंथि चले चलि पवनां तूटै नाद बिंद अरु बाई।
घट हीं भींतरि अठसठि तीरथ कहां भ्रमै रे भाई ॥164॥

By walking on the path the air disintegrates. The unstruck sound, semen and air all become hazy. The 68 pilgrimages are all inside the body. O brother, where all are you wandering.

जोगी होइ पर निंद्या झषै। मद मांस अरु भांगि जो भषै।
इकोतरसै पुरिषा नरकहि जाई। सति सति भाषंत श्रीगोरष राई ॥165॥

The one who criticizes others being a yogi and drinks and partakes of intoxicants as well as eats flesh 7100 generations of his go to hell. Gorakhnath says this is the truth.

अवधू मांस भषंत दया धरम का नास। मद पीवत तहां प्रांण निरास।
भांगि भषंत ग्यांन ध्यांन षोवंत। जम दरबारी ते प्रांणीं रोवंत ॥166॥

Gorakhnath tell the seeker to lead a life of discipline and says the one who eats flesh all compassion and righteousness finish in him. He becomes a drunkard and his life giving breath starts becoming weak. The one who use the alternative to intoxicants , like cannabis, bhang.. their concentration between knowledge and principle breaks in the middle, it gets lost. Such living beings become capable of going to the court of the God of death, Yama.

चालिबा पंथा कै सींबा कंथा। धरिबा ध्यांनं कै कथिबा ग्यांनं।
एकाएकी सिध कै संग। बदंत गोरषनाथ पूता न होयसि मन भंग ॥167॥

Either one should keep walking on the path, or should weave a tale or should meditate or give discourses full of knowledge. By doing these processes continuously and staying with single pointed focus or staying in the company of perfected beings the restlessness of the mind ends

पढ़ि देखि पंडिता ब्रह्म गियानं। मूवां मुकति बैकुंठा थानं।
गाड्या जाल्या चौरासी मैं जाइ। सतिसति भाषंत (श्री) गोरषराई ॥168॥

O learned one! Keep on contemplating on divine knowledge, for without it, all else is unreal. After death, the liberation that is achieved is called getting a place in Vaikunth but in actuality it is like getting a place in a pit or sitting on a pyre and getting into the vortex of the 84 lakh births. This is verily the truth spoken by

Gorakhnath.

आकास तत सदासिव जांण। तिस अभिअंतरि पद निरबांण।
प्यंडे परचांनै गुरमुषि जोइ। बाहुड़ि आबागवन न होइ ॥169॥

The sky element is Shiva himself. The one whose knowledge has developed like this his inner world is full of the desire for liberation. This way, the one who through the knowledge imparted by the Guru knows the body and soul, recognizes it, he becomes free of the cycle of birth and death.

ऊरम धूरम ज्वाला जोति। सुरजि कला न छीपै छोति।
कंचन कवल किरणि परसाइ। जल मल दुरगंध सर्ब सुषाई ॥170॥

The light is fully lit up. The sun aspect cannot be hidden. It's rays start touching the golden lotus–that is the Sahasrara chakra on the crown of the head which absorbs and completely destroys the impurities in the water meaning the illusory bindu dominant water nature and the noxious smell emanating from it.

घटि घटि सूण्यां ग्यांन न होइ। बनि बनि चंदन रूष न कोइ।
रतन रिधि कवन कै होइ। ये तत बूझै बिरला कोइ ॥171॥

Every person does not become knowledgeable merely by listening. Similarly the sandalwood tree is not found in every forest. Therefore the bejeweled accomplishments are achieved by whom (this principle is only understood by the highest seeker).

नींझर झरणैं अंमीरंस पीवणां षटदल बेध्या जाइ।
चंद बिहूंणां चांदिणां तहां देष्या श्रीगोरष राइ ॥172॥

The seeker in the higher realms of practice continuously drinks the divine nectar. This supreme bliss can only be achieved by the one who has pierced the six–petalled lotus through the practice pf pranayama(breath control) and reaches the thousand petalled lotus located in the crown of the head. Such a seeker sees the moonlight without witnessing the moon. He also gets to have a vision of Gorakh.

कै मन रहै आसा पास। कै मन रहै परम उदास।
कै मन रहै गुरू कै ओलै। कै मन रहै कांमनि कै षोले ॥173॥

It is difficult for the mind to remain without support. He is caught in the noose of hope or else stays in total despair or a detached state, either it takes refuge in a woman or takes the shelter of a Guru. It is the Guru who through his grace helps the disciple achieve absolute detachment

दाबि न मारिबा षाली न राषिबा जांनिबा अगनि का भेवं।
बूढी हीं थै गुरबानी होइगी सति सति भाषंत श्री गोरष देवं ॥173॥

One should not exploit the mind. One should also not leave it vacant. One should know the secret of the fire of yoga and the fire of divine consciousness. By doing this, illusion that has been going on since the beginning will turn into the one who liberates. This is the true utterance of Gorakhnath. illusion has a dual form–in the form of ignorance it enmeshes the individual in it 's control and in the form of true knowledge it sets him on the path to enlightenment.

बाहरि न भीतरि नेड़ा न दूर। षोजत रहे ब्रह्मा अरु सूर।
सेत फटक मनि हीरैं बीधा। इहि परमारथ श्री गोरष सीधा ॥175॥

The Supreme Consciousness, the soul is neither outside nor inside, neither close nor far. The creator and the sun kept on looking for him. The white crystal bead was able to pierce the diamond–that is, the soul came to know the secret and got to witness the supreme reality. It is to reach this noble goal that Gorakhnath undertook so many austerities.

आवति पंच तत कूं मो है जाती छैल जगावै।
गोरष पूछै बाबा मछिंद्र या न्यंद्रा कहां थैं आवै ॥176॥

Gorakhnath asks his Guru Matsyendranath, O Baba ! tell me about the one who make this body made of five elements faint and makes one totally unconscious and when it leaves it awakens the consciousness, where does this sleep come from?

गगन मंडल मैं सुंनि द्वार। बिजली चंमकै घोर अंधार।
ता महि न्यंद्रा आवै जाई। पंच तत मैं रहै समाइ ॥177॥

In the sky of the thousand petalled lotus in the mind there is a door to nothingness, shunya. There is pitch darkness the lightening thunders. Sleep comes and goes from there and merges in the body made of the five elements.

ऊभां बैठां सूता लीजै। कबहूं चित भंग न कीजै।
अनहद सबद गगन मैं गाजै। प्यंड पड़े तो सतगुर लाजै ॥178॥

The person full of laziness and procrastination just keeps sitting, he just not reach perfection and the one who sleeps a lot experiences complete disappointment. The yoga practitioner who, under any temptation does not let his mind and consciousness feel fear is the one who constantly hears the sound in the crown chakra. The seeker who is engaged in such a practice becomes better than his Guru.

एकलौ बीर, दूसरौ धीर, तीसरौ षटपट चौथौ उपाध।
दस पंच तहाँ बाद बिबाद ॥179॥

He who stays alone is courageous. Two are patient, if a third one comes, disputes arise. If the fourth one comes there is total chaos and where five or ten gather there a situation of total mayhem presents itself.

एकाएकी सिध नांउं दोइ रमति ते साधवा।
चारि पंच कुटुम्ब नांउ दस बीस ते लसकरा ॥180॥

The one who lives in solitude is the realized one. The ones who live with one or two are saints, if there are four or five then one should consider it a family and if ten or twenty are present consider it an army.

मन मुषि जाता गुरमुषि लेहु। लोही मास अगनि मुषि देहु।
मात पिता की मेटौ धात। ऐसा होइ बुलावै नाथ ॥181॥

The one who is strong of the mind , meaning the one who keeps his mind firm through steady practice, he becomes capable of being a Guru. Such a person should come out of the boundaries of his father and mother and others and become a yogi. The one who goes beyond all kinds of worldly titles is the one who deserves to be called a true yogi and Guru Gorakhnath also gives him credence.

नाद नाद सब कोइ कहै। नादहिं लै को बिरला रहै।
नाद बिंद है फीकी सिला। जिहिं साध्या ते सिधैं मिला ॥182॥

There are many practitioners who talk about the unstruck sound or anhad nada but they are not aware of its real meaning. Rare is the yogi who has heard the anhad nada. The one who has mastered the sound and the bindu semen, his reaching yogic accomplishments is certain.

दरवेस सोइ जो दरकी जांणै। पंचे पवन अपूठां आंणै।
सदा सुचेत रहै दिन राति। सो दरवेस अलह की जाति ॥183॥

He is a 'darwesh' who knows about the 'dar' or the abode, he knows where the abode of God is, he has a knowledge of the brahmrandhra. Through the practice of the control of the breath and by withdrawing the senses into the mind–pratyahara-he is able to withdraw the mind from the sense organs and he is alert day and night. Such a darwesh turns into the supreme reality himself

बैसंत पूरा रमंति सूरा, एक रसि राषंति काया।
अंतरि एक रसि देषिबा बिचरंति गोरषराया ॥184॥

Those who have achieved realization, they sit calmly for there is nothing left for them to do. The ones who are brave, that is, during the time of practice they face all kinds of obstacles bravely and keep the body in an unchangeable state. But Gorakhnath wants to reach the unchangeable state inside and therefore keeps on making efforts.

नाद बिंद बजाइले दोऊ पूरिले अनहद बाजा।
एकंतिका बासा सोधिले भरथरी कहै गोरष मछिंद्र का दासा ॥185॥

The practice of the nada and the bindu are two important resources. The one who perfects these is called a great yogi. The one who practices this becomes used to living in solitude. The one who successfully complete the practice of nada bindu and is verified by Bhartrihari, Matsyendra and Gorakhnath to be a complete saint.

सूर माहिं चंद चंद माहिं सूर। चपंपि तीनि तेहुड़ा बाजल तूर।
भणन्त गोरषनाथ एक पद पूरा। भाजंत भौंदू साधंति सूरा ॥186॥

When the Pingala (representing heat, the sun) and the Ida (representing coolness, the moon) and the the sun meets the moon in the crown chakra and the three qualities of sattva, rajas and tamas are pushed away then the anahat or the instrument of unstruck sound plays up. This way Gorakhnath describes that complete state or accomplishment which is achieved by the brave seekers and without seeking which the foolish seekers run away from the path.

छत्र पवन निरंतर रहै छीजै काया पंजरा रहै।
मन पवन चंचल निजि गहिया बोलै नाथ निरंतरि रहिया ॥187॥

When the chhatra pawan reaches the continuous yogic state without distinction then the body turns feeble, it remains like a skeleton and the gross mind consciousness and the restless sense organs come in one's hand. Nath says that staying like this continuously perfects one's way of living.

According to Yogashastras there are are ten kinds of vayus who carry out various functions in the body. The essence of all these vayus is called chchatra vayu.

इकटी बिकुटी त्रिकुटी संधि पछिम द्वारे पवनां बंधि।
षूटै तेल न बूझै दीया बोलै नाथ निरन्तरि हूवा ॥188॥

When the energy channel Ida meets Pingala in the Sushumna and when in the path of Sushumna air is controlled then the seeker becomes immortal, it 's oil in the form of air does not finish and the wick of life does not extinguish. So, the Nath says that the seeker realizes his true self.

ज्यूं ज्यूं भुयंगम आवै जाइ सुरही धरि नहीं गरड़ रहाइ।
तब लग सिध दुलंभ तोयं अहार बिन व्यापै रोग ॥189॥

The serpent like breath comes and goes and for that the Garuda bird does not reside in the path of Sushumna meaning till the time the breath is not controlled the realization of yoga is difficult.

Because without the diet of water (semen)the body will fall prey to diseases. The seeker consumes a diet of the water and becomes celibate. This is the highest stage and can be reached by the highest stage of pranayama, that is Kumbhak.

ग्यानं सरीषा गुरू न मिलिया चित्त सरीषा चेला।
मन सरीषा मेलू न मिलिया ताथें गोरष फिरै अकेला ॥190॥

The great Yogi Gorakhnath says that there is no Guru greater than knowledge and no disciple greater than consciousness. There are no dear and near ones of the mind. That is why Gorakhnath clarifies that that seeker along with these attributes should live in solitude.

सांग का पूरा ग्यांन का ऊरा। पेट का तूटा डिंभ का सूरा।
बदंत गोरखनाथ न पाया जोग। करि पाषंड रिझाया लोन ॥191॥

The yoga practitioner who is forever wearing ornaments, having special interest in dressing up, away from all knowledge, wanting to partake all kinds of foods can never practice yoga. He can merely attract people by posing as a seeker.

अगनि हीं जोग अगनि हीं भोग। अगनि हीं हरै चौंसठि रोग।
जो इहि अगनि का जाणै भेव। सो आप ही करता आप ही देव ॥192॥

जीवता जोगी अमीरस पीवता अहनिस अषंडित धारं।
दिष्टि मधे अदिष्टि बिचारिबा ऐसा अगम अपारं ॥193॥

The yogi free from the cycle of birth and death drinks the continuous flow of nectar. one should see the invisible God in the visible objects. In this way one can achieve the one beyond reach and abundant God.

जीवता बिछायबा मूंवां वोढिबा कबहु न होयबा रोगी।
बरसवै दिन काया पलटिबा यूं कोई कोई बिरला जोगी ॥194॥

The one who spreads his life breath and wraps the dead body around him meaning he keeps both balanced and uses them as a means can never fall ill. In this manner a rare yogi can transform his body in a day of a year.

सूरजे षायबा चंद्र सोयबा उभै न पीबा पांणी।
जीवता कै तलि मूंवा बिछायबा यूं बोल्या गोरष बांणी ॥195॥

When the right nostril is active one should have food when the left nostril is active one should sleep but one should not drink water in both. For the living i.e. the soul one should spread the dead i.e. the physical body. This means that the body should be used for the development of the soul, says Gorakhnath.

जहां गोरष तहां ग्यान गरीबी दुंद बाद नहीं कोई।
निसप्रेही निरदावै षेलै गोरष कहीयै सोई ॥196॥

Gorakhnath ji says that where there is the abode of the yogi there the world of knowledge can be seen. There is no kind of dualism there nor any kind of partiality. The yogi does not covet anything, he is not desirous of any worldly object. In this manner the yogi who is full of character moves about with abandon in the world of the limitless.

गिगनि मंडल मैंगाय बियाई कागद दही जमाया।
छांछि छांणि पंडिता पीवीं सिधां भाषण षाया ॥197॥

In the ulat bansi technique Guru Gorakhnath says that in the world of meditative practice by virtue of yoga many impossible tasks are also accomplished. The learned partake the buttermilk-the realized seer merely gets to have a taste of the formless God.

गूदड़ी जुग च्यारि तैं आई। गूदड़ी सिंध साधिकां चलाई।
गूदड़ी मैं अतीत का बासा। भणंत गोरषनाथ मछिंद्र का दासा ॥198॥

The yogis carry rags, it 's glory is sung in this sabdi. The past, one who is beyond reach, the universal soul. The realized yogi is also called so because he has himself become the universal soul.

असाध कंद्रप बिरला साधंत कोई। सुर नर गण गंध्रप ब्याप्या बालि सुग्रीव भाई।
ब्रह्म देवता कंद्रप ब्याप्या। यंद्र सहंस्र भग पाई ॥199॥

The one who beyond reach is beyond control. Sugriv thought his brother Bali is dead and took his wife as his own. Both brothers then fought about this. Brahma had intercourse with Saraswati. Indra cheated the wife of Gautam rishi, Ahalya. Gautam rishi cursed his wife and her body had a thousand marks.

अठ्यासी सहंस्र रषीसर कंद्रप ब्याप्या असाधि विष्न की माया।
यंन कंद्रप ईस्वर महादेव नाटारंभ नचाया ॥200॥

The founder of theatre is assumed to be Shiva. Shiva has said that the woman is a form of Vishnu's maya (illusion).

विष्न दस अवतार थाप्या असाधि कंद्रप जती गोरषनाथ साध्या। जनि नीझर झरंता राष्या ॥201॥

The ten incarnations of Vishnu had wives. The moon in the Sahasrara chakra (the energy centre situated at the crown of the head symbolized by the thousand petalled lotus) gives out ambrosia, the flowing ambrosia was protected, protected it from being burnt in the sun (navel chakra).

आसति छै हो पिंड्ता नासति नांहीं अनभै होय परतीति निरंतरि माहीं।
ग्यांन षोजि अमे बिग्यांन पाया। सतिसति भाषंत सिध सति नाथ राया ॥202॥

One cannot carry out spiritual practice by have a feeling of atheism. That is why one should have faith and follow the path of yoga.

माता हमारी मनसा बोलिये पिता बोलिये निरंजन निराकार।
गुरू हमारै अतीत बोलिये जिनि किया पिंड का उधारं ॥203॥

The mother of yogi is his own mind consciousness. The formless supreme consciousness is his father. The Guru is beyond self who has given body in the form of yoga.

आपा भांजिबा सतगुर बोजिबा जोग पंथ न करिबा हेला।
फिरि फिरि मनिषा जनम न पायबा करि लै सिध पुरिस सूं मेला ॥204॥

One should try to break arrogance, one should search for a good Guru.. One should not ignore the path of yoga. One does not get human life again and again. That is why one should daily practice to be in the company of realized beings.

थंभ बिहूंणी गगन रचीलै तेल बिहूंणी बाती।
गुरु गोरष के बचन पतिआया तब द्यौंस नहीं तहां राती ॥205॥

When the faith in Guru Gorakhnath's words was completely established then in the sky without a pillar without oil or wick,the light of knowledge could be seen. That is why for the seeker, there is no question of day and night. That is, he is always walking through the light of knowledge.

षंडित ग्यांनी षर तर बोलै सति का सबद उछेदै।
काया कै बलि करड़ा बोलै भीतरि तत्त न भेदै ॥206॥

The one who has incomplete knowledge speaks harshly and rejects the word of truth. He plucks it and throws it away. In him the real principle has not been absorbed. He has not gained any knowledge. He considers his body as everything. That is why on the strength of his body he uses harsh words.

महमां धरि महमां कूँ मेटै सति का सबद विचारी।
नांन्हां होय जिनि सतगुर षोज्या तिन सिर की पोट उतारी ॥207॥

The ones with glory who do not consider themselves as glorious, politely move about in search of a good Guru, those ones contemplating on the true word have removed the baggage of their actions-karma. They can become seekers.

एक कांमध्येनि बारि सिधि कै गगन सिषर लै बांधी।
लागि जीव ऊपरि बारि सिधि की ल्यौ निरंजन सूं सांधी ॥208॥

At the doorstep of the realized seeker there is a wish fulfilling cow in the form of spiritual realization and profound meditation whom he has tied to the top of the sky. That is his abode. The individual wants to achieve that. He was surrounded by a fence and concentrated totally on the pure one.

आफू षाय भांगि भसकावै। ता मैं अकलि कहां तैं आवै।
चढ़तां पित्त ऊतरतां बाई। तातैं गोरष भांगि न षाई ॥209॥

The one who consumes intoxicants his intellect gets destroyed. By consuming bhang(intoxicant), the bile rises and the air moves downwards, that is why Gorakh does not consume bhang.

म्यंदर छाड़ै कुटी बंधावै। त्यागै माया और मंगावै।
सुन्दरि छाड़ै नकटी बासै। ताते गोरष अलगै न्हासै ॥210॥

The actual seeker leaves the temple and other places as a sequence in his practice and resides in solitude. He discards all illusory and accepted miracles and totally gives up on the objects appearing beautiful from outside. The seeker with this kind of orientation keeps on doing his spiritual practice by singular focus.

त्रिया न सांति बैद र रोगी रसायणी अर जाचि षाय।
बूढ़ा न जोगी सूरा न पीठि पाछैं घाव यतनां न मानैं श्रीगोरषनाथ ॥211॥

If a woman is quiet, a doctor is ill, the one working with chemicals does so without inspecting the components, the yogi is old and the brave one has lots of wounds on his back–then they are all unsuccessful personalities in their respective fields. Gorakhnath says this clearly.

हंड ब्रह्मण्ड चहोड़ीया मानूं बेस्या अंन।
कोई कोई कोरड़ रह गया यूं भाषै नाथ रतंन ॥212॥

Ratannath says that the entire universe is brought up on the grains of the prostitute (illusion) therefore in the reign of illusion rare is the one who is bereft of her influence.

निंद्रा सुपनैं बिंद कूं हरै। पंथ चलंता आतमां मरै।
बैठां षटपट ऊभां उपाधि। गोरख कहै पूता सहज समाधि ॥213॥

The seeker who has made sleep the stuff of dreams, that is, he does not sleep much and is not enchanted by it, the one who is an expert in the protection of his semen, who is not caught up in any particular sect – else his freedom is destroyed by itself. The one who is busy in yogic postures–Gorakhnath aims at such a person and says that he is a sehejyogi–without any support or effort his activities / kriya happen on their own.

सूकै कंठ अरु भूष संतापै। देह बिसर अर निंद्र व्यापै।
बुधि बिन बकै विकल होय जाय। तातैं गोरष भांगि न षाय ॥214॥

By the intake of intoxicants, the throat dries up. Hunger increases. One cannot pay attention to the body. The sleep deepens. The intellect is destroyed. That is why Gorakhnath considers the consumption of bhang as forbidden.

रूसता रूठा गोला-रोगी। भोला भछिक भूषा भोगी।
गोरष कहै सरबटा जोगी। यतनां मैं नहीं निपजै जोगी ॥215॥

अवधू अहार कूं तोड़िबा पवन कूं मोड़िवा ज्यौ कबहु न होयबा रोगी।
छठै छमासि काया पलटंत नाग बंग बनसपती जोगी ॥216॥

O yogi, keep on reducing your diet gradually and continuously and make the movement of air upwards then no disease will come close to you. Every six months make the body pure by yogic kriyas and thus the purpose of a yogi is accomplished.

सूरां का पंथ हास्यां का बिसराम सुरता लेहु बिचारी।
अपरचै पिंड भिष्या षात है अंति कालि होयगी भारी ॥217॥

The yoga practitioner has to walk on that path. Rest is for the one who have submitted themselves to eventual death. O listeners ponder over this thought, the one who has not witnessed the supreme consciousness in his own body and still eats alms, his problems will increase during his the time of death.

उलटी सकति चढ़ै ब्रह्मंड नष सष पवनां षेलै सरबंग।
उलटि चन्द्र राह कूं ग्रहै सिध संङ्केत जती गोरष कहै ॥218॥

When the serpentine Kundalini power upturns and reaches the top of the head then from the toe to the head the entire body is full of air–in the Nath parlance it means the air is eaten up. Then, the crown chakra from where ambrosia flows the moon gulps up the Rahu. Meaning the root lotus and the sun situated there and this makes it possible to drink the nectar. The perfected Yogi Gorakhnath says this.

धरे अधर बिचारीयां धरी याही मैं सोय।
धरे अधर परचा हूवा तब दुतीया नाहीं कोय ॥219॥

When the supreme reality is contemplated upon in this body made of the five elements and it is found in this body itself, in this manner when the supreme reality is witnessed in this body itself then the principle of non-dualism or monism is realized.

जिभ्या इन्द्री एकैं नाल। जो राषै सो बंचै काल।
पंडित ग्यांनी न करसि गरब। जिभ्या जीती जिन जीत्या सरब ॥220॥

He is a true yogi one who has control over his tongue that is, complete control over his eating habits. He is the one who is then saved from the jaws of death. The learned should not be arrogant about his knowledge. He should have control over his tongue.

गोरख कहै हमारा षरतर पंथ। जिभ्या इन्द्री दीजै बन्ध।
लोग जुगति मैं रहे समाय। ता लोगी कूं काल न षाय ॥221॥

Gorakhnath says that his sect talks in a clear and specific manner. The one who has mastered control over his tongue and his sense organs, he can win over death itself.

बरष एक देखिलै हो पंडिता तत एक चीन्हिबा सबदैं सुरति समाई।
गोरखनाथ बोलै भ्रम न भूलिबा रे भाई ॥222॥

In the process of practice, after some time itself one is able to recognize the supreme reality. The one who does not fall in the delusion of the world is a true yogi.

अबूझि बूझिलै हो पंडिता अकथ कथिलै कहांणी।
सीस नवांबत सतगुर मिलीया जागत रैंण बिहांणी ॥223॥

O knowledgable one! Know that is not knowable. Say that which cannot be said. The moment one bows one's head (the emergence of real faith and devotion in one's heart), whose outer sign is the bowing of the head (one has a vision of the perfect Guru and as a result of this continuous waking symbolic of the knowledgable state (this night) symbolizing this life of ignorance breaks into dawn.

विद्या पढ़ि रे कहावै ग्यांनीं। बिनां अविद्या कहै अग्यांनी।
परम तत का होय न मरमी। गोरष कहै ते महा अधरमी ॥224॥

Merely by acquiring knowledge of the sacred scriptures one cannot be called learned. And the one who has not read them cannot be called ignorant. Gorakhnath says that the one who cannot distinguish the ultimate reality all his knowledge has no meaning.

पंथ चले चलि पवनां तूटै तन छीजे तत जाई।
काया तैं कछू अगम बतावै ताकी मूंडूं माई ॥225॥

One should always practice the process of deep breathing. The absolute principle is not away from the body. Because the creator resides within us.

महमंद महमंद न करि काजि महमंद का बौहोत बिचारं।
महमंद साथि पैकंबर सीधा ये लष अजी हजारं ॥226॥

Merely by saying Mohammad God cannot be attained. He should be contemplated upon in meditation. He was a 'paigambar'- a messenger. Pay attention to this.

जीव सीव संगे बासा। बधि न षाइबा रुध्र मासा।
हंस घात न करिबा गोतं। कथंत गोरष निहारि पोतं ॥227॥

The individual soul and the universal soul have only one abode. That is why do not kill for flesh and blood. Do not annihilate any life. Consider everybody as belonging to your own gotra and clan. Gorakh says look at your own children (all creatures are like them).

जीव क्या हतिये रे प्यंड धारी। मारि लै पंचभू भ्रगला।
चरै थारी बुधि बाड़ी। जोग का मूल है दया दाण।
कथंत गोरष मुकत लै मानवा मारि लै रे मन द्रोही।
जाकै बप बरण मास नहीं लोही ॥228॥

O ones having this mortal body! Why do you kill other living creatures, if you have to kill, kill the mind made up of five elements, the deer (mind) who is grazing in your field (intellect). For yes ! the basis of yoga is compassion. Gorakh says for the cause of liberation kill this mind which neither has a body, nor flesh, nor blood or colour.

जिनि मन ग्रासे देव दाण।
सो मन मारिलै गहि गुरु ग्यांन बांण ॥229॥

The mind consciousness which has engulfed both the good and the bad, kill it with the arrow of the knowledge from the Guru.

जोगी सो जो राषै जोग। जिभ्या यंद्री न करै भोग।
अंजन छोडि निरंजन रहै। ताकू गोरष जोगी कहै ॥230॥

He is a yogi who protects yoga, does not use his sense organs like tongue etc. The one who leaves illusion and stays deeply into the supreme consciousness, Gorakh calls him a yogi.

सुंनि ज माई सुंनि ज बाप। सुंनि निरंजन आपै आप।
सुंनि कै परचै भया सथीर। निहचल जोगी गहर गंभीर ॥231॥

The state of profound meditation or Samadhi is the mother, it is the father, it is the pure supreme consciousness. After experiencing the shunya or the Samadhi one achieves stability and the yogi achieves a serious demeanour and becomes pure.

तजौ कुलती मेटौ भंग। अह निसि राषौ ओजुद बंधि।
सरब संजोग आवै हाथि। गुरु राषै निरबाण समाधि ॥232॥

Leave eating kulathi (a kind of heavy lentil), eliminate the habit of consuming bhang, day and night keep the body in control. this way by equanimity yoga will be perfected. And the Guru's grace will protect the nirvana Samadhi–the ultimate realization due to meditation.

अकुच कुचीया बिगसिया पोहा। सिधि परिजलि उठी लागिया धुवा।
कहै गोरषनाथ धुवा प्राण। ऐसे पिंड का परचा जाणै प्राण ॥233॥

The mind which was scattered in various materialist pursuits has now, through the practice of pratyahara–withdrawal of the senses into the mind, has become small and the flower of the individual soul has blossomed by being threaded into a necklace of supreme consciousness. This way perfections blazed and the smoke started rising. This smoke is the prana–the life force or breath (the way the presence of the smoke indicates fire, similarly the rising of the breath upwards into the crown chakra is indicative of achieving perfection in practice) The body has thus been perfected, the signifier of this is the breath.

अवधू यो मन जात है याही तै सब जांणि।
मन मकड़ी का ताग ज्यूं उलटि अपूठौ आंणि ॥234॥

O yogi! This consciousness is going. Everything originates from here, know this. Like a spider's web is upturned, upturn the mind and bring it back.

जे आसा तो आपदा जे संसा तो सोग।
गुर मुषि बिना न भाजसी (गोरष) ये दून्यों बड़ रोग ॥235॥

The ones who nurture hopes and expectations are the ones who have to face obstacles and the ones who doubt have to face sorrow. These two-expectations and sorrow are severe diseases. Without listening to the knowledge imparted by the Guru, they will not be dispelled.

इस ओजुदा मैं मारि लै गोता, कछु मगज भीतरि ष्याल रै।
पंच कटार है भीतरि निमस करि बेहाल रै ॥236॥

If the brain has some power of thoughts then dive into this body because everything is situated here. The five sense organs that support the mind can be killed with a sword which is itself present inside, kill these sensory pleasures totally by it.

ब्यंद ब्यंद सब कोई कहै। महाब्यंद कोइ बिरला लहै।
इह ब्यंद भरोसे लावै बंध। असथिरि होत न देषो कंध ॥237॥

Everybody says 'bindu bindu' but rare is the one who achieves the maha bindu or the supreme consciousness. Without spiritual experience the shukra (semen) that takes the support of the bandh kriya, his body is not seen to have achieved firmness.

उलटै मूल डाल नहीं रहै। फाड़ि कछौटा रात्यौं बहै।
न वोह छीजै ना वोह गलै। ब्यंद नहीं सो भगमुष ढलै ॥238॥

The one who is moving in the opposite direction to the world in pursuit of his spiritual practice, the one who does not know the branches, has forgotten the roots then he gets attracted to illusions and women and in thinking of a woman he loses his celibate state.

His practice may never be perforated, neither should it decrease nor stop, should be so firm that staying in the face of all temptations, he may be saved from decadence, such a one is a true yogi.

बिणि बैसंदर जोति बलत है गुर प्रसादे दीठी।
स्वामी सीला अलुणी कहिये जिनि चीन्हा तिन दीठी ॥239॥

While fire, the light is effulgent and can be seen by me by the grace of my Guru. O master! the one who has adopted the practice of sheelvritti where not even a granule of salt is partaken can witness the light. Sheelvritti is a practice whereby after the collection of the entire crop by the owner of the field, collecting those grains that have fall down on the ground during the process and subsisting on them is called sheelvritti.

ऊजल मीन सदा रहै जल मैं सुकर सदा मलीना।
आतम ग्यांन दया विणि कछु नाहीं कहा भयौ तन पीणा ॥240॥

In the clear, pure waters the fish resides. The dirty pig becomes uncomfortable in water and becomes unhappy. Similarly if the person claiming self–realization is devoid of love and compassion then even after making his body feeble through yoga, he does not gain respect and he becomes useless for the society.

धोतरा न पीवो रे अवधू भांगि न षावौ रे भाई।
गोरष कहै सुणो रे अवधू या काया होयगी पराई ॥241॥

The yoga practitioner is barred from eating intoxicants such as bhang-dhature. If there is no control over this then it will not take time for the body to destruct.

सांइ सहेली सुत भरतार सरब सिसटि कौ एकौ द्वार।
पैसता पुरसि निकसता पूता ता कारिण गोरष अवधूता ॥242॥

Gorakhnath has assumed the entire female race to be his mother and has embraced renunciation.

राष्या रहै गमाया जाय सति सति भाषंत श्री गोरषराय।
येकै कहि दुसरै मानी गोरष कहै वो बड़ों ग्यानी ॥243॥

By protecting a thing, it stays else if something is not protected, if one loses it, it goes away, it is destroyed. This is the true utterance of Gorakhnath. The one who says one thing but considers it as a symbol to mean something else is a knowledgable soul according to Gorakhnath.

(**Comment** – it seems that these two sabdis have half a portion, possibly the first half emphasizes on celibacy and the second talks about the tradition of yogis to express their thoughts through symbolic language.)

च्यंत अच्यंत ही उपजै च्यंता सब जुग षीण।
जोगी च्यंता बीसरै तौ होई अच्यंतहि लीन ॥244॥

Worry sprouts up without notice. The entire world is becoming weak by worry. Yogi forgets all worries. And in this manner merges in the worriless (beyond worry supreme consciousness).

गिरही को ग्यांन अमली का ध्यांन। बूचा को कान बेश्या को मान बैरागी।
अर माया स्यूं हाथ या पांचा को एको साथ ॥245॥

The attainment of supreme knowledge by the householder, the meditation done by an addict, a prostitute desirous of respect and the mendicant inclined towards material objects–these five can never attain liberation. All these are of the same type.

गिरही होय करि कथै ग्यांन, अमली होय करि धरै ध्यान।
बैरागी होय करै आसा, नाथ कहै तीन्यों षासा पासा ॥246॥

The householder can never be the knower of absolute knowledge. The one who is addicted to intoxicants cannot meditate. The one who has renounced everything should not expect anything from anybody.

रांड मुवा जती, धाये भोजन सती धन त्यागी।
नाथ कहै ये तीन्यौ अभागी ॥247॥

Nath says three kinds of people are unfortunate indeed–the one who turns into a yogi after the death of his wife, the hermit who has become one to partake of food given by people and the one who has given up everything after the destruction of his wealth.

पढ़ि पढ़ि पढ़ि केता मुवा कथि कथि कथि कहा कीन्ह।
बढ़ि बढ़ि बढ़ि बहु घट गया पारब्रह्म नहीं चीन्ह ॥248॥

So many people kept on studying holy scriptures and eventually died. So many left their bodies elucidating on the holy scriptures. What could they achieve-many people tried many kinds of techniques for spiritual practice but could still not realize the supreme principle.

सति सति बोलै गोरष राणा।
तीनि जणै का सङ्ग निवारौ नकट बूचा काणा ॥249॥

Gorakhnath says one should not keep the company of people without a nose, ears or eyes.

कदै न सोभै सुन्दरी सनकादिक के साथि।
जब तब कलंक लगाइसी काली हांडी हाथि ॥250॥

Women do not look appropriate with saints. Because the possibility of infamy always persists in their company. They are like a vessel with soot.

पासि बैठी सोभै नहीं साथि रमाई भुंडि।
गोरष कहै असतरी कहा सलह कह मुण्डि ॥251॥

The same meaning as implied above.

जरणा जोगी जुगि जुगि जीवै झरणा मरि मरि जाय।
षोजै तन मिलैं अविनासी अगह अमर पद पाय ॥252॥

The feeble yogi, the one capable of digesting the semen as well as the supreme realization–that is one who stabilizes it–lives till many eras. He searches for the imperishable in the body. He achieves the supreme state.

जप तप जोगी संजम सार। साले कंद्रप कीया छार।
येहा जोगी जग मैं जोय। दूजा पेट भरै सब कोय ॥253॥

The one who is into chanting and penance, considers self-restraint as the main objective, who has destroyed thoughts of desires from his childhood itself, one should consider such a one to be a yogi, the rest are just feeding their stomachs.

जोगेसर की इहै परछ्या, सबद बिचार्‌या षेलै।
जितना लाइक बासणा होवैं, तेतौ तामै मेल्है ॥254॥

The test of the God of yoga is that he thinks of the word and acts accordingly. He imparts as much knowledge to the disciples as they deserve.

चापि भरै तो बासण फूटै बारै रहै तौ छीजै।
बसत धणेरी बासण बोछी कहो गुर क्या कीजै ॥255॥

When the vessel of the body is filled to the brim with food the possibility of its breakage arises and the danger of an empty vessel breaking is also a reality. Similarly in this sequence of being full and the empty the doubt remains about what knowledge the Guru imparted to his disciple.

अवधू सहजै लैणा सहजै दैणा सहजै प्रीती ज्यौ लाई।
सहजै सहजै चलेगा रे अवधू तौ बासण करैगा समाई ॥256॥

Guru Gorakhnath addresses the yogi and says that the biggest sign of a seeker is to receive naturally and to give naturally. The yogi who moves in a natural way like this, the vessel of his body get filled wih the principle of spiritual practice.

तूंबी में तिरलोक समाया त्रिवेणी रबि चंदा।
बूझौ रे ब्रंभ गियानी अनहदनाद अभंगा ॥257॥

All the three worlds are absorbed in the musical instrument of the yogi. Along with this, the pure three pronged 'triveni' and the effulgence of the sun and the moon also merge in his spiritual practice.

सत्यो सीलं दोय असनांन त्रितीये गुर बाधक।
चत्रथे षीषा असनान पंचमे दया असनान।
ये पंच असनान निरमला निति प्रति करत गोरख बाला ॥258॥

त्रियाजीत ते पुरिषा गता मिलि भानंत ते पुरिषा गता।
बिसासघातगी पुरिषा गता कायरौ तत ते पुरिषा गता।
अभष भषंते पुरिषा गता। सबद हीण ते पुरिष गता।
उदिक राषंत ते पुरिषा गता। पर त्रिया राचंत ते पुरिषागता।
सति-सति भाषत गोरष बाला। इतना त्यागि रहो निराला ॥259-60॥

The ones who in return for control over their sense organs want to win over women, in other words they are won over by women. The protection of semen without spiritual experience leads to nothing. For the purpose of yoga, he should be celibate in all aspects.

पंडित भंडित अर कतवारी। पलटी सभा बिकलता नारी।
अपढ बिपर जोगी घरबारी। नाथ कहै रै पूता इनका सङ्ग निबारी ॥261॥

Nath says O son one should leave the company of a handicapped singer,a rag-picker, a dissolved assembly, an over-eager woman.

राति गई अधि राति गई बालक एक पुकारै।
है कोई नगर मैं सूरा बालक का दुःख निवारै ॥262॥

Many nights of ignorance went by. A beginner in yoga practice helplessly kept crying for a knowledgeable master who would put an end to his sorrows and give him an introduction to the absolute principle.

दिसटि पड़ै ते सारी कीमति कीमति सबद उचारं।
नाथ कथै अगोचर बाणी ताका वार न पारं ॥263॥

The spoken word is certainly very precious but its value is there only when the supreme principle hinted in the words is seen. Nath speaks such a language which cannot just be absorbed by sense organs.

सबद हमारा षरतर षांडा, रहणि हमारी सांची।
लेपै लिषी न कागद माडी, सो पत्रीं हम बाची ॥264॥

Guru Gorakhnath gives an introduction to his sect and says our word or sabdi is fast, expresses the right principle, our way of life is simple, natural and true-it is full of truthfulness. This is not the topic for an essay nor can it be written on a paper. The spiritual practice of a yogi is the text–which is done and then read, not read and then done.

मन बांधूंगा पवन स्यूं पवन बाधूंगा मन स्यूं।
तब बोलैगा कोवत स्युं।
मन तेरा की माई मूंडू, पवना दउं र बहाई।
मन पवन का गम नहीं, तहाँ रहै ल्यौ लाई ॥265॥

When the mind and breath meet then the unstruck sound will be heard. O mind consciousness – I will make the illusions of yours as a pupil and blow away the air because I am mediating at a place where the mind and breath cannot reach.

कोण देस स्यूं आये जोगी, कहा तुम्हारा भाव।
कौण तुम्हारी बहण भाणजी, कहां धरोगो पाव ॥266॥

O yogi ! from which country have you come? where do you desire to go? who is your sister and niece? where will you set foot? where will you go? who will you demolish?

पछिम देस स्यूं आये जोगी, उतर हमारा भाव।
धरती हमारी बहण भाणजी, पापी के सिरि पाव ॥267॥

I have come from the region of illusion. I am desirous of reaching the supreme consciousness. Kundalini energy is my sister and niece (who is begged to open the door upwards and we kill the sinner, we donate to the householder sister and niece. Yogi asks for alms from it, kundalini is a form of energy, it is maya. The web of a householder's life make illusion more and more tangible) gross and because of which the Kundalini falls asleep. The grossness of illusion has to be broken and the Kundalini has to be awakened. The Kundalini is supposed to reside in the Manipur chakra. Manipur chakra and the Kundalini in its contact is also called the earth.

सकति अहैड़ै मिस रिध, कोस बल स्यूं बागो।
गोरष कहैं चालती मारूं, कान गुरू तौ लागो ॥268॥

In this energy there was a commotion but I am also the disciple of my Guru I can kill it in motion. I can end the restless mind.

नाथ कहै मेरा दून्यौ पंथ पूरा। जत नहीं तौ सत का नीसूरा।
जत सत किरया हरणि हमारी। और बलि बाकलि देवि तुम्हारी ॥269॥

Nath says both my sects are complete. Physical restraint and the firm resolve of the heart cannot move without each other. This is our way of life–the brave cannot stay without the two.

कथणी कथै सों सिष बोलिये, बेद पढ़ै सौ नाती।
रहणी रहै सो गुरु हमारा, हम रहती का साथी ॥270॥

The one who narrates stories, keeps on elaborating and interpreting sacred scriptures–he is the student of the yogi, the one who studies the Vedas is the yogi's grandson and thus is on the third pedestal. The one who shows how life has to be led by example–is the master, the Guru. In this manner, the person who lives by example is worthy of being called a Guru.

रहता हमारै गुरू बोलिये, हम रहता का चेला।
मन मानैं तौ संगि फिरै, नहितर फिरै अकेला ॥271॥

In spiritual practice the one who integrates all of them in his being, he is the Guru and the rest are his pupils. If one feels like one can live together, else practice is possible in solitude also

दरसण माई दरसण बाप। दरसण माहीं आपै आप।
या दरसण का कोई जाणै भेव। सो आपै करता आपै देव ॥272॥
जिनि जाण्या तिनि षरा पहैचाण्या, वा अटल स्यूं लो लाई।
गोरष कहै अमें कानां सुणता, सो आंष्यां देष्या रै भाई।
बैठां बारै चलत अठारै, सूतां तूटै तीस।
कईथन करंतां चौसटि तूटै, क्यौं भजिवौ जगदीस ॥273॥

The breaths are twelve, thirty and sixty four. By these actions the breath breaks up whereas through the ajapa–japa one should have used these in remembering God's name.

So by all these actions, how can God be realized

नासिका अग्रे भ्रूमंडले अहनिस रहिबा थीरं।
माता गरभि जनम न ओयबा, बहुरि न पीयबा पीरं ॥275॥

The main sign of a yogi is to direct his breath at the tip of his nose and through breath control lead a life of patience. In this manner, the yogi who is always involved in his spiritual practice achieves the supreme state–nirvana–and is free from the continuous cycle of birth and death.

VERSES

Raag Ramagri

[1]

चारि पहर आलंगन निंद्रा, संसार जाइ बिषिया बाही।
ऊभी बांह गोरषनाथ पुकारै, मूल मे हारौ म्हारा भाई ॥टेक॥
अमावस पड़िवा मन घट सूंनाँ, सूंनाँ ते मंगलवारे।
भणता गुंणता ब्राह्मण बेद विचारै, दसमी दोष निबारै ॥1॥
पड़वा आनन्दा बीजसि चंदा, पांचौं लेबा पाली।
आठमि चौदसि ब्रत एकादसी, अंगि न लाऊं बाली ॥2॥
संमी सांझैं सोइबा मंझैं जागिबा, तृसंधि देणां पहरा।
तीनि पहर पर दोइ घट जाइबा, तिहां छै काल चा हेरा ॥3॥
बांमां अंगे सोइबा जमचा भोगबा संगे न पीवणां पांणीं।
इमतौ अजरांवर होइ मछिंद्र, बोल्यौ गोरष बांणीं ॥4॥1॥

The great yogi Gorakhnath addresses the human being caught up in the attractions of the world and the mind infatuated by material objects and says that losing the source (the consciousness of the human beings) is like being defeated in life. The no moon night (darkness), pareva and Tuesdays are all being spent like despondent days, in this manner the Brahmin kept on discussing the holy scriptures and talking about auspicious dates but still could not understand the meaning of life, just kept talking about auspicious and inauspicious dates.

The astrologers who talk about ashtami (eighth day of a

fortnight) and chaturdashi (fourteenth day of a fortnight) say that ekadashi (the eleventh day of the bright fortnight and the dark fortnight) is the purest of all days, they enumerate the process of prayers thrice a day, they sleep at night, wake up in the middle of it and talk about all kinds of auspicious and inauspicious dates. It is not possible for an individual to achieve liberation by these methods. Here by pranayama (deep breathing exercises) at an every three prahar(prahar is one–eighth of a day) one has to enter two bodies. This way, six time presents itself at one go.

Sleeping with a woman at night, engaging in sexual intercourse, cessation of yoga happens and the age lessens, such words are spoken repeatedly by Gorakhnath's Guru Machchendranath.

[2]

छाँटै तजो गुरू छाँटै तजौ तजौ लोभ मोह माया।
आत्मां परचै राषौ गुरुदेव सुन्दर काया ॥टेक॥
कांन्हीं पाव भेटीला गुरू, बिद्यानग्र सैं।
ताथैं मैं पाइला गुरू, तुम्हारा उपदेसैं ॥1॥
एतैं कछू कथीला गुरु, सर्वै भैला भोलै।
सर्ब रस षोईला गुरु बाघंनी चै षोलै ॥2॥
नाचत गोरषनाथ घूंघरी, चें धातैं।
सबैं कमाई षोई गुरू, बाघनीं चै राचैं ॥3॥
रस-कुस बहि गईला, रहि गई छोई।
भणत मछिंद्रनाथ पूता, जोग न होई ॥4॥
रस-कुस बहि गईला रहि गईला सारं।
बदंत गोरषनाथ गुर जोग अपारं ॥5॥
आदिनाथ नाती मछिन्द्रनाथ पूता।
षटपदी भणींलै गोरष अवधूता ॥6॥2॥

O Guru ! leave greed, attachment and illusion separate i.e. do not touch them. O Gurudev! keep knowing the atma or the individual spirit so that this beautiful body remains extant, is not destroyed. Met the Kanhapaav of Vidyanagar. It is from him that I came to know that you are caught in this web of women. Because of being related to the Guru, the message of Kanhapaav has been called a discourse. All that has been said meaning your downfall has been due to a delusion. You have lost the nectar of immortality in the lap of a tigress. The tigress is maya – illusion. Gorakh says O Guru you have started dancing to the rhythm of the tinkling anklets of the tigress and in the love for illusion you have lost all your spiritual earnings.

[3]

सुणौं हो मछिन्द्र गोरष बोलै, अगम गवंन कहूँ हेला।
निरति करी नैं नीकां सुणिज्यौ, तुम्हे सतगुर मैं चेला ॥टेक॥
कांमनी बहतां जोग न होई, भंग मुष परलै केता।
जहाँ उपजै तहाँ फिरि आवटै, च्यंतामनि चित एता ॥1॥
द्वादश षोड़ि षटांणां नौसत, जीव सीव ना बासा।
चौदह ब्रह्मांड नौ एक दंम है, हम हीं जाइ निरासा ॥2॥
पवन का नीर ले अंबर धोवै स्वासैं उसासै आया।
भणत गोरषनाथ इम होइ निरंतर, बीजैं बटक समाया ॥3॥3॥

Addressing his Guru Matsyendra who is caught up with undue attachment the great Yogi Gorakhnath says that moving towards the impassable place is the supreme duty of the yogi. It is good to be free from all desires of the world but this is not being made possible. The one who makes it possible I Gorakhnath am ready to be his disciple. Living with a woman it becomes very difficult to undergo the process of yoga. The mere thought of sexual union with a woman destroys all spiritual practice. For a person overcome by physical passion to go to the reproductive organ for intercourse is so shameful. This worry troubles the yogi day and night. In the dwadash linga (sun) there is no individual soul or the universal soul. in the fourteen worlds only the strength of the breath is seen. On this path one cleans the sky with the water in the form of air, that is, by the practice of breathing the yogi washes away all the sins, troubles. In this context Gorakhnathji says that the tree is hidden in the seed. The universal soul has the seed of the individual soul. This is the vision of the cosmos and the individual cosmos (body).

[4]

बोल्या गोरष घर जोई,
ये तत बूझै बिरला कोई, मेरे ग्यांनी ॥टेक॥
जोज्यौ जोज्यौ रे जहूँबा,
बन जोज्यौ तत्त राष्यौं तरियाली।
आसण इन्द्री जेणै आप बसि राष्यां,
तेणै पाया सर्ब निरंतर, मेरे ग्यांनी ॥1॥
मन माँहें तेणैं तन तार्‌यां,
मन बिसवासैं मिलणां।
मन मैं कुंभ कलस रस भरिया,
तेणैं मनवै अलष लाषाया, मेरे ग्यांनीं ॥2॥
पै र जोई नै एद्धा पुरिष पधार्‌या,
पुरिष नी पारिषा पाई।
पुरिषै मिलि पुरिष रस राष्या,
पुरिषैं पुरिष निपाया, मेरे ग्यांनी ॥3॥
जिहि घरि चंद सूर नहिं ऊगै,
तिहिं धरि होसी उजियारा।
तिहां जे आसण पूरौ तौ सहज,
का भरौ पियाला, मेरे ग्यांनीं ॥4॥
मन मांहिला हीरा बीधा सो सोधीनै लीणां,
सो षांणां सो पीवणां मछिंद्र।
प्रसादैं जती गोरष बोल्या,
बिमल रस जोई जोई नैं मिलंणा, मेरे ग्यांनीं ॥5॥4॥

The one who welcomed the seer, the soul in his heart and in this manner obtained an introduction with the soul, that person by contact with the soul experiences supreme bliss. And in this manner, through the supreme soul he gives rise to his own the voice of conscience, the eternal spirit. He experiences the supreme reality.

Where without the rise of the sun and the moon there is the light of supreme spirit at the place sitting in a yogic asana gives a natural flowing joy.

The self knowledge that one attains is like a diamond(bindha) that the seeker obtains. That is his diet. He sees that(knowledge) and obtains natural bliss.

[5]

गोरष जोगी तोला तोलै,
भिड़ि भिड़ि बाधीलै रतन अमोलै ॥टेक॥
आछै आछै बिंद न पड़िबा कंध।
लाष तोला मोल जाये जे एक षिसै बिंद ॥1॥
जैसी मन उपजै तैसा करम करै।
कांम क्रोध लोभ लै संसार सूंनां मरै ॥2॥
गगन सिषर आछै अंदर पांणीं।
मरतां मूढां लोकां मरम न जांणीं ॥3॥
पूनिम महिला चंदा जिम नारी संगै रहणां।
ग्यांन रतन हरि लीन्ह परांणां ॥4॥
आदि नाथ नातो मछिंद्र नाथ पूता।
ब्यंद तोलै राषीले गोरष अवधूता ॥5॥5॥

The Yogi Gorakh does business with great care and inspection. He keeps the most precious stones (semen and the supreme reality) safely by tying them into a cloth and knotting it. If the bindu is there or if the bindu is indestructible then the body (shoulders etc) would not be destroyed. In the higher reaches–the brahmrandhra-part of the Sahasrara–the crown chakra the ambrosia keeps flowing from the moon(and without the help of yoga it is just soaked up by the sun at the root chakra–the mooladhar) the result is that it keeps becoming weak. The condition of man, though actually complete, is the same when he lives with a woman.

[6]

सोनां ल्यौ रस सोनां ल्यौ, मेरी जाति सुनारी रे।
धंमणि धमीं रस जांमणि जांम्या,
तब गगन महा रस मिलिया रे ॥टेक॥
आपैं सोनां नै आप सुनारी, मूल चक्र अंगीठा।
अहरणि नाद नैं ब्यंद हथौड़ा, घटिस्यूं गगन बईठा ॥1॥
अषै आरण नै विषै कोइला, सहज, फूक दो नलियां।
चंद सूर दोऊ समि करि राष्या आपै आप जु मिलिया ॥2॥
रती का कांम मासे की चोरी, रती मैं मासा चोरै।
मासा चोरि रहै मासे मैं, इहि बिधि गरथैं जोरै ॥3॥
अरधे सोनां उरधै सोनां, मध्ये सोनम् सोनां।
तीनि सुन्यं की रहनीं जानैं, ता घटि पाप न पुंनां ॥4॥
उनमनि डांडी मन तराजू, पवन कीया गदियांना।
आपै गोरषनाथ जोषण बैठा, तब सोनां सहज समांनां ॥5॥6॥

I am a goldsmith by caste. Take the gold of self-realization, ambrosia from me. By the breathing practice which resembles the sound from a blast furnace I perfected the ajapa japa. By the ajapa japa the restless mind is stilled. By this then in the crown of the head the supreme experience, the ambrosia of yoga is experienced.

In our reach is our body which is a gross, small thing, from this, one should take the great self realization principle and should reside there. In this one should save the wealth (of spirit) the wealth is stored in the knot (granthi).

[7]

जांणानैं जोसी जोओ नै विचारी, पहलां पुरिष कै नारी जी ॥टेक॥
बाइ नहीं तहूं वां बादल नाहीं, बिन थाभां बाबै मंडप रचीया।
तिहां आप उपांवन हारी जी ॥1॥
बाप नहीं होतौ तिह्यां बैठणड़ै रे, माता बाल कुंवारी जी।
पीवनैं पौढ्यो माझौ पालनैं, तिहां हूँ हीं ज हिडोलँन-हारी जी ॥2॥
ब्रह्मा बिष्न नैं आदि महेस्वर, ये तीन्यूं मैं जाया।
इन तिहुँवां नी मैं घर घरणीं, द्वैकर मोरी माया जी ॥3॥

गंग जुमन मोरी षाटलड़ी रे, हंसा गवन तुलाई जी।
धरणि पाथरणौं नैं आभ पछेवड़ौ, तौ भी सौड़ी न माई जी ॥4॥
षांडतडी मांझौ जनम बदीतौ, चांवल सांबि न सारी जी।
मछिंद्र प्रसादैं जती गोरष बोल्या, ये तत जोओ बिचारी जी ॥5॥7॥

O learned one ! see and contemplate whether a man was born first or a woman, first it was God or illusion. The supreme consciousness has created the chamber without pillars where there is neither air nor clouds, there the one who gives birth – illusion is there. When the father was not there, then also she was present. This mother–illusion–is a child maiden. She rocked her owner in the cradle. Brahma, Vishnu and Maheshwar are all born from illusion. I, maya, illusion am the housewife in the homes of these three. In both their hands my illusion resides (whatever work they do, is through my illusion). Ida and Pingala nerves are my charpoy and the prana or life force is the blanket. The earth is the stone and the water (that is, the entire universe) is my part. That is also not enough for me to spread my sheet. The entire life went by being pounded in the vessel and still the rice could not be cleaned up similarly the human beings bound in the shackles of karma cannot find relief from sorrow. The process of cleaning the rice from the husk is called sieving. In this the sieve is quickly moved to the left and the right by which the clean rice grains come to the fore. By the grace of Machchandarnath, Gorakh says that try to contemplate on this principle.

[8]

चाल्योरे पांचौ भाइला तेणैं बन जाइला,
जहाँ दुष सुष नांव न जानिये ॥टेक॥
षेती करौं तौ मेह बिन सूकै।
बनिज करौं तौ पूंजी तूटै ॥1॥
अस्त्री करौं तो घर भंग ह्वैला।
मिंत्र करौं तौ बिसहर भैला ॥2॥

जुवटै षैलौं ती बैठड़ौ हारौं।
चोरी करौ तौ प्यंडड़ौं भारौं ॥3॥
बन षंड जांऊं तौ बिरछ न फलना।
नगरी मैं जाऊंतौ भिष्या न मिलनां ॥4॥
बोल्या गोरषनाथ मछिंद्र का पूता।
छाड़ि नैं माया भया अवधूता ॥5॥8॥

O brothers five! (five sense organs) let us go to the forest where there is no pleasure or pain. Here everything converts into either pleasure or pain. The eternal spirit, the atma is the best God. He is the Guru, he is the absolute principle Shiva. It is inside the body. People do not know how to serve it but run to appease other deities all in vain. The nine doors have the nine hands. In the triveni, the God of the universe is there. And in the brahmrandhra, the tenth door–Kedarnath, Shiva–the absolute supreme consciousness is there. If one is able to obtain the real principle of the path of yoga, Gorakhnath says that one can traverse the sorrows of the world.

[9]

गुरदेव स्यंभ देव सरीर भींतरिये।
आत्मां उत्तिंम देव ताही की न जांणौं सेव।
आंन देव पूजि-पूजि इमही मरिये ॥टेक॥
नवे द्वारे नवे नाथ, तृबेणीं जगन्नाथ,
दसवें द्वारि केदारं ॥1॥
जोग, जुगति सार तौ भौ तिरिये पारं।
कथंत गोरषनाथ विचारं ॥2॥9॥

O desires of mine! Wind up your business. The prana purush has taken birth. It means that the consciousness and the breath have come together (this coming together has been made possible due to pranayama–the deep breathing technique) the awakened yogi is now busy with the efforts towards the soul. He has to enter the city in the form of the body. The outgoing and incoming breath is like chanting which does 21,600 chants or japas every day. The vital life breath or prana flows freely in the Ida, Pingala and Sushumna nerves (energy channels).

[10]

मनसा मेरी ब्यौपार बांधौ, पवन पुरषि उतपनां।
जाग्यौ जोगी अध्यात्म लागौ, काया पाटण मैं जांनां ॥टेक॥
इकबीस सहंस षटसां आदू, पवन पुरिष जप माली।
इला प्यंगुला सुषमन नारी, अहनिसि बहै प्रनाली ॥1॥
षटसां षोडि कवल दल धारा, तहां बसै ब्रह्मचारी।
हंस पवन ज फूलन पैठा, नौ सै नदी पनिहारी ॥2॥
गङ्गा तीर मतीरा अवधू, फिरि फिरि बणिजां कीजै।
अरध बहन्ता उरधैं लीजै, रवि सस मेला कीजै ॥3॥
चंद सूर दोऊ गगन बिलूधा, भईला घोर अंधारं।
पंच बाहक जब न्यंद्रा पौढ्या, प्रगढ्या पौलि पगारं ॥4॥
काया कंथा, मन जोगोटा, सत गुर मुझ लाषाया।
भणंत गोरषनाथ रूड़ा राषौ, नगरी चोर मलाया ॥5॥10॥

According to yogis a person the total number of breaths a person takes in a day is 21, 600. Along with these breaths the natural sounds of soham accompanies in process of inhalation and exhalation- it is also called ajapa japa–this is happening automatically with the breath. We have to deliberately take our attention there. The flow has broken from the subtle to form the gross. The Swadhisthan chakra (energy centre situated above the organ of generation) and Vishuddhi chakra (energy centre situated behind the throat region) are formed in this flow. In this flow and in these chakras is the abode of the celibate and the soul. The nine hundred rivers, i.e. the entire system of nerves is like the lady who goes to fetch water and then pours the flow (of breath) on the hans (swan) individual and the branch of the soul blossoms and the Ida nerve produces the cool fruit watermelon (symbolizing the knowledge that bestows coolness and tranquility), so one should trade this fruit again. The downward flow (of ambrosia or breath) should be brought upwards into the abode of the supreme consciousness and the sun and the moon nerves should be made to come together

Because of the predominance of the Sushumna in the Brahmrandhra the other two energy channels–Ida and Pingala are lost and there is darkness (symbolically speaking) the five sense organs thought night had set in and slept off. The main door could be seen and the way inside could also be accessed, that is, the way to a spiritual life opened up.

The consciousness (mind) is a yogi and the body is his rag. This secret was told to me by my Guru. Gorakhnath warns to keep this secret guarded safely because many thieves are roaming about in the city.

[11]

अवधू बोल्या तत बिचारी, पृथ्वी मैं बकबाली।
अष्टकुल परबत जल बिन तिरिया, अदबुद अचंभा भारी ॥टेक॥
मन पवन अगम उजियाला, रवि ससि तार गयाई।
तीनि राज त्रिविधि कुल नांहीं, चारि जुग सिधि बाई ॥1॥
पांच सहंस मैं षट अपूठा, सप्त दीप अष्ट नारी।
नव षंड पृथी इकबीस मांहीं, एकादसि एक तारी ॥
द्वादसी त्रिकुटी यला पिंगुला, चवदसि चित मिलाई।
षोड़स कवल दल सोल बतीसौ, जुरा मरन भौ गमाई ॥2॥
दसवैं द्वार निरंजन उनमन बासा, सबदैं उलटि समांनां।
भणंत गोरषनाथ मछींद्र नां पूता अबिचल थीर रहांनां ॥3॥11॥

The yogi contemplated and then spoke about the supreme principle which is considered worthless on this earth. In this enumeration of the supreme principle 16 dates including the full moon night and the no moon night are used to describe yoga. Some dates are not clearly specified. It is a matter of great surprise that one should swim the Ashtukul mountain without the help of any water. Ashtukul mountain is the gross physical body and the water is the subtle illusion. In the physical body there is both illusion And the soul. When he separates from water (illusion) remains no doubt of a person attaining liberation. By the restraint on the mind and breath one could achieve impassable light in front of which the sun, moon and the stars hide, the rule of the previous empires ceases to be. On the fourth, In the world there is are loud drumbeats of attainments, spiritual perfection. On the fifth, there is placement in the crown chakra. On the sixth, one turned inwards. On the seventh the lamp of divine light was lit. on the eighth the Kundalini power became activated. Ninth, the nine-parts earth and 21 universe are in the body itself. The tenth is described in the end. On the eleventh–ekadashi–there is total deep meditation practice–Samadhi. Twelveth Ida- Pingala have merged in trikuti with Sushumna. Fourteenth the consciousness has merged with the supreme consciousness. On the full moon or no moon night–the 16 petalled lotus and the mastery over Vishuddhi chakra the yogi has received the 32 signs and has crossed the fear of death – and fear of old age and death. Tenth–by the unmani Samadhi–turned pure and in the tenth door merged in the word from which had originated (the son of Matsyendra disciple) Gorakh says that in this manner got stabilized in one's roots.

[12]

ॐ नमो सिवाई बाबू ॐ नमो सिवाइ।
अह निसि बाइ मंत्र कौणें रे उपाइ ॥
भ्यंने भ्यंने अष्यरे जे देवै रे बुझाइ,
ताका मैं चेला बाबू सो गुरू हमार ॥टेक॥
ॐकार आछै बाबू मूल मंत्र धारा,
ॐकार ब्यापीले सकल संसारा।
ॐकार नाभी हृदै देव गुर सोई,
ॐकार साधे बिना सिधि न होई ॥1॥
नादैं लीन ब्रह्मा नांदै लीना नर हरि,
नादैं लीना ऊमापती जोग ल्यौ धरि धरि।
नाद हीं तौ आछै बाबू सब कछू, निधांनां,
नाद हीं थैं पाइये परम निरवांनां ॥2॥

बाई बाजै बाई गाजै बाई धुनि करै,
बाई षट चक्र बेधै अरधैं उरधैं मधि फिरै।
सोहं बाई हंसा रूपी प्यंडै बहै,
बाई कै प्रसादि ब्यंद गुरमुष रहै ॥3॥
मन मारै मन मरै मन तारै मन तिरै।
मन जै अस्थिर होइ तृभुवन भरै।
मन आदि मन अंत मन मधें सार।
मन ही तैं छूटै बाबू विषै विकार ॥4॥
सक्ति रूपी रज आछै शिव रूपी ब्यंद।
बारह कला रव आछै सोलह कला चन्द।
चारि कला रवि की जे ससि घरि आवै।
तौ सिव सक्ती सँमि होवै, अन्त कोई न पावै ॥5॥
एही राजा राम आछै सर्वे अंगे बासा।
येही पांचौं तत बाबू सहजि प्रकासा।
ये ही पांचौं तत बाबू समझि समांनां।
बदंत गोरष इम हरि पद जांनां ॥6॥12॥

Om Namah Shivay. Salutations to Lord Shiva. Salulations to Lord Shiva. The breath keeps on moving in the body day and night and continuously and automatically the natural chant of soham goes on in the body. Who produced this mantra (the one who makes me explain the various letters of this mantra is my Guru and I, his disciple) says Gorakhnath.

The natural mantra of the breath–sohum-has its roots in Om. Om has lead to the flow of all creation. Omkar mantra is present in the entire universe. Omkar resides in the navel (swadhistan chakra) in the heart (anahata) the 16 or 12 petalled lotus. Omkar is the deity, Omkar is the Guru. Without practicing Omkar, perfection cannot be reached.

The root omkar in it's outer expressed form of sound is Brahma, Vishnu and Mahesh who are engrossed and absorbed. Protect it well and accept this naad/ primeval sound and practice yoga. Naad is home to everybody.

It is the sound of the breath. Piercing the six chakras the breath rises up, moves down and generally spreads all over. Soham, hanso– this mantra in the form of breath is flowing in every body. Because of the result of breath the semen stabilizes in the brahmarandhra– the crown chakra.

It is the mind, the consciousness that kills. The mind itself is a tool to subdue (kill it's desires). It is the mind that elevates and the mind that gets elevated. If the mind becomes stable the three worlds can be emancipated. The mind is in the beginning, the mind is at the end and the mind is in the middle. Implying that essentially mind is the eternal principle. The various material temptations that disturb the mind can only be controlled by the mind.

The blood is a form of Shakti – supreme spiritual power and the bindu – the supreme semen is a form of Shiva. The outer twelve aspects are of the sun (situated in the muladhar chakra and adept in soaking up ambrosia) and sixteen aspects of the moon (situated in the Sahasrasara chakra and leading to a free flow of divine ambrosia. At present the aspects of the sun are prominent which means Shakti or illusion are prominent. if the four aspects of the sun merge in the moon and Shiva and Shakti will merge) and will receive that supreme experience which has no end.

This ultimate experience which can be reached , this principle is King Rama (meaning it is a form of the soul) which resides in every organ of the body. This naturally throws light on all the principles. The five elements cannot stay without it and after the realization all the five elements merge in it. Gorakhnath says, in this manner supreme reality comes to be known.

[13]

अवधू जाप जपौ जपमाली चीन्हौं, जाप जप्यां फल होई।
अगम जापं जपीला गोरष, चीन्हत बिरला कोई ॥टेक॥
कवल बदन काया करि कंचन, चेतनि करौ जपमाली।
अनेक जनम नां पातिग छूटै, जपंत गोरष चवाली ॥1॥
एक अषीरी एकंकार जपीला, सुंनि अस्थूल दोइ वांणी।
प्यंड ब्रंह्मांड समि तुलि ब्यापीले, एक अषिरी हम गुरमुषि जांणीं ॥2॥

द्वै अषिरी दोई पष उधारीला, निराकार जापं जपियां।
जे आप सकल सिष्टि उतपंनां, ते जाप श्रीगोरषनाथ कथियां ॥3॥
त्रिअषिरी त्रिकोटी जपीला, ब्रह्मकुंड निज थांनं।
अजपा जाप जपंता गोरष, अतीत अनुपम ग्यांनं ॥4॥
चौ अक्षिरी चतर वेद थापिला, चारि षोंणी चारि वांणी।
मछिंद्र प्रसादै जती गोरष बोल्या, अजपा जपिला धीर रहांणी ॥5॥13॥

O perfectly enlightened yogi! Recognize the string of prayer beads and chant that mantra by which you receive the result that obtains from actual experience of the supreme reality. That impassable chant that Gorakh did is known only to a rare few.

The lotus chakra is the mouth, the body (beads of the string) are gold and consciousness (chaitanya) is the entire string of beads. Gorakh says that if one chants like this, the sins of many past births are washed away. The seeker chants mantras verbally. Those letters of the mantras have different numbers. For example the 12 letter mantra, the 16 letter mantra but the mantra that Gorakhnath chants has no relation to the outer voice that is why the words one lettered, two lettered take on a different meaning altogether. For him, the void and the gross, the one pertaining to the soul and the outer voice related, the non-dual supreme reality which unifies the outer and inner voice, the one that is spread in the individual body and the universal body evenly, that chanting is the one word mantra chanting. This one letter chanting has been obtained by us through the mouth of the Guru.

The two letter chanting is that both the aspects of this world and the other world, the formless and the one with form, the subtle and the gross–have been elevated. This way, the chant that has given rise to the entire creation, it has been enumerated by Gorakhnath.

In the trikuti–the interval between the eyebrows–the space where the forehead and the start of the nose meet is the place of the supreme consciousness and the soul. By the ajapa japa(effortless chanting) Gorakhnath has received the unique knowledge and this is the three letter mantra.

The creator Brahma has produced four kinds of beings–the one which germinates, the one that is produced by hot moisture, the egg-born and the one born from the womb, and he produced four kinds of vaani (voice, Speech–sehej, sanjam, supai and ateet). staying between them and chanting ajapa japa and staying stable and calm–this is the four letter mantra–Gorakhnath writes this with the blessings of his Guru Matsyendranath.

[14]

रमि रमिता सौ गहि चौगांनं, काहे भूलत हौ अभिमांन।
धरन गनन बिचि नहीं अंतरा, केवल मुक्ति मैदांन ॥टेक॥
एक मैं अनंत अनंत मैं एकै, एकै अनंत उपाया।
अंतरि एक सौं परचा हूवा, तब अनंत एक मैं समाया ॥1॥
अहरणि नाद नै ब्यंद हथौड़ा, रवि ससि षालां पवनं।
मूल चापि डिढ आसणि बैठा, तब मिटि गया आवागवनं ॥2॥
सहज पलांण पवन करि घोड़ा, लै लगांम चित चबका।
चेतनि असवार ग्यांन गुरू करि, और तजौ सब ढबकाई ॥3॥
तिल कै नाकै तुभवन सांध्या, कीया भाव विधाता।
सौ तौ फिर आपण हीं हूवा, जाकौं ढूंढण जाता ॥4॥
आस्ति कहूँ तौ कोइ न पतीजै, बिन आस्ति (अनंत सिध) क्यूं सीधा।
गोरष बौलै सुणौ मछिंद्र हीरै हीरा बीधा ॥5॥14॥

Play the game of polo with the supreme consciousness Rama. Why do you forget in arrogance ? there is no difference between the earth and the sky. Not believing in this difference, meaning, to have an undifferentiated vision is the ground for kaivalya liberation.

In one supreme reality the entire limitless universe resides. And in the limitless universe, there is only one supreme reality that resides. That alone has given birth to this limitless universe. When one meets that supreme reality in one's heart, then the entire limitless universe merges into one.

The Anahata nada is the anvil and the semen is the hammer. The Ida, Pingala nerves are the blowpipes to blow the air. Sit firmly in an asana that controls the movement of the Muladhara chakra and work like a blacksmith which will lead to the cessation of the act of coming and going in this world.

The effortlessness is the saddle, breath is the horse, the rhythm is the rein, the soul is the rider and in this manner leave everything apart and pursue knowledge, acquire it.

I articulated the three worlds, prepared a goal, saw everything, inspected all but I could not find the supreme reality which was hidden in a sesame seed. But when God produced that emotion in my heart which I was on a search to find out I became that only.

When I say that the supreme reality exists, nobody believes me but if it does not exist then why do so many seekers undergo difficult penance to achieve it. That real thing is, O Machchandar (Matsyendranath) that all these practices have a goal–that of piercing a diamond with a diamond, the individual soul should merge with the universal soul. It means that God in the form of supreme reality exists that is why the seekers undertook so much trouble.

[15]

ततबणिजोल्यौ तत बणिजील्यौ, ज्यूं मीरा मन पतियाई ॥टेक॥
सहज गोरषनाथ बणिज कराई, मोरे मन उड़ियानी आई ॥1॥
सुरहट घाट अम्हे बणिजारा, सुंनि हमारा पसारा।
लेण न जाणौं देण न जाणौं एद्वा बजण हमारा ॥2॥
भणंत गोरषनाथ मछिंद्र का पूता, एद्वा बणिज ना अरथी।
करणीं अपणीं पार उतरणां, बचने लेणां साथीं ॥3॥15॥

Do the business of the Truth in a way that my faith is strengthened that there is purity in the business. Gorakhnath engages in the trade of natural , true knowledge. The five sense organs are the buffalo, and the nine openings are cows for whom a warehouse or store of natural emotion has been made which means their tendencies have also become natural. My mind is taking a high flight.

I am a trader of high standards. I have spread the supreme void – meaning ‘shunya’there is nothing to sell and the other meaning of 'shunya' is supreme consciousness. I do not know how to take nor do I know how to give, this is how our trade is in which there is no need to give and take. The disciple of Machchandar says that the meaning of such a trade is that by the support of the words of the Guru, attain liberation.

[16]

मांहरा रे बैरागी जोगी, अहनिसि भोगी जोगणि संग न छाड़ै।
मानसरोवर मनसा झूलंती आवै, गगन मंडल मठ माँडै रे ॥टेक॥
कौंण अस्थांनिकि तोरा सासू नैं सुसरा, कौंण अस्थांन क तोरा बासा।
कौंण अस्थानंक तू नै जोगणि भेटी, कहां मिल्या घर बासा ॥1॥
नाभ अस्थांन-क मोरा सासू नैं सुसरा, ब्रह्म अस्थांन-क मोरा बासा।
इला प्यंगुला जोगण भेंटी सुषमन मिल्या घर बासा ॥2॥
कांम क्रोध बाली चूंनां कीधा, कंद्रप कीया कपूरं।
मन पवन दो काथ सुपारी, उनमनीं तिलक सींदूरं ॥3॥
ग्यांन गुरू दोऊ तूबा अम्हारे, मनसा चेतनि डांडी।
उनमनी तांती बाजन लागी, यहि विधि तृष्णां षाडीं ॥4॥
एण सतगुरि अम्हे परणांब्या, अबला बाल कुवांरी।
मछिंद्र प्रसाद श्रीगोरष बोल्या, माया नां भौ टारी ॥5॥16॥

Our yogi who has renounced all (the mind) stays engaged in sensuous pleasures all the time. The mind in the form of a yogi never leaves the side of the yogini. In the pond of the mind, the desires come dancing away and make a home for themselves in the crown of the head.

O yogi, which place do your mother and father-in-law belong to, from where do you come, where did you meet the yoginis, which place did you get to reside

My in-laws stay in the navel (Manipur chakra). I am a resident of the brahm randhra (crown of the head) meaning that I am myself the absolute principle, god. By doing Ida and Pingala pranayam I met the yogini and I got to stay in the Sushumna.

In the navel or the Manipur chakra the Kundalini energy lives, it is believed, this energy source, through the illusion the universe has been created. That is why it is considered the abode of Brahma and Savitri. They are called the in-laws because they give rise to gross illusion.

Yogi uses the illusion in the form of the mind in a way that it does not get strengthened. He burnt away anger and lust like ash or camphor or the God of love, Kamdev. The mind and breath–they became betel nut and catechu and made a vermillion of it for the pure consciousness state- turiya.

This means getting the illusion have a taste of illusory objects and thus making one's illusory existence experience the supreme reality.

Knowledge and the Guru are two tents and the conscious desire is the pole of the tent. The threads of pure consciousness on this tent broke into a rhythm. in this way we destroyed desires. The maiden illusion has been married to me by my Guru, so I have become the master, the owner of illusion. And all fear of illusion has been cast away.

[17]

तत बेली लो तत बेली, लो, अवधू गोरषनाथ जांणीं।
डाल न मूल पहुप नहीं छाया, बिराधि करै बिन पांणी ॥टेक॥
काया कुंजर तेरी बाड़ी अवधू, सत गुर बेलि रूपांणीं।
पुरिष पांणती करै शणियांणौ नीकैं बालि घरि आंणी ॥1॥
मूल एद्वा जेद्वा ससिहर अवधू, पांन एद्वा जद्वा भांणं।
फल एद्वा जेद्वा पूनिम चंदा, जोउ जोउ जांण सुजांणं ॥2॥
बेलडियां दौं लागी अवधू, गगन पहूती झाला।
जिम जिम बेलीं दाझबा लागी, तब मेल्है कूं पल डाला ॥3॥
काटत बेली कूंपल मेल्ही सींचतड़ां कुमलाये।
मछिंद्र प्रसादैं जती गोरष बोल्या, नित नवेलड़ी थाये ॥4॥17॥

O enlightened yogi ! Gorakhnath knows the creeper that is the truth. This creeper does not have any branches, no roots, no flowers, no shadow and it grows without water. O yogi, in your body, is this garden where the good master has planted this creeper.

The farmer in the form of breath irrigates it a lot and as a result brings the beautiful plant home. It's source is like the moon – that is, it's source is in the crown chakra, in the moon situated there and its leaves are like the sun. The moon represents the cool flowing knowledge and the sun represents the fiery sun. This means that the home of maya or illusion is also the supreme truth. This illusion has its roots in the Sahasrara or crown chakra and in the Muladhar chakra its entire development takes place. It 's fruit is like the full moon. If someone takes complete benefit from it then he gets to have the divine nectar (in the form of moon) only the enlightened ones can know this.

When this creeper catches the fire of worldly sorrows it is so formidable that it's flames reach the sky but as the fire spreads the creeper starts moving (the symbolic meaning is that the fire of emotion is conducive for the spread of illusion. The higher the fire of thirst in the world, the more the human being gets entangled in it. This creeper cannot be cut despite continuous efforts. But if one waters it will cool ambrosia of knowledge from the moon, it starts drying up. But this creeper cannot be destroyed forever. Illusion can end for a person but it will continue to tie the world in knots. Every single person has to disentangle themselves. This way the illusion in the form of the creeper is always thriving it stays stable)by the grace of his Guru Matsyendranath Gorakh says this.

[18]

बूझौ पंडित ब्रह्म गियांनं, गौरष बोलै जाण सुजांनं ॥टेक॥
बीज बिन निसपती मूल बिन बिरषा पांन फूल बिन फलिया।
बांझ केरा बालूड़ा, प्यंगुल तरवरि चढ़िया ॥1॥
गगन बिना चंद्रम बाह्मांड बिन सूरं, झूझ बिन रचिया थानं।
ए परमारथ जे नर जांणैं, ता घटि परम गियांनं ॥2॥
सुंनि न अस्थूल ल्यंग नहीं पूजा, धुंनि बिन अनहद गाजै।
बाड़ी बिन पहुप पहुप बिन साइर, पवन बिन भृंगा छाजै ॥3॥
राह बिन गिलिया अगनि बिन जलिया, अंबर बिन जलहर भरिया।
यहु परमारथ कहौ हो पंडित, रुग जुग स्यांम अथरबन पढ़िया ॥4॥

ससंमवेद सोहं प्रकासं, धरती गगन न आदं।
गंग जमुन बिच षेलै गोरष, गुरू मछिंद्र प्रसादं ॥5॥18॥

Learned one! Try to understand the supreme knowledge. The one which is the right knowledge, Gorakh calls it the supreme knowledge. Knowledge or the supreme truth has originated without a seed – it has no cause. It is a tree without any source or roots, it blossoms without leaves or flowers, that is, the rules of nature do not bind it. It is the child of a barren woman. It is the moon without the sky, it is the sun without the universe, it is the battle without the ground. The one who knows this supreme truth, the ultimate knowledge arises in his body.

He is neither a void nor is he grossly physical, he does not have any signs nor is he worshipped. Without any sound, the anahata nada strikes away. It is the flower without a garden, the pollen without the flower and the fragrance without the air which is spread all around, the air makes the fragrance reach the bumble-bee. They are hovering around the flowers.

It swallows up without the planet Rahu. It burns without fire. Without the sky, clouds gather. O learned pundits, you the ones who have read the Rigveda, Yajurveda, Sama veda and Atharva veda. Describe this spiritual meaning. What is the definitive meaning ?how do you make it happen?. The experience of the supreme reality without any support is not the work of any cause. These words are pointing towards the destruction of the world of illusion and the experience of bliss which is a pointer towards the experience of the supreme consciousness. This is the self generating self illumined soham which is neither on earth or on sky or in the water. It can also mean the one which does not have a beginning. By the grace of his Guru Matsyendranath Gorakh is playing in the Sushumna which is in the middle of Ganga (Ida) and Yamuna (Pingala)

[19]

बदंत गोरषनाथ दसबीं द्वारी सुर्ग नैं केदार चढ़िया।
इकबीस ब्रह्मण्ड ना सिषर ऊपरि, ससमवेद ऊचरिया ॥टेक॥

द्वादस दल भींतरि रवि सक्ती, ससि षोड़स सिव थांनं।
मूल सहंसर जीव सींब धरि उनमनी अचल धियांयनं ॥1॥
नाद अनाहद गरजै गेणं, पछिम ऊग्या भांणं।
दक्षिण डोबी उत्तर नाचै, पाताल पूरब तांणं ॥2॥
चंद सूर नीं मुंद्रा कीन्हीं, धरणि भस्म जल मेला।
नादी ब्यंदी सींगी आकासी, अलख गुरू नां चेला ॥3॥
तीन सै साठि थेगली कंथी, इकवीस सहंस छ सै धागं।
बहतरि नाड़ीं सुई नवासी, बावन बीर सीया लागं ॥4॥
इली सोधि धरि प्यंगुली पूरी, सुषमनी चढ़ असमांनं।
मछिंद्र प्रसादै जती गोरष बोल्या, निरंजन सिधि नैं थानं ॥5॥19॥

Gorakh says that he has climbed to the tenth door (brahmrandhra) to the abode of Shiva- the place for heaven and liberation. And above the twenty one universes am pronouncing the experience with the self. The sun situated in the Muladhar chakra has 12 aspects and is the abode of Shakti and the moon has 16 aspects and the abode of Shiva in the crown chakra–so the Muladhar converges in the Sahasrara. And the individual soul merges with the universal thought in deep meditation.

In the sky- trikuti–the anahata nada is making a sound. The sun has risen in the west (sushumna) it means the process of meaning the moon has started. In the south (the power of the Muladhar and the Swadhishthan chakra is dancing in the North, that is, the crown chakra. The nether world (patala loka) Swadhishthan is being drawn to the East, that is towards the direction of the knowledge meaning towards the crown chakra, is happening.

The sun and the moon (Ida and Pingala) both the energy channels have been closed and Sushumna has been opened. This is our mudra. We put the ash of the earth (worldly pleasures) in the water (to rub on the body, thus the yogi is rubbing ashes) in this manner the ones who give prominence to the nada or the sound, or the one who give importance to protection of celibacy or the ones who give importance to playing the rhythm of Shringi nada similar to Anahata nada to the ones who focus on the trikuti all become the disciples of the guru.

Nath yogis believe that there are 360 bones in the human body. These bones are the various patches from which the tatters are sown. A person breathes 21,600 times a day are the threads by which the patches are sown together. 72 nerves. 89 needles are there and 52 brave consciousness is the tailor. Ida nerve is sown into the Pingala completely. And then should move completely into the Sushumna into the sky. In this way by the grace of his Guru Matsyendranath, Gorakh has told about the place of pure consciousness.

[20]

आंबलियौ थलि मौरियौ ऊपरि जींव बिजौरे फलियौ।
सो फल षातां लागै मीठौ, जांणै रे जिन गुरु प्रसादै दीठौ ॥टेक॥
ऊँट सिचाणैं जब ग्रह्यौ जाइ कैरो डाली बैठो।
बांझै बेटा जनमियूं नैणें पुरिष न दीठौ ॥1॥
लाकड़ डूबै सिल तिरै, देषतां जग जाइ।
ऊट प्रनालै बहि गयो, सुसिल्यो पौली न माइ ॥2॥
डूंगरि मंछा जलि सुसा पांणीं मैं दौं लागा।
अहरट बहै तुसासवां, सूलै कांटा भागा ॥3॥
एक गाइ नौ बछड़ा, पंच दुहेबा जाइ।
एक फूल सोलह करंडियां मालनि मन मैं हरिष न माइ ॥4॥
पगां बिहूनड़ै चोरी कोधी, चोरी नैं आंणी गाई।
मछिंद्र प्रसादै जाति गोरष बोल्या, दूझै पाणी न ब्याई ॥5॥20॥

The mango ripened at its place but the fruit that came out was the fruit of the Neem tree. That fruit of the neem tree tastes sweet. Meaning the supreme spirit situated at the Muladhar chakra (the tasty and healthy mango or gooseberry) has been superimposed by illusion (the neem fruit has ripened) but (the ones who know it and then eat find sweetness in it also, so even in an illusory world one can experience the bliss of the experience of the divine). Only the one who has the blessings of his Guru can have the experience of this divine sighting. When the mind (camel) was caught by the eagle (God of death) then he went and sat at the branch of the thorny tree (world). Once caught up in illusion the mind falls into the cycle of birth and death and rebirth and therefore under the rule of Yama- the God of death and starts believing this sorrowful world as an object of joy.

The barren woman (illusion) did not touch, leave alone touch did not as much look at the purush (supreme reality) and still begot a son(divine experience). when the human being who is caught up in the web of illusion is separated from it then he realizes his true self. The wood (those who get excited by the water of this world) they drown and the stones who are not affected (stay stable). Similarly the gross illusion flows away in the current and then subtle illusion then cannot even enter the door therefore the effect of the gross and the subtle illusion is nullified.

The fish (mind) reaches a high state in the mountain. It ceases to have an effect on the individual soul in the water and the water (the world of illusion) is destroyed in the end. Meaning at first the discriminative intelligence is developed to differentiate between truth and untruth, illusion and ultimate reality and thereafter untruth or illusion is destroyed. Then the wheel for drawing water from the well is made for the thirsty ones, the devotees experience the deepest satiation after the divine experience. In this way the thorn is destroyed.

There is a cow (soul)who has nine calves/(nine openings) but those who drink away it's spiritual power(reduce) and the five sense organs drink away its milk. The meaning is that the body does not let the development of spiritual powers. But by the practice of yoga, a flower is obtained which is being filled in 16 vessels. Meaning the moon with 16 aspects has the ambrosia of supreme bliss by which the gardener (soul) became very happy.

We stole without our feet and brought the cow, meaning received the divine experience. She cannot produce offspring again. Means the cycle of birth and death was brought to a nought. By the grace of Machchandar Gorakh talks of this secret.

[21]

गोरष लो गोपलं लो, गगन गाइ दुहि पोवै लो।
मही बिरोलि अंमी रस पोजै, अनभै लागा जीजै लो ॥टेक॥
ममिता बिनां माइ मूइ, पिता बिनां मूवा छोरू लो।
जाति बिहूँनाँ लाल ग्वालिया, अहनिस चारै गोरू लो ॥1॥
अनहद सबदैं संष बुलाया, काल महादल दलिया लो।
काया कै अंतिर गगन मंडल में, सहजै स्वामी मिलिया लो ॥2॥
ऐसी गावत्री घर बारि हमारै, गगन मंडल मैं लाधी लो।
इहि लागि रह्या परिवार हमारा, लेइ निरंतरि बांधी लो ॥3॥
कानां पूछां सींग बिबरजित, बर्न बिवरजित गाई लो।
मछिंद्र प्रसादै जती गोरष बोल्या, तहां रहै ल्यो लाई लो ॥4॥21॥

Gorakhnath is a cowherd. He takes milk from the cow (divine experience) and drinks it. He churns the buttermilk and drinks ambrosia which is the essence of the supreme consciousness, he partakes the essence and discards the rest. This way he is fearless (after attaining experience of the supreme consciousness he has no fear of the world) after the destruction of attachment the illusion is also destroyed. And the father (ego, pride) - after he is gone his offspring also die. By playing the conch-shell of the Anahata nada(unstruck sound) he has defeated the big army of death. Because of this inside the body itself in the sky (akash tatva) very naturally the person has become the supreme reality.

At our doorstep a cow is tied who we got in the sky (crown of the head, brahmarandhra) my entire family with the sense organs are busy in the devotional service of this cow, they are brought up in its absence because God or supreme consciousness is the abode of everything. It has been tied to the continuum. This cow is bereft of ears, horns, tail and is devoid of any colour. Gorakhnath says that by the grace of Machandar we stay deeply involved in the experience of the divine there.

[22]

अवधू ऐसा ग्यांन बिचारी, ता मैं झिलिमिलि जोति उजाली ॥टेक॥
जरां जोग तहां रोग न ब्यापैं, ऐसा परषि गुर करनां।
तन मन सूं जे परचा नांहीं, तौ काहे को पचि मरनां ॥1॥
काल न मिट्‌या जंजाल न छुट्‌या, तप करि हूवा न सूरा।
कुल का नास करै मति कोई, जै गुर मिलै न पूरा ॥2॥
सप्त धात का काया पींजरा, ता माहिं जुगति बिन सूवा।
सतगुरु मिलै तो ऊबरै बाबू, नहीं तौ परलै हूवा ॥3॥
कंद्रप रूप काया का मंडल, अँबिरथा कांइ उलींची।
गोरष कहै सुणौं रे भौंदू, अरंड अँमीं कत सीचौं ॥4॥22॥

O enlightened yogi ! contemplate on such knowledge where the effulgence of light can be seen. Where there is yoga, diseases do not crop up. One should carefully choose a Guru so that one does not fall ill from doing yoga wrongly. If one could not experience supreme consciousness from the mind or body by yoga practice then why should one even face unneccesary destruction. If one does not find a complete Guru, one should not destroy one's clan, should not leave one's family to do yoga because by making someone inadept as Guru the fear of death does not vanish and the web of the world cannot be cast aside. By doing such an incomplete penance, a seeker does not become brave.

This body is a cage made by seven sheaths where the human being is trapped like a bird that does not know a way out.

By meeting a good master one can find redemption else destruction is imminent. God has given the human being such a beautiful body , has given him a form as beautiful as the God of love Kamadeva. Why waste it on worthless pursuits? O foolish one! By learning yoga from non- qualified Gurus is like watering a castor plant with ambrosia.

[23]

आऊं नहीं जाऊं निरंजन नाथ की दुहाई।
प्यंड ब्रह्मंड षोजंता, अम्हे सब सिधि पाई ॥टेक॥

काया गढ़ भींतरि नव लष खाई।
दसवैं द्वारि अवधू ताली लाई ॥1॥
काया गढ़ भींतरि देव देहुरा कासी।
सहज सुभाइ मिले अबिनासी ॥2॥
बंदत गोरषनाथ सुणौ नर लोई।
काया गढ़ जीतैगा बिरला कोई ॥3॥23॥

It is the grace of the pure Nath. My coming and going has ceased. I have found the universe in this body and have achieved all the accomplishments. In this body which is like a fort there are nine lakh pits. The nine openings and the impressions of the 84 lakh births defeating which one reaches the 19th door or gateway which is the brahmrandhra and which is locked and it is important to open that with the help of kundalini energy, all the temples and pilgrimages are inside this fort like body and there I have found the indestructible God who met me very naturally. Gorakhnath says O humans! Rare is the one who wins over the fort like body.

[24]

पवनां रे तूं जासी कौंनैं बाटी।
जोगी अजपा जपै त्रिबेणीं, कै घाटी ॥टेक॥
चंदा गोटा टोका करिलै, सूरा करिलै बाटी।
मूंनी राजा लूगा धोवै, गंग जमुन की घाटी ॥1॥
अरधैं उरधैं लाइलै कूंची, थिर होवै मन तहां थाकीले पवनां।
दसवां द्वार चीन्हिले, छूटै आवा गवनां ॥2॥
भणत गोरषनाथ मछिंद्र ना पूता, जाति हमारी तेली।
पीड़ी गोटा काढ़ि लीया, पवन षलि दीयां ठेलीं ॥3॥24॥

O breath ! which way will you go ? In the triveni also called trikuti–the intersection between the forehead and the start of the nose- at that place the yogi is busy in ajapa japa–effortless chanting–so that path is closed. Make the moon as a soap cake and the sun the wooden board on which clothes are beaten clean by the washerman. in this way, situated in the Sushuma, the King of Yogis washes the clothes (his body)

By exhalation and inhalation are both locked. Only by kevali kumbhak the mind is stabilized and the breath gets tired, witnessing God in the tenth door makes one leave the cycle of birth and death. Machandarnath's disciple Gorakhnath says that I am the oil seller. By squeezing the sesame seeds we have extracted the oil and threw away the outer husk of the seed.

[25]

अवधू गागर कंधै पांणींहारी, गबरी कंधै नवरा।
घरका गुसांई कौतिग चाहै, काहे न बंधौ जौरा ॥टेक॥
लूँण कहै अलूंणां बाबू, घृत कहै मैं रूषा।
अनल कहै मैं प्यासा मूवा अनं कहै मैं भूखा ॥1॥
पावक कहै में जाडण मूवा, कपड़ा कहै मैं नागा।
अनहद मृदंग बाजै, तहां पांगुल नाचन लागा ॥2॥
आदिनाथ बिहवलिया बाबा, मछिंद्रनाथ पूता।
अभेद भेद भेदीले जोगी, बंदत गोरष अवधूता ॥3॥25॥

The owner of the house (soul) wants to see the play, so why will Yama not be tied up (meaning the soul ties the Yamaraj or God of death and makes him dance, makes a monkey dance).

That supreme soul or the one who has achieved self-realization, is the cause of all causes for him there is no cause from those causes, salt says infront of him that I am not salty, asks for salty taste from him, says he is not capable of providing him with one. Ghee (clarified butter) says that it is dry. The air says that it is thirsty, the grains say that they are hungry, fire says that it is dying with cold and cloth says that it is naked. Whatever attraction or influence various objects have, they have no effect on the soul.

This state is reached when the soul plays the musical instrument called mridang and matching rhythm with it is the handicapped soul which has started to think of itself as different from the sense organs and that is why is shorn of any form and is also handicapped because of the bliss of the vision all his sense organs have become useless.

The one whose grandfather Guru is the first yogi Lord Shiva and the one who is the son-disciple of Machchandhar, that perfectly enlightened yogi Gorakhnath says that he has found the secret to non-dualism.

[26]

अवधू अहूँठ परबत मंझार, बेलडी माड्यौ बिस्तार।
बेली फूल बेली फल, बेलि अछै मोत्याहल ॥टेक॥
सिष्टि उतपनीं बेली प्रकास, मूल न थी, चढ़ी आकास।
उरध गोढ कियौ विसतार, जांण नै जोसी करे विचार ॥1॥
आईसौ भील पारवी हाथ नहीं, पाई प्यंगुलो मुष दांत न काहीं।
ह्यों ह्यों मृघलौ धुणहीं न तहीं, घंटा सुर तिहां नाद नाहीं ॥2॥
भीलड़ै तिहां ताणियौ बांण मन हीं मृघलौ बेधियौ प्रमांण।
ह्यौं ह्यौं मृगलौ वेधियौ बांण, धुण ही बांण न थी सर तांण ॥3॥
भीलड़ीं मातंगी रांणी, मृघलौ आंणीं ठांणीं।
चरण बिहूँणौं मृघलौं आंण्यौ सीस सींग मुष जाइ न जांण्यौ ॥4॥
भणत गोरषनाथ मछिंद्र नां पूता, मार्‌यो मृष भया अवधूता।
याहि हियाली जे कोई बूझै, ता जोगी कौं तृभुवन सूझै ॥5॥26॥

Enlightened one! The creeper of illusion has spread like a coil around this body which is like a mountain. It is blossoming a lot. The fruit of muktaphal also grows here. From the light of the creeper the entire creation took birth. This creeper has no roots. In reality it is not the truth but a lie. Still it has climbed up the sky. It has spread itself upwards towards the crown of the head. O astrologers reflect about this.

The soul is a kind of a hunter who does not have any hands. It is invalid from the feet. It's mouth has no teeth, he does not have a bow and arrow still it killed the deer (mind). For bringing the deer under his control he does not have a rhythmic tune and to drive them away he has no sound or bell etc

Still the tribal bheel threw an arrow and as he wished he pierced the deer completely. The arrow hit the deer. He was killed, he was killed, the arrow that he had set forth was not an arrow, so without an arrow and without a bow the hunter killed the deer (mind).

The happy tribal woman brought the footless deer home. None of his body parts–the head, horns or tail were there. The disciple of Machandar, Gorakh says that the mind that was killed became a detached yogi. The one who understands this with all his heart, will gain the knowledge of the three worlds.

[27]

अवधू ऐसा नग्र हमारा, तिहाँ जोवौ ऊजू द्वारं।
अरध उरध बजार मड्या है, गोरष कहै बिचारं ॥टेक॥
हरि प्रांण पातिसाह साह विचार काजी।
पंच तत ते उजहदांर मन पवन दोऊ, हस्ती घोड़ा गिनांन ते अषै भंडारं ॥1॥
काया हमारैं सहर बोलिये, मन बोलिये हुज दारं।
चेतनि पहरै कोटवाल बोलिये, तौ चोर न झंकै द्वारं ॥2॥
तीनिसै साठि चीरा गढ़ रचीले, सोलह षणिलै षाई।
नव दरवाजा प्रगट दीसै, दसवां लष्या न जाई ॥3॥
अठारह भार कोट कठंजरा लाइलै, बहतर कोठडी निपाई।
नव सुत्र ऊपरै जंत्र फिरै, तब काया गढ़ लिया न जाई ॥4॥
अनहद घड़ी घड़ियाल बजाइ लै परम जोति दुइ दीपक लाई।
काम क्रोध दोइ गरदनि मारिलै, ऐसी अदली पातिसाही, बाबै आदम चलाई ॥5॥
तहां सत्य बीबी संतोष साहिजादा, षिमां भगति द्वै हाई।
आदिनाथ नाती मछिंद्र नाथ पूता, काया नगरी गोरष बसाई ॥6॥27॥

O enlightened yogi look at the door to our city. Gorakh says this upon reflecting, our city is such that it has a market which has the wares of inhalation-exhalation on display. The owner of the prana–vital life breath is Hari–who is the king there, the thoughts are the priests, the five elements are the prime minister. The mind is the elephants and horses. The knowledge here is indestructible.

This city is the city of the body, the mind is there, consciousness is sitting on guard as a senior most police officer. If a watch is kept regularly, thieves will not even be able to peep there. The body in the form of a fort has been built by the 360 stones (bones) Mool Garbhawalli Granth. The 16 foundation are (the big toe of the feet, the base, the rectum, the spine, upward abdominal, navel, heart, throat, uvula, the root of the tongue, the roof of the tongue –palate, the root of the teeth, the tip of the nose, the base of the nose, the place between the eyebrows, the forehead– these are the sixteen pits. Like it is important to cross the pits to enter the fort similarly, for realizing the yogic power care of these foundations is very important. The nine doors of this fort can be seen but the 10th door, the brahmrandhra in the crown of the head cannot be seen.)

The fort was fortified with the wooden cages made from several trees and 72 dungeons were made, the way in olden times wooden rooms used to have shade similarly this body has the shade of various nerves. The word 18 and 18 times saint has come up a lot of times in saint literature and is used for trees and plants. There are believed to be 72,000 nerves in the body, of them 72 are the main ones. The are chains at the nine doors and equipments galore so this fort like body cannot snatched away therefore the nine doors have been closed. The sensory pleasures cannot enter inside.

The Anahata nada keeps on playing the gong of the clock, meaning it has warned the people at every step. Two lamps – one with attributes and the other attributeness (nirgunn) were lit up. The neck of lust and anger was strangulated. Such was the reign of Baba Adam.

Truth is the wife of the emperor, contentment is the prince, forgiveness and devotion are the two mid-wives. The grandson–disciple of Lord Shiva and the son-disciple of Matsyendranath Gorakhnath has, in this manner, set up the city of the body.

[28]

ईकीस ब्रह्मंड भाठी चिगावै, पीवत सदा मतिवालं।
मनसा कलालिनि भरि भरि देवै आछा आछा मद नां प्यालं ॥टेक॥
अमृत दाषी भाठी भरिया, ता मधैं गुड़ झकोल्या।
मन महुवा तन धाहुवा, बनासपति अठारै मोल्यां ॥1॥

भ्रमर गुफा मैं मन थरि ध्यानैं, बैस्या आसण बाली।
चेतनि रावल यह भरि छाक्या, जुग जुग लागो ताली ॥2॥
तृकुटी संगम कृपा भरिया, मद नीपज्या अपारं।
कुसमल होता ते झड़ि पड़िया, रहि गया तहाँ तत सारं ॥3॥
एवहां मद श्री गोरष केवट्र्या, बदंत मछींद्र ना पूता।
जिनि कैवट्र्या तिनि भरि भरि पीया, अमर भया अवधूता ॥4॥28॥

In the twenty one universes, ambrosia flows from the oven, partaking of which the yogi is always in a trance. Desires fill a full cup of liquor. The grapes of ambrosia experience were filled in the oven. some jaggery was also put into it. The mind gave space to mahua- the butter tree, other 18 types of herbs were also put into it.

The brahmrandhra sat immovable in an asana. In this way the consciousness in the form of Rawal had a lot of liquor and the clapping that ensued stayed for centuries.

All the impurities that were there separated and the essence – only the liquor came up. Sri Gorakhnath took out such a liquor from the oven. Completed yoga.

The son-disciple of Machcharnath says that the one who took out the liquor also drank copious quantities of it and that yogi became immortal.

[29]

सति सति भाषंत श्री गोरष जोगी, अमे तौ रहिबा रंगै।
अलेष पुरसि जिनि गुर मुषि चीन्ह्यां, रहिबा तिसकैं संगैं ॥टेक॥
सतजुग मधे जुग एक रचीला, बिसहर एक निपाया।
ग्यांन बिहूणां गण गंध्रप अवधू, सब हीं डसि डसि षाया ॥1॥
त्रेता जुग मधे जुग दोइ रचीला, राम रमाइंणा कीन्हां।
नर बंदर सब लड़ि लड़ि मूये, तिन भी ग्यांन न चींन्हां ॥2॥
द्वापर जुग मधे जुग तीनि रचीलै, बहु डम्बर बहु भांर।
कैरों पांडौ लड़ि लड़ि मुये, नारद कीया संघारं ॥3॥
कलिजुग मधे जुग चारि रचीला, चूकिला चार बिचारं।
घरि घरि दंदी घरि घरि बादी, घरि घरि कथण हारं ॥4॥

चौहु जुग मधे जुग चारि थापिला, ग्यांन निरालंब रहिया।
मछींद्र प्रसादैं जती गोरष बोल्या, कोई बिरला पांर उतरिया ॥5॥29॥

Sri Gorakhnath says that he is speaking the truth that he stays happy in the colour. The one who has recognized the supreme consciousness through the teachings of his Guru, one should stay with such a person.

[30]

ऐसा जाप जपौ मन लाई, सोहं सोहं अजपा गाई ॥टेक॥
आसण दिढ करि धरौ धियानं, अहनिस सुमिरौ ब्रह्म गियानं।
जाग्रत न्यंद्रा सुलप अहारं, काम क्रोध अहंकार निवारं ॥1॥
नासा अग्र निजु ज्यौ बाई, हड़ा प्यंगुला मधि समाइ ॥2॥
छसै संहस इकीसौं जाप, अनहद उपजै आपहि आप।
बंक नालि मैं ऊगै सूर, रोम रोम धुनि बाजै तूर ॥3॥
उलटै कमल सहंस्रदल बास, भ्रमर गुफा महि जोति प्रकास।
सुणि मथुरा सिव गोरष कहै, परम तत ते साधु लहै ॥4॥30॥

O yogi, chant with concentration so much so that without the sound of sohum the ajapa japa takes place.

Sit on a firm mat and meditate and remember supreme knowledge day and night. Eat less. Resolve lust, anger and arrogance.

The prana vayu pervades the Ida and Pingala and the tip of the nose (the prana vayu resides till 12 fingers outside the nostrils) at the door of such breath when 21,600 chants happen–implying that the process of breathing becomes the process of chanting then the Anahata nada is produced by itself. Then in the Sushumna the sun rises and the musical instrument turi plays in every pore of the body–meaning the Anahata is experienced. it upturns and finds a home in the crown chakra and in the cave (brahmarandhra) the light becomes lit. in this way, O Mathura, listen, the seekers who practice like that described above achieve the supreme principle.

[31]

जागा जोगी कनक रावलिया, गुरुदेव मेंहलौ बूठौ।
षोजतां षोजता सतगुरु पाया, सहजै नैं भावै तूठौ ॥टेक॥

उतर देंस मैं मेंह बड़क्या, दक्षिण आचल छाया।
पूरब देस थीं पाणिन बिछूटी, पछिम खेत्र में पाया ॥1॥
मन पवना धोरी जोतावो, सतनां सांतीड़ा समधावो।
दया धर्म नां बीज अणावो, इणीं परि षेत्रे जावो ॥2॥
षातां न षूटै, देतां न निठै, जम बार नहीं जाइ।
मछींद्र प्रसादै जती गोरष बोल्या, नित नवेरड़ौं थाइ ॥3॥31॥

The Kanak Rawal yogi awakens (the Rawal yogis are a kind of yogi). Kanak means Gold thereby signifying excellence, it can also mean something in the sense of alchemy and could also point towards the habit of the yogis to have cannabis and thorn apple. The Guru has burst like a cloud, he is satisfied with the natural self. In the northern country (either in the trikuti or the brahmrandhra) the clouds thundered and then totally spread in the south. In the East (Ida, Pingala) the flow of water was released and reached the West, that is, towards Sushumna. Till the field in the form of body by the buffalo in the form of breath. It will give rise to such an abundant produce that will not end even after eating, not end after giving and will prevent you from going to Yama's door.

By the blessings of Machandar the yogi Gorakh says that this kind of farming will always remain new.

[32]

जीव सीव ना संगै, बासा, ना बधि षाइबा रे रुध्र मासा ॥टेक॥
घाव न घातिबा हंस गोतं, बंदत गोरषनाथ निहारि पोतं ॥1॥
मारिबा रे नरा मन द्रोही, जाकै बप बरण नहीं मास लोही ॥2॥
सब जग ग्रासिया देव दाणं, सो मन मारीबा रे गहि गुरु ग्यांन बांण ॥3॥
बसू क्या हतिये रे प्यंड धारी, मारिये पंच भू मृघला जे चरै बुधि बाड़ी।
जोग का मूल है दया दांनं। भणत गोरषनाथ ये ब्रह्म ग्यांनं ॥4॥32॥

The individual spirit and the supreme spirit are residents of the same place. That is why one should not kill and eat meat or blood. Do not assault the swan (soul) who belongs to the same family as yours. When you strike him, look at your own child. He is like your own child O humans. Instead of living beings one should kill this mind which is a traitor, which has no body, no complexion, no flesh, no blood. This mind has swallowed the deities as well as demons, the entire world. Why do you slaughter those animals which have a body, kill the mind which is like a deer , made of five elements, kill that deer that eats up the flower bed of the intellect. The essence of yoga is compassion and giving, Gorakhnath expresses this divine knowledge.

[राग असावरी]

[33]

ऐसा रे उपदेस दाषै श्री गोरष राया,
जिनि जग चतुर बरन रह लाया ॥टेक॥
पढ़िलै ससंवेद। करिलै बिधि नषेद।
जांणिलै भेदांनभेद। पूरिलै आसा अमेद ॥1॥
बिषमी संधि मंझारी। संझाया पंचौ वषत सारि।
रहिबा दसवैं दुवारि। सेइबा पद निराकार ॥2॥
जपिलै अजपाजाप। बिचारिलै आपै आप।
छूटिला सबै बियाप। लिपै नहीं तहाँ पुनि पाप ॥3॥
अहो निसि समा ध्यांन। निरंतर रमेबा राम।
कथै गोरषनाथ ग्यांन। पाइया परम निधांन ॥4॥33॥

Gorakhnath who distributed work among the four classes, gives this discourse that instead of studying the Vedas, study your own self- achieve that which has the power to be fully tested or experienced by itself. One has to follow the principles, know the secret of secrets, have to fulfill all hopes. Do the holy namaz five times in the heterogenous joints, one should stay in the 10th door or cranial aperture and worship the formless. Chant the ajapa japa. Reflect on the supreme spirit. Doing this will make all the diseases and designations, titles go far away. No merit or sin stays there. Day and night one should be equally absorbed in meditation or should stay in a doubt free state of solutions and continuously think of the name of Rama. Gorakhnath expresses the knowledge by which he got the supreme state of divinity.

[34]

गुर कीजै गहिला निगुरा न रहिला,
गुर बिन ग्यांन न पायला रे भाईला ॥टेक॥
दूधैं धोया कोइला उजला न होइला,
कागा कंठैं पहुप माल हंसला न भैला ॥1॥
अभाजै सी रोटली कागा ले जाइला,
पूछौ म्हारां गुरू नै कहां वैसि षाइला ॥2॥
उतर दिस आविला, पछिम दिस जाइला,
पूछौ म्हारा सत गुरू नै, तिहां बैसि षाइला ॥3॥
चीटी केरा नेत्र मैं गज्येंद्र समाइला,
गावडी के मुष मैं बाघला बिवाइला ॥4॥
बारें वरसैं बंझ व्याई, हाथ पाव टूटा,
वंदत गोरषनाथ मछिंद्र ना पूता ॥5॥34॥

Seek a Guru who is full of grave knowledge. Do not remain without a Guru. O brother, knowledge cannot be obtained without a Guru. Coal does not get fair even if it is washed with milk. If you put a garland of flowers in the crow's neck, he would still not become a swan.

He has come from the North direction (brahma randhra or cranial aperture) the supreme spirit is his abode. And the western direction (sushumna energy channel) is from where he will go. He sits there- meaning the path where it leads to–in the brahmarandhra he eats his meal–meaning he experiences the supreme spirit.

In this way the elephant has entered the eyes of the ant. Which means that the subtle spiritual form has merged in the gross physical form. In the mouth of the cow the tigress enters meaning that spiritual knowledge enters the physical life to destroy it.

The barren girl was married at 12 but in child birth it 's hands and feet are broken, she has become useless–these are the words of the disciple of Matsyendranath–Gorakhnath. The life of illusion is not fruitful, that is why it is called barren. By a deep penance knowledge can come to the fore in this illusory life itself, this is the act of giving birth by the barren woman. When true knowledge rises to the fore then illusion becomes powerless, and this is what is meant by the breakage of its hands and feet.

[35]

कहा बुझै अवधू राई गगन न धरनीं,
चंद न सूर दिवस नहीं रैंनी ॥टेक॥
ॐकार निराकार सूछिम न अस्थूलं,
पेड़ न पत्र फलै नहीं फूलं ॥1॥
डाल न मूल न वृष न बेला,
साषी न सब्द गुरू नहीं चेला ॥2॥
ग्यांनें न बिनसै आवै न जाई,
जुरा न मरण वांकै बाप न माई ॥4॥
भणत गोरषनाथ मछींद्र नां दासा,
भाव भगति और आस न पासा ॥5॥35॥

O yogi why do you ask? There is no sky, no earth, no moon, no sun, no day, no night. The supreme spirit is formless. No adjective can be used to describe it. It is neither gross nor subtle, neither branches nor leaves. It is neither a creeper nor a tree, it does not have a verse or a word. It is neither a master or a disciple, it is neither in knowledge nor in meditation. Neither in yoga nor in practical application, neither in merit nor in sin, neither in liberation nor liberated. It is neither born nor destroyed, neither comes nor goes (beyond the cycle of coming and going). It neither has old age or death or a father or a mother. The student of Machandar, Gorakh says that neither is he in devotion or caught in the web of desires.

[36]

आवो माई धरि धरि जावो,
गोरष बाला भरि भरि खावो ॥टेक॥

झरै न पारा बाजै नाद,
ससि हर सूर न बाद बिबाद ॥1॥
पवन गोटिका रहणि अकास,
महियल अंतरि गगन कविलास ॥2॥
पयाल नीं डोबी सुनि चढ़ाई,
कथंत गोरषनाथ मछींद्र बताई ॥3॥36॥

O mother, come and take alms from every house with the instruction that O child Gorakh, eat to your heart's full (all the women of the world are like mothers for Gorakhnath, who look after him, he does not look at any other way at women lest he may lose control over his sperm. That is why his sperm is stable and does not fall. Deep inside him the Anahata nada keeps in playing. There is congruence between the sun and the moon) there is no quarrel. Because of the power of breath he resides up in the sky (brahmarandhra) the brahmnarandhra high as Kailash mountain is for him on earth (body), similarly the Kundalini energy residing in the nether world (Swadhisthan chakra) has risen to the supreme void(brahmarandhra). Gorakh says his Guru Machandar has told him this.

[37]

कैसें बोलौं पंडिता देव कौनै ठांई,
निज तत निहारतां अम्हें तुम्हें नाहीं ॥टेक॥
पषांणची देवली पषांण चा देव,
पषांण पूजिला कैसें फटीला सनेह ॥1॥
सरजीव तेड़िया निरजीवी पूजिला,
पाप ची करणीं कैसे दूतर तिरीला ॥2॥
तीरथि तीरथि सनांन करीला,
बाहर धोये कैसें भीतरि भेदीला ॥3॥
आदिनाथ नाती मछींद्रनाथ पूता,
निज तत निहारै गोरष अवधूता ॥4॥37॥

O learned ones how should I tell where the deities reside. By witnessing the real self I do not remain I and you do not remain - we become one, all differences end. You build a temple of stone and place an idol of stone there. How can affection and compassion arise in you?

You pluck living flowers and leaves to place them before lifeless idols and worship it. So by committing this sin how can you hope to crossover from this world (you bathe in holy pilgrimages. How can water that cleanses externally enter inside and cleanse the soul) the grandson –disciple of the first Yoga Guru Lord Shiva and the son-disciple of Machchardarnath, Gorakh only witnesses his own soul.

[38]

पंडित जण जण बाद न होई, अणबोल्या अवधू सोई ॥टेक॥
पत्रे ब्रह्मा कली बिसना, फल मधे रुद्रम् देवा।
तीनि देव का छेद किया, तुम्हें करहु कौंन की सेवा ॥1॥
येक डंडी दुडंडी त्रियडंडी भगवांन हूवा।
बिष्न कौ तिन पार न पायौ, तीरथां भ्रमि भ्रमि मूवा ॥2॥
येक काल मुहां जटा धारी, ल्यंग उपासिका हूवा।
महादेव कौ तिन पार न पायौ, राष रौलि रौलि मूवा ॥3॥
चारि महाधर बारह चेला, येकंकारी हूवा।
कायम कौ तिन पर न पायौ, जोति बालि बालि मूवा ॥4॥
चौदसियांनै पूनमिया, जैन ब्रतधारी हूवा।
अरहंत कौ तिन पार न पायौ, केस लौंचि लौंचि मूवा ॥5॥
येक मुलांनम् दोई कुरानंम्, ग्यारह षुरसाणी हूवा।
अलह कौ तिन पार न पायौ, बंग देइ देइ मूवा ॥6॥
नौ नाथ नै चौरासी सिधा, आसणधारी हूवा।
जोग कौ तिन पर न पायौ, बन षंडां भ्रमि भ्रमि मूवा ॥7॥
पंच तत्त की काया विनसी राषि न सक्या कोई।
काल दवन् जब ग्यांन प्रकास्या, बदंत गोरष सोई ॥8॥38॥

O learned Brahmin, here one does not enter into deep philosophical discussions with everybody. The enlightened yogi is the one who does not speak because the bliss of profound meditation cannot be described in words.

The leaf has Brahma, the creator, the bud has Vishnu the preserver and the fruit has Rudra or Lord Shiva, so in this manner when you offer leaf, flower, fruit then there is a difference in the three. So tell me whose devotee are you?

The four perfected beings possibly being talked about here are Sanak, Sanandan, Sanatan and Sanatkumar. In the Chandogya Upanishad Sanatkumar has given the discourse of monism which ultimately leads to enlightenment to Narada. the other three can be considered like him. The twelve disciples are Narada, Janak, Yagyavalkya, Lomash, Markandeya, Vyas, Vashisht, Shukra, Jadbharat, Dutt, Gaudpada and Shankar.

Maula and Allah are one but those who read the Quran have made them into two and the Muslim community has been divided into Shia and Sunni. by the eleven Khorasanis, maybe Nabis are implied. But the Nabis have been twelve and one of them was a native of Khorasan.

[39]

भणंत गोरषनाथ काया गढ़ लेबा,
काया गढ़ लेवा जुगे जुगी जीवा ॥टेक॥
काया गढ़ भींतरि नौ लख षाई,
जंत्र फिरै गढ़ लिया न जाई ॥1॥
ऊँचे नीचे परबत झिलमिलि षाई,
कोठड़ी का पांणी पूरण गढ़ जाई ॥2॥
इहां नहीं उहां नहीं त्रिकुटी मँझारी,
सहज सुनि मैं रहनि हमारी ॥3॥
आदिनाथ नाती मछिंद्रनाथ पूता,
कायागढ़ जोतिले गोरष अवधूता ॥4॥39॥

Gorakhnath says that one should make one's body as a citadel and in this manner live long for various eras altogether. In this body (fort) there are nine lakh pits (nine openings) which create a lot of obstacles inside. The citadel is protected with an instrument.

This citadel cannot be taken. The fort is at a very far off, difficult to reach place. There are many big mountains there. The water that reaches the citadel is kept in a safely guarded warehouse. Here it means the trikuti or the brahmarandhra from where the flow of nectar provides nourishment to the entire body (not here, not there but in the middle of the trikuti is our natural abode) meaning we have laid control over the warehouse supplying water to the entire citadel- in this manner the grandson-disciple of Lord Shiva and the son-disciple of Machandar Gorakh has won over the entire citadel.

[40]

बदंत गोरष राई परसि ले केदारं,
पांणी पीओ पूता तृभुवन सारं ॥टेक॥
ऊँचे ऊँचे परबत विषम के घाट,
तिहां गोरषनाथ कै लिया सेबाट ॥1॥
काली गंङ्गा धौली गंङ्गा झिलिमिलि दीसै,
काउरू का पांणीं पुनि र गिर पईसै ॥2॥
अरधैं जोगेस्वर उरधैं केदारं,
भोला लोक न जानैं मोष दुवारं ॥3॥
आदिनाथ नाती मछींद्र नाथ पूता,
काया केदार साधीले गोरष अवधूता ॥4॥40॥

Gorakhnath says that touch the peak of Kedar mountain. Become the one who touches the supreme-consciousness. Lord Shiva is not just important for his sighting, but he is also touched. O son reach the brahmarandhra (cranial apparatus) and drink the nectar which is the essence of the three worlds.

Reaching there is difficult. There are high mountains and deep valleys there. But Gorakh has turned them into plains. The black Ganga (Yamuna, Pingala nerve) and the Dhauli Ganga (Ganga, Ida) both meet Sushumna at the trikuti and have obtained a form of light. The Kanwariyas had gone to distribute the water of Gangotri and Yamunotri. It implies that the flow of ambrosia that falls down and gets destroyed , that enters the mountain again. The ambrosia that is soaked by the sun again becomes upward moving. The individual (who can become the God of yoga through yogic practice) his place is down and the Kedar (Shiva, Supreme spirit) its place is upwards in the brahmarandhra (cranial apparatus). the foolish ones do not know about the door to liberation. But the grandson disciple of Adinath Lord Shiva and the son-disciple of Matsyendranath enlightened Yogi Gorakh has accomplished the stable Kedar in his body.

[41]

कासौं सूझौं अवधू राइ, विपष न दीसै कोई।
जासौं अब झूझौ रे आत्मा राम सोई ॥टेक॥
आपण हीं मछ कछ अपण हीं जाल,
आपण हीं धीवर आपण हीं काल ॥1॥
आपण हीं स्यंघ बाघ आपण हीं गाइ,
आपण हीं मारीला, आपण हीं षाइ ॥2॥
आपण हीं टाटीं फड़िका, आपण हीं बंध,
आपण हीं मृतग, आपण ही कंध ॥3॥
न्हाइबे कौं तीरथ न पूजिबे कौं देव,
भणंत गोरषनाथ अलष अभेव् ॥4॥41॥

O King of yogis, who should I fight a battle with... I cannot see any adversary. The one whom I fight with is my own soul in the form of Rama, this soul is itself the tortoise and itself the fish and the one who is trapping them is the fisherman himself, death itself. The lion and the tiger are the illusion and the cow is the individual which they have come to kill. He kills his own self and eats. He is himself the structure of bamboo and himself the thatched roof tied on it and himself the bond to tie it. He is himself the killer and himself the body. There is no pilgrimage outside the soul where one can take a purifying bath and no deity which can be worshipped. Gorakhnath says the soul cannot be seen by the eyes, nobody knows its secret.

[42]

मेरा गुरु तीनि छंद गावै,
ना जाणौं गुर कहां गैला, मुझ नींदडी न आवै ॥टेक॥
कुम्हारा कै घरि हांडी आछै, अहीरा के घर सांडी।
बमना कै घरि रांडी आछै, रांडी सांडी हांडी ॥1॥
राजा कै घरि सेल आछै, जंगल मधे बेल।
तेली के धरि तेल आछै, तेल बेल सेल ॥2॥
अहीर कै घरि महकी आछै, देवल मध्ये ल्यंग।
हाटी मधे हींग आछै, हींग ल्यंग स्यंग ॥3॥
एकैं सुत्रैं नाना बणियां, बहु भांति दिखलावै।
भणंत गोरषि त्रिगुणीं माया सत गुरु होइ लषावै ॥4॥42॥

My Guru explains the same principle thrice and in three different ways. Separation from such a priceless Guru is making me restless. My sleep and hunger have vanished. The separation from my Guru is giving me sorrow. Guru taught me that illusion is spread out everywhere. Everybody is tied to it within their limits– they are not happy. Illusion is everywhere. In the potter's home it is in the form of the unbaked vessel, in the milkman's house it is n the form of the cream of milk. In the Brahmin's house illusion is spread in many varied forms. In the King's palace it is in the form of weapons. In the forest it is in the form of valuable flora and i. spread in all directions,for the trader of oil illusion is present in the form of oil in his house. In this manner illusion has become oil-flora and weapons. In the house of the milkman it is the container of milk and in the temple it is in the form of Shiv-linga. In the market it is present in the form of a asafoetida (a fragrant herb), therefore it is present in the form of asafoetida in the market, linga idol in the temple and milk in the milk trader's house. The illusion mother has just one thread in which she ties everybody and forces them to dance to her tunes. Gorakhnath says she is full of the three qualities of sattva, rajas and tamas and inturn also influences them. The illusion full of these three gunas or qualities can only be pointed out by a Guru and there is no other solution.

[43]

गुरुजी ऐसा करम न कीजै, ताथैं अमीं महारस छीजै ॥टेक॥
दिवसैं बाघणि मन मोहै राति सरोवर सोषै।
जाणि बूझि रे मूरिष लोया घरि घरि बाघणी पोषै ॥
नदी तीरै बिरषा नारी संगै पुरषा अलप जीवन की आसा।
मनथैं उपज मेर षिसि पड़ई ताथैं कंध बिनासा ॥1॥
गोड़ भए डगमग पेट भया ढीला, सरि बगुलां की पंषियां।
अमीं महारस बाघणीं सोष्या घोर मथन जैसी अषियां ॥2॥
बाघनी कौं निदिलै बाघनीं कौं बिंदिलै बाघनीं हमारी काया।
बाघनीं घोषि घोषि सुंदर षाये भणत गोरष राया ॥3॥43॥

They say that Machcharnath went to the beauties of Singhaldweep to achieve perfection in yoga and got attached to them and decided to stay put there. Gorakh addresses him and says O Gurudev do not engage in such activities which lead to the weakening and destruction of nectar in the body. The man who stays with a woman is like a tree that is there on the bank of a river. It 's life is not too long. The city of illusion attracts the mind and through the discharge of semen at night soaks up the reservoir of nectar. In this way, foolish people rear a tigress knowingly. The moment such a thought is created in the mind, from the mount Meru (signifying the peak–the upward opening of the sushumna-the brahmarandhra or the cranial apparatus) throws down the nectar. This leads to the destruction of the body. And whenever some kind of attachment or love develops in the mind for a woman at the same time the nectar starts falling down. When the tigress illusion who has the eyes which are capable of churning the mind soaks up the nectar then the feet stumble, the stomach loosens and the hair on the head become white like the egret.

[44]

भोगिया सूते अजहूँ न जागे।
भोग नहीं रे रोग अभागे ॥टेक॥

भोगिया कहैं भल भोग हमारा।
मनसई नारि किया तन छारा ॥1॥
एक बूंद नर नारी रीधा।
ताही मैं सिध साधिक सीधा ॥2॥
भोगिया सोइ जी भगथैं न्यारा।
राजस तामस झरै न द्वारा ॥3॥
भणत गोरखनाथ सुणो नर लोई।
कथणीं बदणीं जोग न होई ॥4॥44॥

The pleasure seekers are sleeping, they have not yet awakened. O unfortunate one, this is not the real pleasure, this is a disease. The hedonistic ones they that their pleasure is good. By wanting to be with a woman they have burnt up their body. In this drop (of pleasure) men and women died again and again and by practicing it the seekers got perfection. The one staying away from woman gets real pleasure and the gunas of rajas and tamas have no influence on him that is why from his sense-organs the nectar or semen does not flow down in waste.

[45]

मारौ मारौ स्रपनीं निरमल जल पैठी,
त्रिभुवन डसती गोरषनाथ दीठी ॥टेक॥
मारौ स्रपणीं जगाईल्यो भौरा,
जिनि मारी स्रपणीं ताकौ कहा करै जौंरा ॥1॥
स्रपणीं कहै मैं अबला बलिया,
बहा बिष्न महादेव छलिया ॥2॥
माती माती स्रपनीं दसौं दिसि धावै,
गोरषनाथ गारड़ी पवन बेगि ल्यावै ॥3॥
आदिनाथ नाती मछिंद्र नाथ पूता,
स्रपणीं मारिलै गोरष अवधूता ॥4॥45॥

Enter the pond of pure water and kill the snake of illusion. Gorakhnath has seen her biting the three worlds. The wise say that in water the poison of the snake does not affect one. The seeker who has partaken the divine nectar is also not affected by illusion. Kill the serpent and those desirous of the nectar of the thousand-petalled lotus, the bumble bee cave (brahmrandhra-cranial apparatus) and its resident (the bumble bee–super consciousness, the soul)– awaken it for it has killed the serpent. What can the God of death do to such a one. The serpent says that she is powerful. She has tricked Brahma, Vishnu and Mahesh. In this manner the strong-headed serpent keeps running in all the ten directions but Gorakhnath says that the air (garuda bird) catches her and brings her to her place quickly by which she can be controlled. The grandson-disciple of Shiva and the son-disciple of Machandarnath Gorakhnath enlightened yogi has killed the serpent. Gorakh yogi says that you should also kill the serpent in the same way.

[46]

थान दे गोरीए गोरष बाला माई बिन प्याले प्याला।
गिगांन ची डाल्हीला पालंषू गोरषबाला पौढ़िला ॥टेक॥
देव लोक ची देव कंन्या, मृत लोक ची नारी,
पाताल लोक ची नाग कन्या, गोरषबाला भारी ॥1॥
माया मारिली मावसी तजीली, तजीला कुटंब बन्धु,
सहंसर कवल तहाँ गोरषबाला जहां मन मनसा सुर संधू ॥2॥
आसा तजीला तृसनां तजीला तजीला मनसा माई,
नौ षंड पृथ्वी फेरि ने आलौं गोरष रहीला मछिंद्र ठांई ॥3॥46॥

O maiden ! keep the place vacant for the child Gorakh, give him place. He has drunk from the cup without the cup and drunk the liquor without the liquor. The palanquin of knowledge is kept and Gorakhnath lies inside it. The celestial nymphs of the heaven, the women of this earth and the serpent-maidens of the nether world find it difficult to attract Gorakh towards them. He has killed illusion, has left his home, renounced his family. The abode of Gorakh is in the thousand petalled lotus where there is a congruence of the mind, desires and breath. All three merge eventually. Gorakh has renounced illusion in the form of hope, thirst and desire and the nine parts of earth again he has come to the place of Machandar under his shelter–meaning he has sought shelter in the crown chakra or sahasrara which is the place of the supreme consciousness which is the ultimate Guru, he lives there.

[47]

नाथ बोलै अमृत बांणी बरिषैगी कंबली भीजैगा पांणीं ॥टेक॥
गाड़ि पडरवा बांधिलै षूंटा, चलैं दमांमां बाजिले ऊँटा ॥1॥
कउवा की डाली पीपल बासै भूसा के सबद बिलइया नासै ॥2॥
चले बटावा थाकी बाट, सोवै डुकरिया ठौरै षाट ॥3॥
ढूकिले कूकर भूकिले चोर, काढै धणीं पुकारै ढोर ॥4॥
ऊजड़ षेड़ा नगर मझारी तलि गागरि ऊपर पनिहारी ॥5॥
मगरी परि चूल्हा धूंधाइ, पोवणहारा कौं रोरी खाइ ॥6॥
कांमिनि जलै अगीठी तापै, बिचि बैसंदर थरहर कांपै ॥7॥
एक जु रढिया रढती आई, बहू बिवाई सासू जाई ॥8॥
नगरी कौ पांणीं कूई आवै, उलटी चरचा गोरष गावै ॥9॥47॥

Nath speaks the words that are eternal–like ambrosia - kambali (the physical mental karmas which usually save the yogi from getting drenched in the rainfall of ambrosia) now have become pure and in the form of ambrosia like good karma are falling over the existence built by bindu. Imprudence which is the offspring of the animal of illusion,cow of illusion (tie that imprudence down), illusion acts as a strap to tie down the individual. The Anahata nada is heard, it is being heard continuously, because of the sound of Anahata is continuously being beaten at the camel (representing the gross mind) it is being beaten like an instrument. The crow (the imprudence, low mind that cannot distinguish between good and evil)-when this crow sits on a high branch (elevated state) then peepal (a sacred tree representing experiencing the supreme reality) speaks. The mouse who has heard the subtle word of the spiritual life, now hearing him the cat (which is illusion which was earlier strong but has turned weak now) has run away. The traveller on the path of knowledge walks but gets tired. Because walking on the path of knowledge leads to liberation and there is nothing to do after liberation. Illusion which had made spiritual life its cot and was sleeping soundly over it has grown weak and is now sitting up in that place. Till now the mind was guarding like a dog and supreme knowledge was running away like a thief. Now that dog(the traitor mind) has gone into hiding and its place has been taken up by knowledge which keeps on driving away thoughts of the material world. This thief (is the bark of self-realization) the wood is kept, it is not burning. By having an experience of self-realization he has lost all heat and trouble and the place where all objects were kept to burn is burning itself implying maya or illusion coming into contact with whom the entire world used to burn, is now burning itself, it is destroyed. The city of illusion built of sense organs, nine openings has now turned desolate, now it does not get food from material things. This city (body) has the pot below and the woman who fetches water is above it. The soul's (woman who does the work of fetching water) above is the brahmarandhra (crown of the head) and the kundalini energy (earthern water pot) by which one experiences supreme bliss–that is in the Muladhar Chakra. All the differences have been created by illusion–illusion creates those material objects and destroys them as well just like the one who makes a chapatti also eats it up. But now the stage is different. The one who has made the chapatti (illusion) is being eaten up by the chapatti. By having the realization of the supreme consciousness all illusions are destroyed.

In normal circumstances, the stove (individual soul suffers due to troubles) burns and the woman (illusion) heats up the stove but after realizing the supreme reality the woman (illusion) is being heated by the stove, the burnt illusion is shivering in the flames of realization of supreme, divine consciousness because it fears being completely burnt. The one who makes a firm decision has come, such a stage comes when the daughter-in-law gives birth to the mother-in-law. The material entanglement is the daughter in law. She enchants the individual soul or her husband (jeevatma) the individual soul is the son of universal consciousness. By sincerity and diligence the material entanglement gave birth to divine consciousness. This is what is meant by the daughter-in-law giving birth to the mother-in-law.

The way water is taken out of the well to reach the cities, similarly Kundalini emerges emerges out of the supreme consciousness and into the Muladhar chakra. by the practice of yoga the yogi upturns it and makes it reach its original source. This is like making the water from the city return to the well. Gorakh sings such an opposite discussion.

[48]

भग राकसि लो, भग राकसि लो, बिंणं दंतां जग षाया लो।
ग्यांनी हुता सु ग्यांन मुष रहिया, जीव लोक आपै आप गंवाया लो ॥टेक॥
दिन दिन बाघिनी सींया लागी, राति सरीरै सोषै।
विषै लुबधी तत न बूझै, घरि लै बाघनीं पोषै ॥1॥
भणंत गोरषनाथ द्वै कर जीड़ी। भिड़ै आगैं चावड़ तोड़ी।
चांमैं चांम घसंता लोई, दिन दिन छीजै काया,
आपा परचै गुर मुषि न चिन्हैं, फाड़ि फाड़ि बाघर्णी षाया ॥2॥
बाघनीं उपाया बाघनी निपाया बाघनी पाली काया।
बाघनी डाकरै जौरियों पाषरै, अनभुइ गोरष राया ॥3॥48॥

Beauty is a demoness, beauty is a demoness. It has no teeth yet has eaten up the world. The knowledgable one takes the support of knowledge and saves himself from becoming fodder for beauty. But the ordinary group of people of the world lose their soul themselves. The tigress keeps sleeping in the morning meaning it is not an enemy at that time but it exploits the body at night. The human being attracted to sensual pleasures does not know this principle and that it why he keeps the tigress in his own home and rears her. Due to intercourse people's bodies are growing weaker by the day. They have not received true knowledge from the mouth of the Guru. That is why the tigress (illusion) tears them up and eats them. This tigress has given birth to the body, it has nourished it. She keeps on roaring next to Yama–the God of death–this is what Gorakh has experienced.

[49]

रूपे रूपे करूपे गुरदेव, बाघनीं भोले भोले,
जिन जननीं संसार दिषाया, ताकौं ले सूते षोले ॥टेक॥
गुरू षोजौ गुरदेव गुरूषौजौ, बदंत गोरष ऐसा,
मुषते होइ तुम्हें बंधनि पड़िया, ये जोग है कैसा ॥1॥
चांम हीं चांम घसंतां गुरदेव दिन दिन छीजै काया,
होठ कंठ ताकुला सोष काढ़ि मिजालू षाया ॥2॥
दीपक जोति पतंग गुरदेव, ऐसी भग की छाया,
बूढ़े होइ तुम्हें राज कमाया नां तजी मोह माया ॥3॥
बदंत गोरषनाथ सुनहु मछंदर तुम्हें ईश्वर के पूता,
ब्रह्म झरंता जे नर राषै, सो बोलौ अवधूता ॥4॥49॥

She resides in beauty, also in ugliness, O Guru (Matsyendranath) the tigress (illusion) is present in an innocent form. She appears innocent when viewed from outside, her terrible form is hidden because of this outer innocence and look at this improper behaviour–the mother who showed the world, who gave birth to one (Gorakhnath considers all women as mothers) men sleep in the lap of women.

O Guru please search for a real Guru- this is the statement from Gorakhnath. You are in bondage even after being liberated, what kind of yoga (union) is this. The body becomes weaker day by day due to intercourse. The lips, throat and palate are all sucked up and the bone marrow is also eaten up by this tigress. A life full of physical gratification destroys a man just as the flame of the earthen lamp destroys the insect hovering above it. Listen to the words of Gorakhnath–you are the son of God, the son-disciple of Adinath Lord Shiva, why have you forgotten yourself? Do you not know that the man who protects the semen from falling he is verily the enlightened yogi.

[50]

सरवा रे सरवा त्रिभुवन ते गरवा। पांणी तैं पतला पहुप तैं हलवा ॥टेक॥
काया थै मन जांन न देह। राति दिवस अभि अंतरि लेह।
मन मुद्रा कै रूप न रेष। जगत रूप मन हीं मन देषि ॥1॥
उलटैगा पवनां तब काया कौं गहैगा। काच गहे कंचन ह्वै रहेगा।
यहु तन साच साच का घरवा। रुध्र पलट अमींरस भरवा ॥2॥
अतीत पुरस ग्यानं पद परसै। अविचल होइ सरीरं दरसै।
जुरा मृतु काल का भछिण। निसपति जोगी जोगी का लक्षिण ॥3॥
गरड़ भुवंगम संमि करि सूता। देव द्वार रस मरदौं पूता।
मर्दत मर्दत ह्वै है पीठी। ते बात गोरष प्रतषि दीठी ॥4॥50॥

The soul which assumes all forms is the heaviest and the most excellent in all the three worlds. It is also thinner than water and lighter than the flower.

One should not let the mind go outside the body.. With effort one should make it inward looking. The bodily mudra (gesture) is not of much use, one should have a mudra of the mind, while closing the openings of the body does not make one's yoga practice perfect but yoga is perfected by closing the mind because yoga is the cessation of movements in the consciousness. When the breath goes in opposite direction, that it when it goes downwards and after the practice of deep breathing, pranayama, it will enter the universe (crown chakra) then it will accept the body. Such a yogi if he touches glass by hand. It will turn into gold.

This body is actually the house of truth whose blood has changed and instead ambrosia flows there. The purusha or the supreme consciousness that can be known by the highest knowledge can also be visible when the body is stable. In this manner when the yogi has obtained mastery over old age, death then it should be considered a sign of nispatti yogi meaning he attains a state of being one with body, mind and self.

When the prana (breath) and the kundalini energy become one in the crown of the head then the mind consciousness goes to sleep then I will reach the brahmrandhra (cranial capacity) and rub the mind (of the child) with ambrosia. This way by rubbing it will become subtle–this has been seen by Gorakhnath himself–he has experienced it.

[51]

बांधौ बांधौ बछरा पीओ षीर।
कलि अजरावर होय सरीर ॥टेक॥
आकास की धेन बछा जाया।
ता धेन कै पूछ न पाया ॥1॥
बारह बछा सोलह गाई।
धैनु दुहावत नैनि बिहाई ॥2॥
अचरा न चरै धेन कटरा न षाई।
पंच ग्वालियां कौ मारण धाई ॥3॥
याही धेन का दूध जु मींठा।
पीवै गोरषनाथ गगन बईठा ॥4॥51॥

The calf (the sun situated in the muladhar chakra which keeps on drying up the ambrosia). This mind is a signifier of a low, restless, traitor kind of nature. Till the time the sun soaks up the ambrosia, the tendency of the mind is outward looking. by this your body will become immortal in this age of the Kali. Due to yoga practice the moon situated in the crown chakra meets the sun in the root chakra then the falling down of the ambrosia ceases and the seeker can himself drink it. The supreme consciousness is present in the form of a seed in all the energy channels (chakras) therefore the sun in the root chakra is called a calf and that supreme consciousness or has originated from the moon of the crown chakra. That is why he is the calf of the cow which is the moon or is a form of supreme consciousness. The main source of the mind is also the soul.

It will be easier to partake of (the milk) of bliss. This partaking of ambrosia from the moon in the crown chakra is possible due to the experience of the divine or in profound meditation or in the crown chakra or in the meeting place of the forehead and the beginning of the nose. This cow neither has a tail or feet.

The calf is outside and the moon with 16 aspects is the cow.

The night was spent milking this cow (this means daybreak has happened, the night has passed–there is the dawn of knowledge and the darkness of ignorance has gone).

This cow is stable and calm, because experience of supreme consciousness is not restless. (the five sense organs are the five milkmen who want to keep this cow) experience of supreme consciousness, this drinking of ambrosia (under their control, she runs to hit them). The milk of this cow is sweet. Gorakhnath drinks it while sitting in the sky.

[52]

आवै संगैं जाइ अकेला। ताथैं गोरष रांम रमेला ॥टेक॥
काया हंस संगि ह्वै आवा। जाता जोगी किनहूँ न पावा ॥1॥
जीवत जगमैं मूवां मसांणं। प्राण पुरिस कत कीया पयाणं ॥2॥
जांमण मरणां बहुरि बिओगी। ताथै गोरष भैला जोगी ॥3॥52॥

The individual soul, the human being comes into this world with a body but goes (dies) alone. That is why Gorakh is busy with his God Rama (he did not get entangled in the world). Along with the physical body, the swan (soil) also comes along. But when the body is leaving this world, nobody knows where the soul goes and in what form. What was there in the world in an alive state became the graveyard upon death, but where does the prana the life breath go (that is why Gorakhnath has become a yogi and is free from the cycle of birth and death).

[53]

चेला सब सूता नाथ सतगुर जागै।
दसवै द्वारि अवधू मधुकरी मांगै ॥टेक॥
सहजैं षपरा सुषमनि डंडा।
पांच संगाती मिलि षेलैं नव षंडा।
गंग जमन मधि आसण बालौ।
अनहद नाद काल भै टालौ।

गगन मंडल मैं रमूं अकेला।
उरध मुषि बंक नालि अमीरस झेला।
कथंत गोरषनाथ गुरु उपदेसा।
मिल्यां संत जन टल्या अंदेसा ॥53॥

The whole world is a disciple of Nath (is a disciple of supreme consciousness). Realizing the ultimate truth is knowledge. That is why Gorakhnath is called the sadhguru. Only the supreme consciousness is awake. Human beings also awaken but on awakening they too become the supreme consciousness itself, they are not counted as a part of the world, there remains no difference between the Guru and the disciple. That is why the Nath stays awake while the entire world sleeps. That enlightened Nath yogi does not set out to beg for alms in the world. He asks from the ambrosia in the brahmarandhra- the crown of the head, he tastes the ambrosia. This Nath yogi has the container of natural knowledge. He carries the staff of the Sushumna. The five sense organs do not oppose him, they are his supporters. They do not create obstacles in the experience of supreme consciousness. The Nath yogi along with them keep playing in the nine openings, the sense organs also become refined and take part in the divine bliss. You should also take a posture between the Ida and the Pingala, listen to the Anahata nada- the unstruck sound and let go of the fear of death. By the instruction of my Guru I kept on moving alone in the brahmrandhra or the trikuti. And take out the ambrosia from the upward moving Sushumna and taste it. In this manner Gorakhnath repeats the discourse given by his Guru. After meaning saints and sages, all doubts vanish.

[54]

रे मन हीरै हीरा बेधिला, तौ काया केणैं जाई।
गिनन सिषर चंदा रहिबौ समाई ॥टेक॥
सात पांच तीनि तव धरि लै उपाई।
बिपरति करणी करिलै ज्यूं थिर ह्वै बाई ॥
बाई जब थिरि ह्वै महारस सीझै।
कोट्यां मधे गुरू देवा गोटा एक बूझै ॥1॥

कांने रातां डौरौं गाटा किणि मीर मूले।
सदा अभ्यास रहै जोगी गंगा जमुन कूंले ॥
गंगा जमुना कूंले पैसि करिले असनांनं।
चांपीला मूले अवधू धरीला धियांनं ॥2॥
मेर डंड थिरि करै स्यौ सक्ती जोड़ै।
कोई गुरू आराधीला जो ब्रह्म गांठि छोड़ै ॥
छूटै जब ब्रह्म गांठि भरिये मेर नाला।
सहजैं पांचै चूरा भया पूरण कला ॥3॥
चंदा गोटा षूटा करि लै सूरिज करि लै पाटी।
अह निसि धोबी धोवै त्रिवेणी की घाटी।
तलै एक चंदा गोटा पाटी गोटा आछै।
भौजल नदी पारि उतरीया सिध गोरष भाछै ॥4॥54॥

O mind ! when the diamond was pierced that is when the individual soul met the universal soul, the soul met the supreme consciousness then why should anybody go towards the physical body that one should be inward looking rather than outwards looking. Stay merged with the top of the sky, that is, the moon in the brahmrandhra–crown of the head, stay merged with the soul. Have control over the five elements, sense-organs and the three gunas (qualities) and the nine openings. Do not stay under their control. Practice the viprit karni mudra so that the prana stabilizes. By the stabilizing of air (prana), the ambrosia will become manifest. O Gurudev, one in crores has the knowledge of the magic pill. By the use of which the ambrosia becomes perfect. O lord ! listening from the ears, seeing from the eyes is all this the main object or a resource of yoga. Do not fall in the trap of external things but o yogi you should practice pranayama or breath control and in this way become pure. Contract the muladhar and sit in meditation.

Keep the spine erect and join the Shiv and Shakti. Pray to an accomplished yogi who can free you from your brahma granthi (perineal knot)-it is a spiritual blockage. When the Ida and Pingala merge in the Sushumna through pranayama then all the five elements are destroyed, they no longer have an effect on us thus the full moon rises. The Sahasrara moon is a peg and the Muladhar sun is the washboard on which the washerman throws clothes again and again to wash, the seeker gets rid of the impurities of illusion. This washboard etc is available to us as humans. In this way Gorakh yogi says that he crosses the river of life.

[55]

जागौ हो जोगी अध्यात्म लागौ जागतड़ा मूल मे हारौ म्हारा भाई रे।
अंदरि बैठो अपणौ साहिब, देषै सोधै सकल कमाई रे ॥टेक॥
दासी नैं नारी अरु घर द्वारी, तुम्हे बेस्यां न करम न कीज्यो रे।
बिधवा नारी नौ संग करेस्यौ, तौ रोमि रोमि नरक पड़ीस्यो रे।
एक बूँदि कै कारणि आप सवारथि, तुम्हें बाल हत्या फल लेस्यौ रे।
नर नारी दोन्यूं नरकि पड़िस्यौ, घाणी घालि पड़ैस्यौ रे।
अंजनि भूला निरंजन चूका तुम्हें लीयां सालि मे बालौ रे।
मछिंद्र प्रसादै जती गोरष बोल्या जीती सारि न हारौ रे ॥55॥

O yogi, wake up and start working towards your spiritual realization. No not forget the source of this awareness O brother mine. Our god is residing inside us and inspecting all our good and bad karmas. O yogi, keeping a female servant, a woman, household and a house by a yogi is like entering prostitution. If you keep the company of widows every pore of your being will rot into hell implying great suffering. For this selfishness for just a drop of semen you will get the punishment that accrues to the murderer of a child. Both men and women will fall in hell. If you stay attached to the body and forget the supreme spirit you will burn up the acquired harvest. By the grace of Matsyendranath, Yogi Gorakhnath says that do not lose a winning battle.

[56]

चलि रे अबिला कोयल मौरी, धरती उलटि गगन कूँ दौरी ॥टेक॥
गईयां बपड़ी सिघ नै घेरै। मृतक पसू सूद्र कूँ उचरै।
काटै ससत्र पूजै देव। भूप करै करसा की सेव।

तलि करि ढकणी ऊपरि झाल। न छीजैगा महारस बंचैगा काल।
दीपक बालि उजाला कीया। गोरष कै सिरि परबत दीया ॥56॥

Mango is an illusion. When it blossoms then the koel bird (mind) is delighted and goes and perches on the mango tree branch but when there is the dawn of knowledge the situation reverses. With the dawn of knowledge the outward looking tendencies of the mind stops and instead of searching for bliss outside he realizes bliss inside himself. He becomes the centre of joy himself because the foundation upon which the mind consciousness is built is the blissful supreme consciousness itself. This is the koel's chirping. Now the one who has experienced the supreme bliss also receives the same bliss in his illusory aspect (mango). This entire creation has originated from the sky and the supreme void and it dissolves in the void for the one who has experienced this supreme reality. Kundalini energy is the symbol of the earth or the creation whose abode is the Manipur chakra. The Kundalini energy rises up due to yoga practice and goes towards the brahmrandhra (cranial apparatus near the crown of the head) for the ignorant his restless outward looking tendency is like a lion who along with six more enemIes like ego etc has surrounded the peaceful serene nature (cow). But after the success of the spiritual practice this illusory nature in the form of a lion has become weak and is now tied to spirituality, it has been defeated. The ones who do not have self-realization they are like dead animals. The God of death Yama (shudra) drags them away but when they cut the cord of animal-ness in them (ego, pride etc) then the person becomes a jivanmukta–one free from the continuous cycle of birth and death and they, in turn, drag Yama, he is in their control, he cannot do anything against the person. After the realization of the supreme reality the need to worship any god is no longer relevant instead the gods come and worship such a seeker because supreme reality is above everything else. Now there is no need to kill animals for sacrifice but the weapons themselves have been cut, meaning they have been rendered useless. If the lid is removed and the vessel upturned the food will fall down. And by turning the vessel upside down upon fire will not cook any dish. But this is a special circumstance. Here we are being instructed to master the viprit mudra by which the head (lid) is downwards and the fire (kundalini energy) is upwards. This saves the ambrosia that is falling down and destructing and death will be averted. This knowledge of the Naths is called kalvanchini vidya. In this manner Gorakh lit the light (of supreme reality), but his head became heavy instead of becoming light. An entire mountain was kept on his head because he realized that he himself is the cause of creation- the supreme consciousness and on becoming liberated I have to now joyously liberate the world.

[57]

सांभलि राजा बोल्या रे अवधू। सुणौ अनोपम बांणी जी।
निरगुण नारी सूं नेह करंतां। झबकै रैणि बिहांणी जी ॥टेक॥
डाल न मूल पत्र नहिं छाया। विण जल पिगुला सीचै जी।
बिण ही मढीयां मंदला बाजै। यण बिधि लोका रीझै जी ॥1॥
चींट्यां परब्रत ढोल्या रे अवधू। गायां बाघ बिडाऱ्याजी।
सुसलै समदां लहरि मनाई, मृघां चीता माऱ्याजी ॥2॥
ऊझड़ मारगि जाता रे अवधू, गुर बिण नहीं प्रकासा जी।
जीत्या गोरष अब नहीं हारै, समझि ररालै पासा जी ॥3॥57॥

The yogi gave a discourse, O king, beware. Listen to my unique discourse. They have spent their life loving and sleeping with illusion (woman) illusion is as untrue as a tree which has no branches, no roots, no leaves, no shadow, it is watered by an invalid and that too without water. Still people stay eager to eat its fruit. It is like the musical instrument mridang whose two opposite sides do not have the covering flap (so how can one beat fingers on either side) the pleasure of illusion is fake like the sound of the mridang without the outer flaps on either side. This way people get enamoured by illusion. O yogi in this way the ant (illusion) pushed the elephant (supreme soul) down. The cow (the feeble illusion) made life terrible for the tiger (strong soul). Illusion started to control the waves of the sea. Made it agree to its wishes. The deer (sense organs) have killed the cheetah (self principle) the sense organs are gaining strength and the soul is becoming weaker. Controlled by illusion, everywhere people are walking the rocky path but they cannot find light without the Guru, they stay in darkness. Gorakhnath will play the dice after deliberation now, he will not lose the game he already won.

[58]

तुझि परि वारी हो अणघड़ीया देवा।
घड़ी मूरति कूं सब कोई सेवै, ताहि न जांणै भेवा ॥टेक॥
तू अबिनासी आदू कहीए, मीहि भरोसा पड़ीया।
सब संसार घड्या है तेरा, तू किनहूँ नहि घड़ीया ॥1॥
दस औतार औतिरीया तिरिया, बै पणि राम न होई।
कमाई अपणी उनहूँ पाई, करता औरै कोई ॥2॥
तूं पूरण ब्रह्म पुरष प्रिथमी का, सूरति मूरति सारा।
श्रवणां सुण्यां न नैनां देष्या, तेरा घड़णैं हारा ॥3॥
तूं तौं आप आप तैं हूवा, तूं देष्यां उजियारा।
गोरष कहै गुरू कै सबदां तूं हीं घड़नै हारा ॥4॥58॥

This Couplet is easy to comprehend hence it's meaning has not been given.

(राम रामगरी)

[59]

मन रे राजा राम होइलै नृदंद,
मूलै कमलै साजि लै रचिचंद ॥टेक॥
अनहद भौरी भवैं तृबेणीं कै घाट,
पीयलै महारस फाटिलै कपाट ॥1॥
चंदा करिले षूटा सूरजि करलै पाट,
नित उठ धोबी धोवै, तृबेणीं के घाट ॥2॥
भरिलै नाड़ी षोड़ी, पूरिलै बंक नालि।
बंदत गोरषनाथ अवधू, इम उतरिबौ पारि ॥3॥59॥

O mind become the supreme reality and lose all duality. Join the sun in the Muladhar chakra to the moon in the Sahasrara chakra. In the trikuti the Anahata nada is vibrating. Open the gates of the brahmrandhra (cranial apparatus)and drink the ambrosia. Make the moon the beating stick and sun the board or the stone on which the washerman washes clothes. In this way the washerman (spiritual seeker) should wash clothes daily. Meaning he should get rid of the dirt of the individual soul, should keep away illusion. He should fill the nadis full of impurity with pure air and fill the Sushumna energy channel with air. Gorakhnath says O enlightened yogi cross the river of life in this manner.

[60]

गोरष बालूड़ा बोलै सतगुरु बांणीं रे।
जीवता न परण्यां तेन्हैं अगनि न पांणी ॥टेक॥
षीलौ दूझै भैंसि बिरोलै, सासूड़ी पालनड़ै बहुड़ी हिंडोलै ॥1॥
कोयल गोरी आंबौ बास्यौ गगन मछलड़ी बगलौ ग्रास्यौ ॥2॥
करसन पाकु रषवालू षाधू, चरि गया मृघला पारधी बांधू ॥3॥
सींगी नादै जोगी पूरा, गोरषनाथ परन्यां तिहां चंद न सूरा ॥4॥60॥

The child Gorakhnath speaks the words of his Guru. Gorakh has married the supreme reality. For this there is no fire or water that is needed.

Earlier the mind in the form of buffalo seemed tied to the nail of illusion and was giving out the milk of the sensory pleasures. But now the low nature of the nail of illusion seems to have vanished and it has adopted a sattvic luminous self and is giving out the milk of knowledge and the intelligence in the form of a buffalo is churning it and taking out the essence or butter of supreme knowledge. Illusion is the mother-in-law. In the physical world, the individual being is the son of illusion. He has married the supreme reality. So supreme reality is the daughter-in-law of illusion. Upon the advent of this experience of supreme reality illusion turns weak like a child. According to Nath yoga the experience of supreme reality or the divine also nourishes the body like a mother nourishes a child. This supreme reality is now cradling the mother- in-law in a cradle. The mind (koel bird) which was earlier delighted on the ripening of the mango fruit (illusion) now, due to turning inwards is herself blossoming with the experience of the divine and the illusory existence of the spiritual seeker is also seeped in that bliss now. The fish (consciousness) has reached the sky which was in the water earlier has now swallowed the heron earlier it was the opposite. The profound meditation is the field of the yogi. He has not let ego, pride, arrogance enter this field and all these have been destroyed by the deep meditative state. So the field ate its keeper in this way. The grazing deer (mind and sense-organs) which was so restless earlier has now left that restlessness and has tied down time/ death itself. Till now yogi used to do Anahata nada. Now Anahata nada is pervading the yogi. Earlier he was hollow without the experience of supreme reality and now after the experience that comes from Anahata nada he has become complete. Gorakhnath says with the highest effulgence–the param jyoti – there is a bond of love, there is no sun or no moon there.

(आरती)

[61]

नाथ निरंजन आरती गाऊं।
गुरदयाल अग्यां जो पाऊँ ॥टेक॥
जहां अनंत सिधां मिलि आरती गाई।
तहां जम की बाच न नैड़ी आई।
जहां जोगेसुर हरिकूं ध्यांवै।
चंद सूर तहां सीस नवांवै।
मछिंद्र प्रसादै जती गोरषनाथ आरती गावै।
पूर झिलमिलि दीसै तहां अनत न आवै ॥61॥

If I have the blessings of my kind Guru then I may get to sing the praises of the supreme truth the pure supreme consciousness. Where the enlightened yogi are engaged in complete surrender to God, there is no fear of Yama or death. Where the lord of yoga sits in deep meditation, even the sun and the moon bow down there–it means God controls both of them and eventually both the moon and the sun, that is, the moon that gives out ambrosia and the sun that is a part of the Muladhar chakra and which soaks the ambrosia, they both come under the control of the yogi. By the blessings of Matsyendranath Gorakh sings the praise of God. He can see the light of the supreme one. In that state everything is in harmony.

[62]

नाथ निरंजन आरती साजै। गुर के सबदूं झालरि बाजै ॥टेक॥
अनहद नाद गगन मैं गाजै। परम जोति तहां आप बिराजै ॥
दीपक जोति अषंडत बाती। परम जोति जगै दिन राती ॥
सकल भवन उजियारा होई। देव निरंजन और न कोई ॥
अनत कला जाकै पार न पावै। संष मृदंग धुनि बेनि बजावै ॥
स्वांति बूंद ले कलस बंदाऊँ। निरति सुरति ले पहुप चढ़ाऊँ ॥
निज तत नांव अमूरति मूरति। सब देवां सिरि उदबुदि सूरति ॥
आदिनाथ नातीं मछेंद्र ना पूता। आरती करै गोरष औधूता ॥62॥

The Nath yogi sings the praise of the pure supreme consciousness. The words of the Guru are like the rhythmic sounds of the cymbal. In the brahmrandhra the Anahata nada (unstruck sound) is playing. That is where the supreme consciousness is present in the form of light. It is a light emanating from indestructible wicks, it can never blow out. It is lit day and night. It's light spreads across the universe. In that light one can see that beyond the supreme consciousness there is nothing else. It has endless aspects. Nobody can go beyond it. There are various sounds and rhythms coming from the conch, the drum, flute etc. May I offer to this earthen pot (the body) the water drop (complete knowledge) after prayers. May I offer it flowers.

Shiksha darshan

ॐ। अबिगत उतपतते ॐ। ॐ उतपतते आकासं। आकासं उतपतते बाई। बाई उतपतते तेज। तेज उतपतते तुया। तुया उतपतते मही। मही रूप देवी का रंग। जल रूप ब्रह्मा का वरण। तेज रूप बिश्न की माया। पवन रूप ईश्वर की काया। आकास रूप नाद की छाया। नाद रूप अबिगत उपाया। सुंनि निरंजन भूचर देव। भूचर का नहीं पाया भेव। अगम अगोचर। अनंत तरवर। अनन्त साषा। ससंवेद परम भेद। भेदां निभेद। आत्मा ध्यांन ब्रह्मग्यांन। षेचरी मूंद्रा। भूचरी सिधि। चाचरी निधि। अगोचरी बुधि। उनमनी अवस्था। अनभै करामाति। अतीत देवता। अबिगत पूजा। अनील आश्रम। अध्यात्म बिद्या। गगन आसन। अमृत प्याला। मनसा माई। पंचभू चेला। मन रावल, पवन भोगी। दसवैं द्वारि प्रांणनाथ जोगी। सहजि आंवणां। अवधू संजमे जांणां। सुषमनां नदी। निहिकेवल जल। तृबेणीं सनांन। तृकाल संझ्या। अजपा गायत्री। अनूपम मंत्र।

निरंजन माला, निराकार ज्वाला। कवल गरजै सबद उजियाला।
छसै सहंस इकबीस मेला। नष सष पवन ले बन्धिबा भेला।
नाद अनाहद निहसबद बांणीं। जीव थैं सीव होइबा प्राणी।
देही बदेही अबिचल थीरं। रुंध्र उलटि फिरि होइबा षीरं।
दिष्टि बिदिष्टा जोइबा नैनं। पवन निरजंन बोलिबा बैनं।
सबद निहसबद तब होइबा थूलं। आदिका आदि सो होइबा मूलं।

नाद ब्यंद गांठिया पवन अकास। पड़ै घट न होइबा नासं।
धरणि गगन परि माघ न कोई। जंत्र चलै तहं काल न होई।
अषंड मढी तहां जोतिबा ध्यांन, जुग जुग ताली कथिवा ग्यांन।
मूल चक्र तहां प्रगटै ज्यंदू, पलटै काया थिर होइ कंधू।
मूल बन्ध बज्र कछोटा पकड़िबा थीरं, सत उडियांणी, बंधिबा बीरं।
जत जगोटा आसण पूरं, अमृत धारा कमंडल होइबा सूरं।
कुंभ पात्रे पीयबा नीरं, चेतनां विभूति अंगि सरीरं।
अजर कथा नहीं बाद विबादं। अनाहद सींगी बाइबा नादं।
संतोष तिलक तहां पद नृबांणं। ब्रह्म कवल टोपीं पहरिबा त्राणं।
मन बैराग मुंद्रा जोई रूपं। बदंत गोरष ए तत अनूपं।
दया दंड तहां तृकुटी ध्यांनं। छिमा लाठी टेकिबा मांनं।
चंद सूर भाटी उजेबा धारं। झूरै गगन तहां होइ मतिवारं।
सो जोग्यंद्र जोग जुगता अबिचल सारं। छछंद मुक्ता भै भ्रमपारं।
दोइ पछि ब्रह्म बिंधबा सूलं। गुर बचन अनाहद मांनिबा मूलं।
अनंत सिधा तहां सारमसारं। निश्चल थीरं तब होई निरालं।
अजाचीक भिक्ष्या आइबि थानं। गुरू मछींद्रनाथ नी सिछ्या पहरिबाकांनं।
अकलप डीबी झोली निरांसं। सजीवन मात्रा बीरजनांसं।
एकांति रहीबा अवधू बेधिबा थूलं। नहिं होवै आवागमन का मूलं।
बारह कला देबी सोलह कल देवं। सुषमनां नारी बंधिबा भेवं।
नौ से जोगणीं चालिबा साथं। बुरिज बहतरि गाइबा नाथं।
नव षंड प्रिथमी मांगिबा भिक्षा। त्रिलोकमधे न होइवी विप्यष्या।
चवदह ब्रह्मंड तहां जोहबा द्वारं। षट दरसन ए पंथ लै सारं।
दार बहनीं ज्यूं होइबा भेवं। असंष दल पंषूडी गगन करि सेवं।
बदंत गोकरष अबिचल जापं। लिपै नहीं तहां पुंन न पापं।
सुंनि ध्यानं सोलह कला समूरण माला। आपण स्यंभू श्रीगोरष बाला।

इती श्रीगोर्ष सिष्या पढंते गुणंते, कथंते करंते, पापे न लिपंते, पुन्ने न हारंते, ॐ नमो सिवाइ, ॐ नमो सिवाइ, गुरु मछींद्रनाथ पादुका नमस्तते। एवं सिक्ष्या दरसण जोग ग्रंथ शास्त्र संपूरण समाप्तः।

Should pick up from the fumes and slowly drop. When removing alcohol first the through the process of evaporation the alcohol rises up and then falls into another vessel through a filter.

In this way the one who partakes of the alcohol (ambrosia) falling from the sky he becomes intoxicated. This means he is completely devoted to yoga, he is Yogindra. Such a yogi stays in the essence (stays with experience, stays immovable in the soul) and crosses all fear and doubt and moves about freely.

Duality is a bird, is dependent on duality. Consider this as sorrow. On the basis of the teachings of the Guru consider the Anhad nada is its source or like the Sanskrit translation says, consider the words of the Guru as Anhada nada.

Being at ease is the thatched roof, no expectations from any one is the small begging bag. By rising upwards and drawing the semen towards the brahmrandhra (cranial apparatus) is like sanjivani–the life giving panacea.

One should stay in solitude. O realized yogi one should pierce the gross element implying one should know the secret behind it. Doing this destroys the reason for the continuous cycle of birth and death. Devi (the female Kundalini energy that has contact with the sun) has twelve aspects and dev (Shiva) has sixteen aspects (moon) which should be controlled by Sushumna and their secret should be known. In this way bring along 900 yoginis (nine nerves), 72 nerves will sing a song. One should ask for alms in the nine sections of the earth, that is, one should keep control over the nine doors. In this way there will be no opposition to your going to the Trikuti, no objection when you reach the brahmrandhra at the top of the head. There one should see the door of the 14 brahmins (home) this sect has taken the essence of the six darshans. Then just like the wood has fire hidden inside it similarly the hidden supreme soul will manifest in you. One should do service to the innumerable lotuses there. There Gorakh is calm and is chanting, there merits or sins do not touch one, in the supreme void he has seen the moon in all the 16 aspects and through perfection in yoga Gorakh who has received the form of a child becomes Shiva himself.

Prann sankali

प्रथमे प्रणऊं गुरु के पाया। जिन मोहि आत्म ब्रह्म लषाया।
सत गुरु सबद कह्यां तै बूझ्या। तुहूँ लोक दीपक मनि सुझ्या ॥1॥
पाप पुंन करम का बासा। मोष मुक्ति चेतहु हरि पासां
जोग जुक्त जब पाओ ग्याना। काया पोजौ पद नृबाना ॥2॥
सप्त दीप नव षंड ब्रह्मण्डा। धरती आकाश देवा रविचंदा।
तजिबा तिहुँ लोक निवासा। तहाँ निरञ्जन जोति प्रकासा ॥3॥
दिवस न रातृ बरषे न मासा। गरजै मेष गगन कविलासा।
अगम सुगम गढ़ रच्या बिनांणीं। अगनि पवन षेह जलं सांणीं ॥4॥
तीस पौलि तेरह प्रबांणी। तीनि गुप्त दस प्रकट जांणीं।
नौ नाटिका कोटड़ी बहतरि। चोर पचास पचीस पंच घरि ॥5॥
चोरा लगा तीनिसै साठी। नौसे षाई नाटिक गांठी
नदी अठारह गंडिक बहई। मगर मच्छ जल पैरत रहई ॥6॥
अहूठ कोटि बनासपती माला। सहज कमल दल पदमनी नाला।
भेदि षट चक्र बसै नांगणीं। कोटणीं सत मोहि फणीं ॥7॥
सबद एक जै प्रगट कहूँ सतगुर होई लषावै।
गुहज्य नाम अमींरस मीठा जो षोजै सो पावै ॥8॥
गंगा जमुना तृबेणीं संधी। अजपा जपौ गावत्री बन्धी।
पदया नीर उरध अस्थांनां। हिरदा पंकज मैं रहै समांनां ॥9॥
नाद बिंद गांठि प्रवांनां। कवण घटि जोति कवण अस्थानां ॥
कहाँ निरजँन बासा कहरीं। कहाँ काली नागनी मीड़क धरहीं ॥10॥

कहाँ जलधर पवनां मेला। उद्र कहाँ बिलइया घेरा।
सींगी नाद कहाँ जोगी पूरा। जीत्या संग्राम पुरिष भया सूरा ॥11॥
पूनम चंदा कैसैं छीनां। रवि ससि फेरि पवन घरि कीनां।
सुपिनैं इंद्री कांम न गहई। ता कारणि जोगेस्वर परलै ढहई ॥12॥
सप्त गांठि सरीर की नारी। अरध उरध मैं लाइलै ताली।
बिच बिच लागी नौ नौ कली। अष्ट कवल बतीस पांषुड़ी ॥13॥
नाद रह्या सरबत्र पूरि। गगन मंडल मैं षोजौ अवधू वस्त अगोचर मूर।
नगर कोटि की बहुविधि गली। सुन्दिर एक राजंदरि खड़ी ॥14॥
पंच महा रिषि तहाँ कुटवाल। तिनकी तृया महा झूझारि।
इनहि मारि जें लागै पंथा। सुन्दिर जीतै लोक सौ कंथा ॥15॥
इला प्यंगुला सुषमनां नाड़ी। छुटै भ्रंम मिलै बनवारी।
पंच तत्त विष अंमृत बसई। गुरूवचन अंमृत भया अंचई ॥16॥

The lamp of knowledge lights up the three worlds.

One should search for salvation inside the body. Leave living life outwardly, leave the desire to look outside of yourself towards material objects and start looking inwards. It is there that the light of the supreme spirit is shining bright. Death cannot even touch it.

The results of day and night, months and years cannot reach there. Fire, air, earth and water together have built this unreachable but accessible fort called the body. Ordinarily this fort is inaccessible but by yogic practice it becomes accessible. This is as high as Mount Kailash. Above this the clouds roar in the sky.

There are many proven doors to reach that world in which ten are visible and three are invisible(the ten visible doors are the nine openings along with the Brahmarandhra. The three invisible door are secret that is why the yogis have not mentioned it in their banis- precepts). It has nine nerves and seventy two mansions. The nerves are considered to be 72,000. Out of them 72 are considered excellent and out of them ten are considered to be the main ones. Here the nerves are the same nine ones barring Sushumna. All of them meet in Sushumna. Their name are Ida, Pingala, Gandhari, Hastijivha, Poosha, Yashasvini, Alambusha, Kuhu and Shankini.

In this house there are fifty (meaning the six chakras whose count of lotus petals add to fifty, twenty-five-twenty prakriti, see further Gorakh Ganesh Goshthi) and the five elements are the thieves. Till the six chakras are pierced the twenty five prakritis cannot be controlled. Meaning –till the time one does not rise above the sense organs one cannot attain perfection in the attainment of a spiritual state.

The 360 bones in the body are like stones by which this fort is built. The main nine nerves in the body are like a pit. There are believed to be 72,000 nerves in the body. Just like there are 84 lakh births of a human being but sometimes we just say 84 the same way it has been said 72 here. Crocodile, fish symbolize materialism and it's sign ego.

The innumerable nerves end in many pores. The pore that arise from them are like a garland of flora. The nerves that are entangled in each other are called kothri above. The main knots are called lotus here through a metaphor. These are the six chakras. The Kundalini energy is based here. That leper (kundalini, illusion) spreads its illusion like hands to mask the truth, does not let anybody reach the truth.

The one word that I am saying expressively can only be shown by a Guru, the ambrosia or nectar is sweet but it is secret. The one who is a real seeker of truth can only get it.

The word 'bandhi' means to be tied or be totally involved. Padya would mean padya neer. Neer would mean semen but the word padya is not clear. Padya–so associated with feet so it would mean that the semen that is lying low should be made to move upwards.

One should bind the nada (sound)and the bindu (semen) should be bound in a proven manner. In which body does the light reside (it's abode is where the pure consciousness resides, maya or illusion is like a black serpent who eats up the frogs-individual soul).

The upward moving breath meets where where does the the cat (illusion) catches hold of the mice (individual) where does the yogi play his anahata nada-singhi nada...plays it in the battlefield after the win and the brave soldier (seeker) becomes a purush (realized soul).

How did the nectar flowing out of the full moon dry up - because the sun has returned the moon and has taken control over the breath. Do not accept the desires of the sense organs even in a dream, do not be inspired by the mind's desires, that is why the God of yoga decides to bring about pralaya or apocalypse which means an apocalypse where the desires of the mind are subsumed.

There are seven knots in the nerves of the body. These refer to the six chakras and the seventh chakra at the crown of the head – Sahasrara. Concentrate on the breath that goes downwards and upwards. In between there are nine buds (nine openings) and eight lotuses (the yogis believe in eight lotuses). The seventh the gyan chakra which has the thousand petalled lotus and the eighth having 21 thousand petalled lotus. See the text–Ashta granth (and has 32 petals).

The Anahata nada or the unstruck sound is filled to the brim. O enlightened seeker! search for the invisible source the Shiva principle in the Brahmrandhra. The body is like a fort with a parafet wall around it and it has many paths. But one woman (kundalini–illusion) is standing at the main gate stopping the way, it does not let one reach the main destination.

In this city there are five great sages (five sense organs) that are the police heads and do not get anyone go inside to meet the king – implying the sense organs create obstacles in the realization of the self. Their wife (mind) is very strong and adept at warfare. The one who kills these five sense organs and walks on the path and also wins over maya (illusion) and along with it the world and the body as well.

Ida, Pingala and Sushumna are the three main nerves through which the vital life force or prana flows. The practice of which clears all doubt and one meets the supreme reality. With the contact with five sense organs the ambrosia remains like poison. When it turns into ambrosia with the words of the Guru, then the disciple partakes it.

इति श्री गोरखनाथ विरंचते प्रांण संकली सरीर विचारण, एवं प्राण संकली जेन्य विचारंत, पापे न लिपंते पुंने न हरंते, मृतलोके भये अस्थित अमर लोकेषु

गछिते। ॐ नमो सिवाई, ॐ नमो सिवाई गुरु मछींद्रनाथ पादुका नमस्तते इती प्राण संकली ग्रन्थ जोग सास्त्र सपूरण समापतः।

Narvai Bodh

सुणौ हो नरवै सुधि बुधि का बिचार।
पंच तत ले उपतनां सकल संसार।
पहलै आरम्भ घट परचा करौ निसपती।
नरवैबोधकथंत श्रीगोरष जती ॥1॥
पहलै आरम्भ छाड़ौ काम क्रोध अहंकार।
मन माया विषै बिकार।
हंसा पकड़ि घात जिनि करो।
तृस्नां तजौ लोभ परहरौ ॥2॥
छांड़ौ दंद रहौ निरदंद।
तजौ अल्यंगन रहौ अबंध।
सहज जुगति ले आसण करौ।
तन मन पवनां दिढ करि धरौ ॥3॥
संजम चितओ जुगत अहार।
न्यंद्रा तजौ जीवन का काल।
छाड़ौ तंत मंत बैदंत।
जंत्रं गुटिका धात पाषंड ॥4॥
जड़ी बूटी का नांव जिनि लेहु।
राज दुवार पाव जिनि देहु।
थंभन मोहन बसिकरन छाड़ौ औंचाट।
सूणौ हो जोगेसरौ जोगारम्भ की बाट ॥5॥

O King! You also listen. Listen to the pure words full of

intellect. The five elements–earth, water, air , fire, ether have given rise to the entire world. The yogi Gorakhnath says that leave the business of the world and meet the soul. The one who gives up anger, ego, illusion, weaknesses is the real sage. Do not be violent. Try to live a life without duality.

और दसा परहरौ छतीस।
सकल बिधि ध्यावो जगदीस।
बहु बिधि नाटारम्भ निबारि।
काम क्रोध अहंकारहि जारि ॥6॥
नैणं महां रस फिरौ जिनि देस।
जटा भार बंधौ जिनि केस।
रूष बिरष बाड़ी जिनि करौ।
कूवा निवांण षोदि जिनि मरौ ॥7॥
टूटै पवनां छीजै काया।
आसण दिढ करि बैसौ राया।
तीरथ बर्त कदे जिनि करौ।
गिर परबतां चढि प्रान मति हरौ ॥8॥
पूजा पाति जपौ जिनि जाप।
जोग माहिं बिटंबौ आप।
छाडौ बैद बणज-व्यौपार।
पढ़िबा गुणिबा लोकाचार ॥9॥
बहुचेला का संग निबारि।
उपाधि मसांण बाद बिष टारि।
येता कहिये प्रतक्षि काल।
एकाएकी रहौ भुवाल ॥10॥
सभा देषि माडौ मति ग्यांन।
गूंगा गहिला होइ रहौ अजांण।
छाड़ौ राव रङ्क की आस।
भिछ्या भोजन परम उदास ॥11॥

सींगी नाद पयानां देहु।
देव कला कै लछिन लेहु।
बग ज्यूं ध्यांन् मांडि जिनि रहौ।
स्वान जती की निंद्रा गहौ ॥12॥
रस रसाइंन गोटिका निवारि।
रिधि परिहरौ सिधि लेहु बिचारि।
परहरौ सुरापांन अरु भंग।
तातैं उपजै नाना रंग ॥13॥
नारी सारी कींगुरी।
तीन्यूं सत गूर पर हरी।
आरंभ घट परचै निसपती।
नरवै बोध कथंत श्री गोरष जती ॥14॥

इति श्री गोरखनाथ विरंचते, नरवै बोध ग्रन्थ, पठंते गुणंते कथंते, पापे न लिप्यंते, पुन्ये न हरंते, ॐ नमो सिवाई ॐ नमो सिवाई गुरु मछींद्रनाथ पादुका नमसतते। इति श्री नरवै बोध ग्रंथ जोग सास्त्र सपूरण समापत।

Self Realization - Atma Bodh

ॐ आसण करि पदम आसण बंधि। पिछलै आसण पवनां संधि।
मन मुछावै लावै ताली। गगन सिषर मैं होइ उजाली ॥1॥
प्रथमि बैसि बाई दर बंधि। पवनां षेलै चौसठ संधि।
नव दरवाजा देवै ताली। दसवां मधें होइ उजाली ॥2॥
ऐसा भुवंगम जोगी करै। धरती साषै अंबर भरै।
गगने सुर पवने सुर तांणि। धरनी का पांणी अंबरि आंणि ॥3॥
ता जोगी की जुगति पिछाणि। मन पवन ले उनमनि आंणि।
मन पवन ले उनमनि रहै। तौ काया जगजै गोरष कहै ॥4॥
चढ़ै महारस अभरा भरै। ऐसा अरम्भ जोगी करै।
उलटी सक्ति चढ़ै बह्मंड। नष सष पवनां षेलै नव षंड ॥5॥
उलटै चन्द्र राह कौं ग्रह। सूरज उलांट केत संग्रहै।
ससि द्वार सरज थिर रहै। तत्व भांण जोगेस्वर कहै ॥6॥
अरधैं जाता उर्धौं गहै। द्वादस पावनां उनमन रहै।
अहनिसि बाई धुंनि मैं बाजै। पछिम द्वारै पवनां गाजै ॥7॥
अभिअंतरि ब्रह्म अगनि परजालै। पेच चोर ले ग्यान संभालै।
जोगी अपणैं घरि दिवाला दीपै। ता जोगी की काया काल न छीपै ॥8॥
हलि हलि पवनां काया गरजै। सूरा होइ अभिअंतरि झूझै।
ग्यान षडग ले झूझिबाद्वारं। अजीत जीतिबा पंच गहि सारं ॥9॥
अष्ट परबत असाध साधिबा। नव दरबाजा दिढ करि बांधिबा।
दसवैं दरवाजे कूची सार। मैमंत हस्ती बांधिबा बार ॥10॥

भींतरि राजा झूझण हार। चुहँदिसि जाता राष्या मार।
राजा झूझै बिषमैं घाइ। मन पवन ले रहै समाइ ॥11॥
मन पवन को बिषमी संधि। चंद सूर द्वै समिकरि बंधि।
नवसै नवासी सायर सोषै। जोगी सोषै सदा भरि षोषै ॥12॥
बिन पुस्तक वंचिबा पुरांण। सुर्स्वती उचरै ब्रह्म गियांन।
अझर सोषै बजर करै। सर्व दोष काया ले हरै ॥13॥
षेरै षोजै लावै बध। तौ अजरावर थिर है कंध।
सोषै पोषै जालैं बालैं। अह निसि ब्रह्म अग्नि परजालै ॥14॥
अहनिसि अगनि पाप कूं षाइ। संधै संधै पवन लुकाइ।
मन है धीर थिर बहै पवनं। सिवपुरी जीता राषै कवनं ॥15॥
ब्रह्म सागर सोषै बध ज्यंद। षीर सागर सोषै अजरांवर कंद।
बजर कछोटा आसण करै। रोग व्याधि षुध्या सब हरै ॥16॥
जड़ी बूटी भूलै मति कोइ। पहल रांड बैद की होइ।
जड़ी बूटी अमर ज करै। तौ बैद धनन्तर काहे मरै ॥17॥
सोनै रूपै सीझे काज। तौ कत राता छांड़ै राज।
पसुवा हाइ जपै नहीं जाप। सो पसुवा मोषि क्यू जात ॥18॥
रिधि सकेलै रौलांणी धरै। गुरु न षोजै मुरिष मरै।
रौलांणीं आगै बैसै फूलि।गुर की बाचा गया जे भूलि ॥19॥
अकल पुरिस कै सकल नियाव। मीठा बोलै झूठा भाव।
सत बोलै सोई सतबादी। झूठ बोलै सो महा पापी ॥20॥
देषत भौंदू बिषिया षाई। झूठा बोलै मरि मरि जाई।
जैसा करै सो तैसा पाय। यकोतर सै पुरिषा नरकि लै जाय ॥21॥
एक पूरिष बहु भांति नारी। सरब निरन्तर आत्मां सारी।
सरब निरन्तर भरि पूरि रहिया। आत्मां बोध सपूरण कहिया ॥22॥
पापै न पुन्ने लिपे न काया। आत्मां बोध कंथत श्री गोरषराया।

The Sun and the moon upturn and bite 'rahu' and 'ketu'. In this way, the God of Yoga, who is bright as the sun due to his knowledge as the the sun becomes stable at the gateway of the moon, meaning that deliberately the union of the sun and the moon is brought on, since it is brought out with stubborn effort, it is a part of Hatha yoga.

The breath goes down should be made to go upwards towards the crown of the head and should stay in the state of thoughtlessness,. When the air rushes through the path of Sushumna and day and night there is a sound that comes our from the breath and the unstruck sound or the anahata nada is heard.

The warrior king (soul) is inside and he has killed the mind who runs in all the four directions and has safely kept him inside.

The king (soul) fights a battle that is difficult (he suffers wounds) but he keeps fighting and keeps the union of the mind and the breath, that is, stays involved in yoga.

The union of the mind and the breath is difficult that is why balance the sun and the moon and bind them by one. The yogi does not get disturbed with the increased amount of sperm. He soaks up the nine hundred and ninety nine oceans (that is, limitless semen) and makes it move upwards and fills the empty space again.

The yogi does not need to read scriptures to educate himself. The Goddess of learning Saraswati herself sits in his heart and talks about supreme consciousness, the yogi should make the opposing semen come under his control by make it move upwards and practices the Vajroli mudra and thereby destroys all the impurities of the body.

The amrit (ambrosia) that is flowing away has to be searched for and through yogic practices like Jalandhar bandh (lock) and prevents its destruction and the body becomes stable. The kand–it is the place behind the root chakra from where the entire web of nerves comes out. Once it become stabilized the body becomes immortal. It should soak the semen (make it move upwards) which will nourish the body and one will experience self-realization and one should let the divine fire burn day and night.

In this manner this fire will burn all the sins day and night, fearing which the breath will sit in each joint and run away. In this way when the breath stabilizes, the mind will also become stable. When that happens who will be able to win the soul who won over the brahmrandhara (seat of Shiva) who can capture it now.

To soak up the sea of supreme consciousness , that is, to move it upwards one has to increase one's life force and by soaking the amrit (ambrosia) the body becomes immortal. One should wear the vajra kaupin and do the vajrasana by which all disease and hunger and thirst will vanish.

If things could be accomplished by gold and silver then why would kings like Bhartrihari and Gopichand leave their kingdom. The human beings that remain in an animal state by not chanting (ajapa japa) how can they achieve salvation?

The one who amasses wealth and keeps a yogini and does not search for a Guru, in this manner that foolish one dies, he–the one who gladly sits in front of a woman but forgets the words of a Guru.

The one who has experienced the supreme consciousness all his conduct becomes complete though he might not speak softly.

इति श्रीगोरष आतमबोध, पठंते करंते गुणंते कथंते। पापि न लिपंते पुंने न रहंते।

ॐ नमो सिवाई ॐ नमो सिवाई गुरु मछिंद्रनाथ पादुका नमस्तते। इति श्रीआतमां बोध ग्रंथ जोग सास्त्र सपूरण समाप्तः ॥

अभै मात्रा जोग

ॐ अकल पंथ, अकलि का मारग, सत भोमि, सहज आसन प्रांण, जोगी, पवन गुटिका, निज भुवन गुफा, सञ्जम कोपीन, मरजादा मेषलीं, निहकेवुल जगौटा, जुगति, उडयांणीं, साच मुद्रा, सील कंथा, षिमांटोषी, जरनां, अधारी, अंतरि गति झोली, धीरज, डंड, बमेक फाहुड़ी तप चक्र, मूल कंमडल, मन उदिक, महा अमृत भोजन, दया, रह रासि, बिचार पुसतक, जिभ्या रसांयन, सरबंङ्गी कला, विद्या बंचणीं, नृपै नग्री, अकल बनषंड, निरास मढी, अतीत, देवता, गिनांन दीपक, अकलप रहनी, आजाचीक भिक्ष्या, सबद सींगी, अनहद कोंगुरी स्याम सरोवर, अमृत प्याला, निहंचल रिर्धी, सति करामाति, मुक्ति सिधि अलेष ध्यांन, अटल समाधि, निराकार तरवर, जुग पलव, अमीं फल।

इती अभै मात्रा संपूर्ण

Fifteen dates

बंदै गोरष एकंकार। पंद्रह तिथि का कह बिचार ॥टेक॥
अमावस दिढ़ आसण होइ। आतम परचै मरै न कोइ।
मूल सहस्र पवनां बहै। बंक नालि तब बहत रहै ॥1॥
पड़िवा है द्वै पष की आदि। सतगुरु सबदां सहज समाधि।
गगन मंडल मैं रहै समाइ। तौ चारि जुग लौं हेलै टलि जाइ॥2॥
दुतिया द्वै कुल उधरन धीर। उनमन मनवां अखलि सरीर।
बाहरि भीतरि एकंकार। गुरु प्रसादै भौ निधि पार ॥13॥
तृतीया तृबेणी करौ स्नान। पाप पुंनि दोउ देउ दान।
तब जोग जुगति पाऔ बिसवास। जुरा मरण नहीं कंध बिनास ॥4॥
चौथे चंचल निहचल करौ। काल बिकाल दूर परहरौ ॥
जम जौरा का मर्दौ मांन। सतगुर कथिया पद निरबांन ॥5॥
पांचमि पंच तत की संधि। माता मैंगल राषौ बंध।
अमीं महारस छिन छिन पीबौ। गुर परसादैं जुगि जुगि जीवौ ॥6॥
छटि षट चक्र बिचारौ सार। रिधि सिधि बुधि मति अषिल भंडार।
अरथ दरब की छाड़ौ आस। काया कांमिनि भेाग बिलास ॥7॥
सातन सतरज तम गुण बंधि। पावौ जीवण मरण की संधि।
अबिहड़ अजर अमर पद गगौ। मन पवन ले उनमन रहौ ॥8॥
आटमि अष्ट भैरौ नवनाथ। अनंत सिधां सौ मिल्यौ संघात।
अचंभ बांणीं कथी न जाइ। झरत महारस गगन समाइ ॥9॥
नवमीं नव निधि काया मंझारि। पाप पुंनि देषौ पट तारि।
बूडै पाप तिरै सत धरम। काया बाहरि जाति न जनम ॥10॥

दसमी दह दिसि लागै बंध। जत सत संजम थिर ह्वै कंध।
धरम करम गुर बाचा लींन ग्यांन बिचषन बाजै बीन ॥11॥
एकादसी अग्यारह रुद्र। मांणक पायो काया समुंद्र।
अलष रतन गुरि दीयौ बताइ। एकादसी तिथि की राइ ॥12॥
द्वादसी दिनकर तपै अकास। पसरै किरण होइ प्रकास।
तहाँ चढ़ि भवरा रह्या समाइ। सतगुरि कथिया चीवन उपाइ ॥13॥
तेरसि तृकुटी समि करि मेलि। चंद सूरज दो संमि करि भेलि।
एक सिंध रूंध्या, नव घाट। सत गुर षौजौ ऊजू बाट ॥14॥
चौदसि चौदह रतन बिचार। काल बिकाल आवता निवारि।
आपैं आप देषौ पट तारि। उतपति परलै काया मंझारि ॥15॥
पून्यं पूगी मन की आस। माया मोह तजि भये उदास।
सोलह कला सूपरण चंद। गर परसाते थिर भया कंधि ॥16॥
पंद्रह तिथि कला को सधि। मछींद्र सादैं थिर भया कंध।
भया थिर तब आछै धीर। अंनत सिधां श्री गोरष पीर ॥17॥

If the yogi remains absorbed in the brahmarandhra (cranial apparatus) then all the four eras can be spent as a child's play that is, from one apocalypse to another apocalypse no body can do any harm to him.

सप्तवार

जोग मूल गहि बारंबार। सतगुरु सबदां सहज बिचार ॥टेक॥
आदित सोधौ आवा गवन। घट मैं राषौ दिढ़ करि पवन।
स्यौ पूजा करि बसवैं द्वारि। तौ गुर पावौं आजित वार ॥1॥
सोमवार मन धरिवा सुंनि। निहचल काया पाप न पुंनि।
ससिहर बरिषै अंबर भरै। तौ सोमवार गुंण एता करै ॥2॥
मंगल बिषमीं माया बंधि। चंद सूर दोऊ समि कर संधि।
जुरा मरण बंचौ भौ काल। तौ गुर पावौ मंगल वार ॥3॥
बुधवार गुर दीन्हीं बुधि। बिवरौं काया पावौ सिधि।
सिव धरि सक्ती पांणीं भरै। तौ बुधवार गुन एता करै ॥4॥
बृसपति वार विषम मन धरौं पांचौं इंद्री निग्रह करौ।
संषणीं लै रूंध्या नव द्वार। तौ गुर पावौ बृसपति बार ॥5॥
सुक्रवार सोधिवा शरीर। कहां बसै अमृत कहाँ बसै षीर।
नव बहतरि पवनां बहै। तौ सुक्रवार गुण बिरला लहै ॥6॥
थावर थिर करि आसण देहु। बारह सोलह गिणि गिणि लेहु।
ससि हर कै घरि आवै भांण। तौ दिन दिन थावर गगँन सनांन ॥7॥
सातौं आंन्यां एकैं रास। काला भौंरा बेधै पास।
प्यंडै प्रांणीं परचा भया। सप्त बार श्रीगोरष कह्या ॥8॥

मछींद्र गोरष बोध

योगियों की जीवन पद्धति पर विचार

गोरषोवाच : स्वामी तुम्हें गुरु गुसांई अम्हें जु सिष।
(सबद एक पूछिबा) दया करि कहिबा मनहि न करिबारोस
आरंभि चेली कैसे रहै। सतगुर होइ सो बूझया कहै ॥1॥

मछिंद्र उवाच : अवधू रहिबा हाटैं बाटैं रूष वृष की छाया।
तजिबा कांम क्रोध तृष्णां संसार की माया ॥
आप सौं गोष्टी अनंत बिचार।
षंडित निद्रा सुछिम अहार ॥2॥

गोरष– स्वांमी कौन देषिवा कौंन विचारिबा, कौंन ले धारिबा सारं।
कौन दोष मस्तक मुडाइबा, कौन ले उतरिबा पारं ॥3॥

मछिंद्र– अवधू! आपा देषिबा अनंत बिचारिबा, तत ले धरिबा सारं।
गुरू का सबद देषि मसतग मुडाइबा ब्रह्म ग्यान ले उतरिबा पारं ॥4॥

गोरष– स्वांमी आदेस का कौन उपदेस, सुंनि का कथं वास।
सबद का कौन गुरू, पूछंत गोरषनाथ ॥5॥

मछिंद्र– अवधू आदेस का अनूषम उपदेस, सुंनि का निरंतर बास।
सबद का परचा गुरू, कथंत मछिंद्र नाथ ॥6॥

गोरष– स्वांमी मनका कौन रूप, पवन का कौंन आकार।
दंम की कौन दसा, साधिबा कौंन द्वार ॥7॥

मछिंद्र– अवध मन का सुंनि रूप, पवन का निरालभ आकार।
दंम की अलेष दसा, साधिबा दसवैं द्वार ॥8॥

गोरष– स्वांमी कौन पेड़ि विन डाल, कौंन पषि बिन सूव।
कौंन पालि बिन नीर, कौंन बिन कालहि मूवा ॥9॥
मछिंद्र– अवधू पवन पेड़ि बिन डाल, मन पंषि बिन सूवा।
धीरज पालि बिन नीर, निंद्रा बिन कालहि मूवा ॥10॥
गोरष– स्वांमीं कौंन बीरज कौंन षेत्र।
कौन सरचंण कौंन नेत्र।
कौन जोग कौंन जुगति।
कौन मोक्ष कौंन मुकति ॥11॥
मछिंद्र– अवधू मंत्र बीरज मति षेत्र।
सुरति श्रवण निरति नेत्र।
ऊरम जोग धूरम जुगती।
जोति मोक्षि ज्वाला मुकति ॥12॥
गोरष– स्वामी कौंन मूल कौंण बेला।
कौण गुरू कौन चेला।
कौंण षेत्र कौंण मेला।
कौंण तत्त्व ले रमै अकेला ॥13॥
मछिंद्र– अवधू मन मूल पवन बेला।
सबद गुरू सुरति चेला।
त्रिकुटी षेत्र उलटि मेला।
नृबांण तत्त्व ले रमौ अकेला ॥14॥
गोरष– स्वामी कौंण घरि चन्द कौंण घरि सूर।
घौंण धरि काल बजावै तूर।
कौंण घरि पंच तत्व समि हरै।
सतगुर होइ सु बूझ्या कहै ॥15॥
मछिंद्र– अवधू मन घरि चंद पवन घरि सूर।
सुन्नि घरि काल बजावै तूर।
न्यांन घरि पंच तत्त्व समि रहै।
सतगुर होइ सु बूझ्याँ कहै ॥16॥

गोरष— स्वांमीं कौंण अमावस कौंण स पड़िबा।
कहाँ का महारस कहाँ ले चढ़िबा।
कौंण अस्थांने मन उनमन रहै।
सतगुर होइ सुबूझ्याँ कहै ॥17॥

मछिंद्र— अवधू रवि अमावस चन्द सु पड़िबा।
अरध का महारस उरध ले चढ़िबा।
गगन अस्थांने मन उनमन रहै।
ऐसा बिचारि मछिंद्र कहै ॥18॥

गोरष— स्वांमीं कु-सबद का कौंण ग्रास।
सु-सबद का कथं बास।
द्वादस अंगुल बाई कौंण मुषि हरै।
सतगुर होइ सु बूझ्यां कहै ॥19॥

मछिंद्र— अवधू कुसबद का सुसबद ग्रास।
सुसबद का निरंतर बास।
द्वादस अंगुल बाई गुरमुषि रहै।
ऐसा बिचार मंछिद्र कहै ॥20॥

गोरष— स्वांमीं आदि का कौंण गुरू।
धरती का कौंण भरतार।
ग्यांन का कौंण अस्थांन।
सुंनि का कथं द्वार ॥21॥

मछिंद्र— अवधू आदि का अनादि गुरू।
धरती का अम्बर भरतार।
ग्यांन का अस्थानं चैतनि।
सुंनि का परचा द्वार ॥22॥

गोरष— स्वांमीं कौंण परचै माया मोह टूटै।
कौंण परचै ससि घर फूटै।
कौंण परचै लागै बंधा।
कौंण परचै थिर है कंध ॥23॥

मछिंद्र– अवधू मन परचै माया मोह टूटै।
पवन परचै ससि घरि फूटै।
ग्यांन परचै लागै बन्ध।
गुरु परचै अजरावर कन्ध ॥24॥

गोरष– स्वांमीं बसै मन कहां बसै पवन।
कहां बसै सबद कहां बसै चंद।
कौंण असथानें ए तत रहै।
सतगुर होय स पूछ्यां कहै ॥25॥

मछिंद्र– अवधू हिरदै बसै मन नाभी बसै पवन,
रूप बसै सबद गगंन बसै चंद।
उरध सथांने ए तत रहै।
ऐसा बिचार मछिन्द्र कहै ॥26॥

गोरष– स्वामी हिरदै न होता, तब कहां रहिता मन।
नाभि न होती तब कहां रहिता पवन ॥
रूप न होता तब कहां रहिता सबद,
गगन न होता तब कहां रहिता चंद ॥27॥

मछिंद्र– अवधू हिरदा न होता तब सुंनि राता मन।
नाभी न होती तब निराकार रहिता पवन ॥
रूप न होता तब अकुलान रहिता सबद,
गगन न होता तब अंतरष रहिता चंद ॥28॥

गोरष– स्वांमी राति न होतीं दिन कहां थैं आया।
दिन प्रसरया राति कहां समाया॥
दिवा बुझांनां जोति कहां लीया बास।
प्यंड न होता तब प्रांण का कौंण बेसास ॥29॥

मछिंद्र– अवधू राति न होत्ती दिन सहजैं आया,
दिन प्रसर्‌यां राति सहजैं समाया।
दिवा बुझांनां जोति निरन्तरि लीया बास,
प्यंड न होता तब प्रांण का सुनि बेंसास ॥30॥

गोरष– स्वांमीं किया मधै कै लष चंद।
पुहुप मधे कहां बसै गंध।
दूध मधे कहां बसै घीव।
काया मधै कहां बसै जीव ॥31॥

मछिंद्र– अवधू काया मधे द्वै लष चंद।
पहूप मधे चेतनि गंध।
दूध मधे निरंतर बसै घीव।
काया मधो सरब व्यापीक जीव ॥32॥

गोरष– स्वामी कहां बसै चंद कहां बसै सूर।
कहां बसैं नाद बिंद का मूर।
कहां होइ हंसा पोवै पांणीं।
उलटी सक्ति आप घरि आंणीं ॥33॥

मछिंद्र– अवधू उरधैं बसैं चंद, अरथैं बसै सूर।
हिरदै बसै नाद बिंद का मूर।
गगन चढ़ि हंसा पीवै पांणीं।
उलटी सक्ति आप घरि आंणीं ॥34॥

गोरष– स्वांमीं कथं उतपन्यों नादं, कथं नाव समभवते।
कौंण ले थापते नादं, कथं नादं बिलीयते ॥35॥

मछिंद्र– अवधू ॐकार उतपतते नादं, नाद सुन्नि समिभवते।
स्रवन ले थापते नादं, नादं निरंजन बिलीयते ॥36॥

गोरष– स्वांमीं नादेन नादिबा बिंदेन बिंदबा,
गगनेन लाइबा आसा।
नाद बिंद दोऊ न होइगा,
तब प्रांन का कहां होइगा बासा ॥37॥

मछिंद्र– अवधू नादे भी नादिबा बिंदे भी बिंदवा,
गगने भी लाइबी आसा।
नाद बिंद दोऊ न होइगा,
तब प्रांण का निरंतर होइगा बासा ॥38॥

गोरख– स्वामी अकार छूटिसी निराकार होइसी,
पवन न होसी पांणीं।
चंद सूर दोऊ न होसी,
तब हंस की कौन सहनांणी ॥39॥

मछिंद्र– अवधू सहज हंस का षेल भणीजै, सुनि हंस का बास।
सहजै हीं आकार निराकार होइसी,
परम जोति हंस का निवास ॥40॥

गोरष– स्वांमीं अमूल का कौंण मूल, मूल का कथं बास।
पद का कौंण गुरू, पूछंत गोरष नाथ ॥41॥

मछिंद्र– अवधू अमूल का सुंनि मूल, मूल का निरन्तर बास।
पद का निरबांन गुरू, कथंत मछिंद्र नाथ ॥42॥

गोरष– स्वांमीं जी कथं उतपदिते प्रांण कथं उदपदिते मन।
कथं उदपदिते बाचा, कथं बाचा बिलीयते ॥43॥

मछिंद्र– अवधू अबगति उतपदिते प्रांण, प्रांण उदपदिते मन।
मन उदपदिते बाचा, बाचा मन बिलीयते ॥44॥

गोरष– स्वांमीं कौंन सरोबर कौंण सनाल।
कौंण मूष होइ बंचिये काल।
लोक अगोचर कैसे लिव लहै।
मन पवन कैसें समि रहै ॥45॥

मछिंद्र– अवधू मन सरोवर पवन सनाल।
उरध मुष होइ बंचिये जंम काल ॥
अरध उरध अगोचर लिव लहै।
मन पवन ऐसै समि रहै ॥46॥

गोरष– स्वांमीं कौंन सो बिषमी कौंण सो संधि।
कौणैं चक्री लागै बंध।
कौंणें चेतनि मन उनमनि रहै।
सतगुर होइसु बूझां कहै ॥47॥

मछिंद्र– अवधू अनली बिमली बिषमीं संधि।
चाकी ऊपरि लागै बन्ध।

सदा चेतनि मन उनमन रहै।
ऐसा विचार मछिंद्र कहै ॥48॥

गोरष– स्वांमीं कहां उतपन्यां व्यापक,
कहां आदि की अस्तुत समाई।
ए तत्त्व कहीं गुरू गुसाई,
जहां हमारी उत्पति रहाई ॥49॥

मछिंद्र– अवधू तिल मधे जथा तेलं,
काष्ट मधे हुतासनं।
पहुप मधे जथा बासं,
देही मधे तथा देवता ॥50॥

गोरष– स्वामी सापणि कुहकै कौंणे भाई।
बङ्क नालि है कौंणें ठांइ ॥
जब यहि पाणी निद्रा करै,
पिण्ड मधे प्राण अपरछन रहै ॥52॥

गोरष– स्वांमी कौंणें चक्रें दिढ़ करि चंद।
कौंणें चक्रै लागै बन्ध ॥
कौंणें चक्रै निपावै निरोध।
कौणैं चक्रै मैं मन प्रमोध॥
कौंणैं चक्रैं धरिये ध्यांन।
कौंणैं चक्रैं लीजै बिश्रांम ॥53॥

मछिंद्र– अवधू अरधै चक्रै दिढ़ करि चंद।
उधैं चक्रैं लागै बन्ध ॥
पछम चक्रैं निपावै निरोध।
हिरदा चक्र मैं मन प्रमोध।
कांठै चक्रैं धरिये ध्यांन।
ग्यानं चक्रैं लीजै विश्रांम ॥54॥

गोरष– स्वांमी कौंन उदैं माया सुन्नि।
नौ ग्रह कैसें पाप न पुन्नि ॥

कौंन ग्रह लै उनमन रहै।
सतगुर होइ सु बुझ्यां कहै ॥55॥

मछिंद्र– अवधू बोलता जैसे माया सुंनि,
नवग्रह बिचारै पाप न पुनि।
सिव सकती ले उनमन रहै।
ऐसा बिचार मंछिद्र कहैं ॥56॥

गोरष– स्वांमी कौंण घर कौंण बास।
कौंण गरभि रह्या दस मास।
कौंण मुषि पांणीं कौंण मुषि अस्तुति षीर।
कौंण दिसा भई उतपति सरीर ॥57॥

मछिंद्र– अवधू अनील गृह अबिगत बास,
अतीत गरभि रह्या दस मास।
मन मुषि पांणीं पवन मुषि अस्तुति षीर,
ओंकार दिसा भइ उतपति सरीर ॥75॥

गोरष– स्वांमीं कौंण नालि सिव संचर्‌या,
कौंण मुषि पईठा जीव।
कौंण गरभि बसंतडां,
कौंण नालि रस पीव ॥59॥

मछिंद्र– अवधू संषनि नालि सिव संचर्‌या,
सुषमनि पईठा जीव।
माता गरभि बसंतडां,
बंक नालि रस पीव ॥60॥

गोरष– स्वांमी कौन सुंनि उतपनां आइ।
कौंण सुंनि सतगुरू बुझाइ
कौंन सुंनि मैं रह्या समाइ।
ए तत्त्वा गुरू कहौ समुझाइ ॥61॥

मछिंद्र– अवधू सहज सुंनि उतपनां आइ।
समि सुंनि सतगुरू बुझाइ ॥

अतीत सुंनि मैं कहूँ समझाइ।
परम तत्त्व गुरू कहौ समुझाइ ॥62॥

गोरष– स्वांमीं कौंण मुषि लागै समाधि।
कौंण मुषि छूटै उपाधि।
कौंण मुषि ले तुरिया बन्ध।
कौंण मुषि अजरावर कंध ॥63॥

मछिंद्र– अवधू मन मुषि बाला लागै समाधि।
पवन मुषि बाला छूटै उपाधि।
सुरति मुषि बाला तुरिय बन्ध।
गुर मुषि बाला अजरावर कन्ध ॥64॥

गोरष– स्वांमी कौंण सोवै कौंण जागै।
कौंण दहदिसि जाइ।
कहां थैं उठंत कहां होइ,
होठ कण्ठ तालुका बजाइ ॥65॥

मछिंद्र– अवधू मन सोवै पवन जागै,
कलपनां दह दिसि जाइ।
नाभी थैं उठंत पवनां,
आगगैं होइ होठ कंठ तालुका बजाइ ॥66॥

गोरष– स्वांमीं कहां थै करै मन गुंण घणां।
कहां थै करै पवन आवागवनां।
कौंण मुषि चंदा नीझर झरै।
कौंण मुषि काल निद्रा करै ॥67॥

मछिंद्र– अवधू हृदा थै मन करै गुंण घणां।
नाभी थैं करै पवन आवागवनां।
आप मुषि चंदा नीझर झरै।
मन मुषि काल निन्द्रा करै ॥68॥

गोरष– स्वांमी कौंण तेज थैं जोति पलटै।
कौंण सुंनि थे बाचा फुरै।

कौंण सुंनि थैं त्रिभुवन सार।
कौंण सुंनि थैं उतरिबा पार ॥69॥

मछिंद्र– अवधू उग्र तेज थैंजोति पलटै।
अभय सुनि थैं बाचा फुरै।
परम सुंनि थैं त्रिभुवन सार।
अतीत सुंनि उतरिबा पार ॥70॥

गोरष– स्वांमी कथं उतपनी षुध्या कथं उतपनां अहार।
कथं उतपनीं निंद्रा, कथं उतपनां काल ॥71॥

मछिंद्र– अवधू मनसा उतपनीं षुध्या, षुध्या उतपनां अहार।
अहार उतपनों निंद्रा निंद्रा उतपनां काल ॥72॥

गोरष– स्वांमी सति सति भाषंत हो गुरू पंडिता,
मन पवन कौंण दिसा।
कौंण द्रिष्टि कौंण बिधि ग्यांन,
नृगंथा पार उंतरिबा किसा ॥73॥

मछिंद्र– अवधू द्रिष्टि थै दिब द्रिष्टि होइबा,
गिनांन थैं बिनांन होइबा।
तथा गुरू सिख की एकै काया,
परचा होइ तौ बिहड़ि न जाया ॥74॥

गोरष– स्वांमी कहां थैं उठंत सास उसासं।
कहाँ परम हंस का बासं।
कौंण घर मन थिर होइ रहै।
सतगुर होइ सु बूझयां कहैं ॥75॥

मछिंद्र– अवधू अरधै उठंत सास उसासं।
उरधैं परम हंस का बासं।
सहज सुन्नि मैं मन थिर रहै।
ऐसा बिचार मंछिद्र कहै ॥76॥

गोरष– स्वामी कैसे आसैं कैसें जाइ।
कैसें चीया रहै समाइ।

कैसें मन तन सदा थिर रहै।
सत गुर होइ सु बूझ्या कहै ॥77॥

मछिंद्र– अवधू सुंने आवै सुंने जाइ।
सुंने चीया रहै समाइ।
सहज सुंनि मन तन थिर रहै।
ऐसा बिचार मछिद्रं कहै ॥78॥

गोरष– स्वांमीं कहां बसै सक्ती कहां बसै सीव।
कहां बसै पवनां कहां बसै जीव।
कहां होइ इनका परचा लहै।
सतगुर होइ सुबझ्यां कहै ॥79॥

मछिंद्र– अवधू अरधै बसै सक्ती उरधैं बसै सीव।
भींतरि बसै पवनां अंतारी बसै जीव ॥
निरंतर इनका परचा लहै।
ऐसा बिचार मछींद्र कहै ॥80॥

गोरष– स्वांमीं कौंण मुषि बैठे कौंण मुषि चलै।
कौंण मुषि बोलै कौंण मुषि मिलै ॥
क्यूँ करि स्वामी नृभै रहै।
सतगुर होइ सुबझ्यां कहै ॥81॥

मछिंद्र– अवध सुरति मुषि बैठे सुरति मुषि चलै,
सुरति मुषि बोलै सुरति मुषि मिलै।
सुरति निरति मैं नृभै रहै।
ऐसा विचार मछिंद्र कहै ॥82॥

गोरष– स्वांमीं कौंण सो सब्द कौंण सो सुरति,
कौंण सो बंध कौंण सो निरति।
दुबध्या भेटैं कैसैं रहे।
सतगुर होइ सु बुझ्या कहै ॥83॥

मछिंद्र– अवधू सबद अनाहद सुरति सोचित।
निरति निरालंभ लागै बंध।

दुबध्या मेटि सहज मैं रहै।
ऐसा विचार मछिंद्र कहै ॥84॥

गोरष– स्वांमीं कौंण सो आसण कौंण सो ग्यान।
किहि बिधि बाला धरै धियांन
कैसे अबिगत का सुष लहै।
सतगुर होइ सु बूझ्यां कहै ॥85॥

मछिंद्र– अवधू संतोष सो आसण बिचार सो ग्यांन।
काया तजि करि धरिये ध्यान ॥
गुरमुष अबिगत का सुष लहै।
ऐसा बिचार मछिंद्र कहै ॥86॥

गोरष– स्वांमी कौंण संतोष, कौण बिचार।
कौण ध्यांन काया कै पार
कैसे इन मैं मनसा रहै।
सतगुर होइ सु बूझ्यां कहै ॥87॥

मछिंद्र– नृभै संतोष अनभै बिचार।
दुह मैं ध्यांन काया कै पार।
गरु मुषि मनसा इन मैं रहै।
ऐसा बिचार मंछिद्र कहै ॥88॥

गोरष– स्वांमीं पाइ बिन कौंन मारग,
चक्षि बिन कौंन दृष्टि।
करण बिन कौंण श्रवण।
मुष बिन कौंण सबद ॥89॥

मछिंद्र– अवधू पाइ बिन बिचार मारग,
चक्षि बिन निरति द्रिष्टी।
करण बिन सुरति श्रवण,
मुष बिन लाय सबद ॥90॥

गोरष– स्वांमीं कौंण सो घोवती कौंण सो आचार।
कौंण जाप मन तजै बिकार।

कौंण भाव थैं नृभै रहै।
सतगुर होइ सुबूझ्यां कहै ॥91॥

मछिंद्र– अवधू ध्यांन सो ब्रह्म आचार।
अजपा जाप मन तजै बिकार।
आतम भाव थै नृभै रहै।
ऐसा बिचार मछिंद्र कहै ॥92॥

गोरष– स्वांमी कौंण सो ॐकौंण सो आप।
कौंण सो माई कौंण सो बाप।
कैसें मन मैं दरियाव रहै।
सतगुर होइ सु बूझ्यां कहै ॥93॥

मछिंद्र– अवधू सबद सो ॐजोति सो आप।
सुंनि सोई माई चेतनि बाप।
निहचल मन मैं दरियाव रहै।
ऐसा बिचार मछिंद्र कहै ॥94॥

गोरष– स्वांमीं कौंण सो चेतनि कौंण सार।
कौंण निंद्रा कौंण काल।
कौंण महि पांचौ तत्त्व समि रहै।
सतगुर होइ सु बुझ्याँ कहै ॥95॥

मछिंद्र– अवधू जोति चेतनि निरमै सार।
जागिबा उतपत निंद्रा काल।
जोति महि पाँचौं तत्त्व समि रहै।
ऐसा बिचार मछिंद्र कहै ॥96॥

गोरष– स्वांमीं कौंण बोलै कौंण सोवै।
कौंण रूप मैं आपा जोवै।
कौंण रूप मैं जुगि जुगि रहै।
सतगुर होइ सु बूझ्यां कहै ॥97॥

मछिंद्र– अवधू सबद बोलै सक्ति सोवै।
अदेष रूप मैं आपा जोवै।

अरूप रूप मैं जुगि जुगि रहै।
ऐसा बिचार मछिंद्र कहै ॥98॥

गोरष– स्वामी कौंण मुषि रहणीं कौन मुषि ध्यान,
कौंण मुषि अमीं रस कौंण मुषि पांन।
कौंण मुषि छेदि बदेही रहै।
सतगुर होइ सु बुझ्यां कहै ॥99॥

मछिंद्र– अवधू सहज मूषि रहणीं सक्ति मुषि ध्यांन,
गगन मुषि, अमींरस चित मुषि पांन।
आसा मुषि छेदि बदेही रहै।
ऐसा बिचार मछिन्द्र कहै ॥100॥

गोरष– स्वांमी कौंण मुषि आवै कौंण मुषि जाइ।
कौंण मुषि होइ काल कौं षाइ।
कौंण मुषि होइ जोति मैं रहै।
सतगुर होइ सु बूझ्यां कहै ॥101॥

मछिंद्र– अवधू सहज मुषि होइ।
आवै सक्ति मूवि होइ जाइ।
निपष होइ काल कौ षाइ॥
निरास मुषि होइ जोति मैं रहै।
ऐसा बिचार मछिंद्र कहै ॥102॥

गोरष– स्वांमीं कौंण सो काया कौंण सो प्रांण,
कौंण पुरिस का करिये ध्यानं।
कौंण अस्थानं घरि काल सौं रहै,
सतगुर होइ सुबूझ्यां कहै ॥103॥

मछिंद्र– अवधू पवन सो काया मन सो प्रांण,
परम पुरिस का धरिये ध्यांन।
सहज अस्थांन घरि काल सौं रहै,
ऐसा बिचार मछिंद्र कहै ॥104॥

गोरष– स्वांमी कौंण सो कूंची कौंण सो ताला,
कौंण सो बूढ़ा कौण सो बाला।

कौंण अस्थांन मन चेतिन रहै।
सतगुर होइ सु बूझ्यॉं कहै ॥105॥

मछिंद्र– अबधू निहसबद कूंची सबद ताला।
अचेत बूढ़ा चेतनि बाला।
ग्यांन अस्थांन मन चेतनि रहै।
ऐसा बिचार मछिंद्र कहै ॥106॥

गोरष– स्वांमी कौंण सो साधिक कौंण सो सिधि,
कौंण सो माया कौंण सो रिधि।
कैसे मन की भ्रांतिज नसाइ।
गुरू गुंसाई कहौं समझाइ ॥107॥

मछिंद्र– अवधू सुरति सो साधिक सबद सो सिधि।
आप सों माया पर सो रिधि।
दुहुँ कौ मेटि निरति मैं रहै।
ऐसा बिचार मछिंद्र कहै ॥108॥

गोरष– स्वांमी कौंण सो सांचा कौंण सो रांग।
कौंण आभूषण चढ़ै सुरंग।
तामैं निहचल कैसे रहै।
सतगुर होइ सुबूझ्यां कहै ॥109॥

मछिंद्र– अवधू ग्यांन सो सांचा प्रांण सो रङ्ग,
जत आभूषण चढ़ै सुरङ्ग।
तामहि निहचल उनमन रहै।
ऐसा बिचार मछिंद्र कहै ॥110॥

गोरष– स्वांमी कौंण सो मंदिर कौंण सो देव।
कहां बैसि करि कीजै सेव।
कौंण सो पाती किहि बिध रहै।
सतगुर होइ सु बूझ्यां कहै ॥111॥

मछिंद्र– अवधू सुनि सो मंदिर मन सो देव।
बैसि निरंतर कीजै सेव।

पांचों पाती उनमनि रहै।
ऐसा विचार मछिंद्र कहै ॥112॥

गोरष– स्वांमीं कौंण सो मंदिर कौंण सो द्वार।
कौंण सो मूरति कौंण अपार।
कौंण रूप मन उनमन रहै।
सतगुर होइ सु बूझ्यां कहै ॥113॥

मछिंद्र– अवधू सुनि सो मंदिर सबद सो द्वार।
जोति सो मूरति ज्वाला अपार।
रूप अरूप मन उनमनि रहै।
ऐसा बिचार मछिंद्र कहै ॥114॥

गोरष– स्वांमीं कौंण सो दीवा कौंण प्रकास।
कौंण बाती तेल निवास।
कैसे दीवा अबिचल रहै।
सतगुर होइ सु बूझ्यां कहै ॥115॥

मछिंद्र– अवधू ग्यांन सो दीवा सबद प्रकास।
संतोष बाती तेल निवास।
दुबध्या मेटि अषंडित रहै।
ऐसा बिचार मछिंद्र कहै ॥116॥

गोरष– स्वांमी कौंण सो बैठा कौंण सो चल्या,
कौंण सो फिर्‍या कौंण सो मिल्या।
कौण सो घरि मैं निरभै रहे।
सतगुर होइ सु बूझ्यां कहै ॥117॥

मछिंद्र– अवधू धीरज बैठा चल्या बिकार।
सुरति सो फिर्‍या मिल्या सोइ सार।
सदा अतीत घरि निरभै रहै।
ऐसा बिचार मछिंद्र कहै ॥118॥

गोरष– स्वांमी कौंण सो जोगी कैसे रहै।
कौंण सो भोगी कैसे लहै।

सुष मैं कैसे उपजै पीर।
तामैं कौन बंधावै धीर ॥119॥

मछिंद्र– अवधू मन जोगी जै उनमनि रहै।
उपजै महारस सब सूष लहै।
रस ही मांहि अषंडित पीर।
सतगुर सबद बंधावै धीर ॥120॥

गोरष– स्वांमी कौंण सु आत्मां आवै जाइ।
कौंण सु आत्मां रहै समाइ
कौण सो आत्मां त्रिभुवन थीर।
कौण परचै बांवन बीर ॥121॥

मछिंद्र– अवधू पवन सो आत्मा आवै जाइ,
मन सो आत्मां सुनिं समाइ।
ग्यांन सो आत्मां त्रिभुवन थीर,
सबद परचै बांवन बीर ॥122॥

गोरष– स्वांमी मन का कौंण जीव,
जीव का कौंण बेसास।
बेसास का कौंण आधार,
आधार का कौंण रूप ॥123॥

मछिंद्र– अवधू मन का पवन जीव,
पवन का सुंनि बेसास।
बेसास का ब्रह्म आधार,
ब्रह्म का अच्यंत रूप ॥124॥

गोरष– स्वांमीं कौंण चक्र थिर होवै कंध।
कौंण चक्र अगोचर बंध।
कौंण चक्र मैं हंस निरोधै।
कौण चक्र मैं मन परमोधै।
कौंण चक्र में लहै सवाद।
कौंण चक्र मैं लागै समाध ॥125॥

मछिंद्र– अबधू मूल चक्र थिर होवै कंद।
गुदा चक्र अगोचर बंध।
मणि चक्र मैं हसं निरोधै।
अनहद चक्र अगोचर बंध।
बिसुध चक्र मैं लहै सवाद।
चंद्र चक्र मैं लागै समाध ॥126॥
गोरष– ए षटचक्र का जांणैं भेव।
सो आपैं करता आपैं देव।
मन पवन साधै ते जोगी।
जुरा पलटै काया होइ निरोगी ॥127॥

पापे न लिप्यते पुन्ये न हरंते ॐनमो सिवाइ ॐ नमो सिवाइ।
श्रीमछिंद्रनाथ पादुका नमस्तते।

रोमावली

सत पिता रज माता तम करि गाड़ी पाई,
लोह मास तुचा नाड़ी ये चारि धात माता की बोलिये,
बीरज हाल गुद्र ये तीनि धात पिता की बोलिये,
ए सप्त धात का शरीर बोलिये।
द्वै हाथ द्वै पैर छाती लिलाट घाट अष्टांग जोग बोलिये।
बंद भेद मुद्रा तीन्यूं साधंति ते सिधा बोलिये।
कौंण बंधि बांधिये, कौंण भेद भेदिये, कौंण मुंद्रा मुंदिये
ए बोलिये घट भीतरि। ते कौंण कौंण।
मन बन्धि बांदिये पवन भेद भेदिये बिंद मुंद्रा मुंदिये।
कौंण बिमल बिचारै कौंण षिरै कौंण झरै।
मन बिमल बिचारै कौंण सूरज षिरै चैद्र झरै।
हिंद पीर जिंद पीर ए बोलिये घट भींतरि। ते कौंण कौंण।
हिंद पीर बोलिये मन, जिद पीर बोलिये पवन।
षेचरी भूचरी गुपत प्रगट। ते कौंण कौंण।
षेचरी बोलिये मन, भूचरी बोलिये पवन,
गुपत बोलिये ग्यान प्रकट बोलिये सरीर।
सरीरारथ परमारथ, गूढ़ारथ। ते कौंण कौंण।
सरीरारथ बोलियो सरीर भेद, परमारथ बोलियो प्रांण भेद,
गूढारथ बोलिजै बिचार।
चारी पीर बोलिजै घट भींतरि। ते कौंण कौंण।

मन मछिंद्रनाथ पवन ईश्वरनाथ, चेतना चौरंगीनाथ,
ग्यांन श्री गोरषनाथ।
चारि तकबीर बोलिजै घट भींतरि। ते कौंण कौंण।
दृष्टि कहै क्यू लीजै दीजै, सुरति कहै क्यूं बोलिये सुणिये,
नासका कहै क्यू संगध बास परमलादि लीजै,
जिभ्या कहै क्यूं षाटी मींठी षाइये।
चारि दिशा बोलिये घन भींतरि। ते कौंण कौंण।
सबद बोलिये उत्तर, पवन बोलिये पछिम,
दृष्टि बोलिये दषिण सुरति बोलिये पूरव।
चारि आप कला बोलिये घट भीतरि। ते कौंण कौंण।
ऊरम धूरम जोति ज्वाला।
ऊरम बोलिये मन, धूरम बोलिये पवन,
जोति बोलिये नेत्र, ज्वाला बोलिये श्रवन।
चारि षांणी बोलिजै घट भींतर। ते कौंण कौंण।
स्वेतरज अंडरज जेरज उदबीरज।
सेतरज बोलिये हाड़ जेरज बोलिये बीरज अंडरज बोलिये नेत्र,
उदबीरज बोलिये रोमावाली।
चारि बांणी बोलिये षट भींतरि। ते कौंण कौंण।
सहज संजम सुपाइ अतीथ।
सहज बोलिये सरीर, संजम बोलिये पवन,
अतीत बोलिये परम पद।
महा मुद्रा महां अजाच नग्री महां जोगणी स्यंभू बोलिये।
जे बांणी षांणीं कौं बिचारै ते निराकार बोलिये,
ॐकार मधे जोति जांणिये
ऊरम धूरम जोति ज्वाला। भेदौ रवि का चार्यूं कला।
मन करि हस्ती विमल जल पीवै।
द्वै पष चीन्है तौ सोलह कला जीवै।
बारह कला सूरज, सोलहा कला चंद।

गुरू जिसका लषावै नहीं चेला तिसका अंध।
बारह कला सूरज की, ताकी गुण घट भींतरि ब्यापै।
ते कौंण कौंण।
चिंता, तरंग 'इ्यंभ, माया, परग्रहण, परपंच, हेत, बुधि, काम, क्रोध, लोभ; दृष्टि ये बारह कला सूरज बारह की बोलिये।
सोलह कला चंद्रमा की ताकै गुण षट भींतरि राषै।
ते कौंण कौंण।
सांति, नृवर्त, क्षिमां, नृमल, निहचंल ग्यांन, सरूप, पद, नृबांण, नृबिष, निरंजन, अहार,निद्रा, मैथुन, बाई, अंमृत ये सोलह कला चंद्रमा की बोलियें।
एचारि कला सूरज की साधै तौ सोलह कला चंद्रमा की पावै।
एती एक रोमांवली ग्रंथ जोग कथितं श्री गोरखनाथ।

Gyan Tilak

ॐ सबदहि ताला सबदहि कूची सबदहि सबद भया उजियाला।
कांटा सेती कांटा षूटै कूंची सेती ताला।
सिध मिलै तो साधिक निपजै, जब घटि होय उजाला ॥1॥

The word is the lock which has imprisoned the supreme consciousness and the word is itself the key with which that lock can be opened and a direct vision of God can be had.

The 'Pranav' word is the first diffraction of the supreme consciousness. That is why it has covered it but by worshipping the 'Pranav', one can witness the supreme consciousness which is not visible externally. That is why it is the key. The word of the Guru also has supreme consciousness hidden in it. The knowledge of supreme consciousness and supreme consciousness itself are not two different things and the difference is clear with the word of the Guru. Just like a thorn is taken out with a thorn and the lock is opened with the help of a key similarly it is from the word that the light of knowledge spreads all around.

अलख पुरुष मेरी दिष्टि समाना, सोसा गया अपूठा।
जब लग पुरुषा तन मन नहीं, निपजै, कथै बदै सब झूठा ॥2॥

By the vision of the absolute spirit or the supreme individual (purusha) his visage consumed my being the result of which was that I was myself soaked up by the supreme spirit. The supreme spirit dissolved in me and I dissolved in the supreme spirit. Till such time the supreme individual, the supreme consciousness does not appear in the body, is not manifest there, till the time we do not experience him in all our being, all spiritual utterances are untrue.

सहज सुभाव भेरी तृष्ना फीटी, सींगी नाद संगि मेला।
यंम्रत पीया विषै रस टार्‌या गुर गारड़ौं अकेला ॥3॥

The thirst, desires that have naturally been destroyed and the Anahata nada, the unstruck sound–the symptom of which is also called singinada that has been accepted by Nathpanth, I have united with supreme consciousness. In this way the conjurer like Guru has removed my poison of worldly desires and brought me to the kaivalya stage of enlightenment.

सरप मरै बांबी उठि नाचै, कर बिनु डैरूं बाजै।
कहै नाथ जौ यहि बिधि जीतै, पिंड पडै तो सतगुर लाजै ॥4॥

The one whose Kundalini energy or shakti-supreme power that has merged in Shiva-the supreme spirit, the one whose illusions have died, his body after partaking the nectar of yoga breaks out in a dance of bliss. Inside him the damru (musical instrument of Shiva) starts playing without the movement of the hands–that is, the Anahata nada starts playing. Nath says, in this manner the seeker who obtains victory over maya or illusion he becomes immortal. If Such a disciple who has reached this level of perfection dies, then it is a matter of shame for his Guru. Because this indicates that the Guru is incomplete himself so what can he teach the disciple.

दरपन माहीं दरसन देष्या, नीर निरंतरि झांई।
आपा माहीं आपा प्रगट्‌या, लखै तौं दूर न जाई ॥5॥

The one who has seen the vision in the mirror, implying the one who has himself witnessed the pure supreme consciousness–just like an object's reflection falls in the water, and the one's whose soul manifested in his own self, such a person need not wander here and there. He achieves stability by himself.

चकमक ठरकै अगनि झरै यूं, दूध मथि घृत करि लीया।
आपा माहीं आपा प्रगट्‌या, तब गुरू सन्देसा दीया ॥6॥

Just like the stone chakmak emits out fire on rubbing, and just like curd is churned to take out ghee (clarified butter) similarly when the soul appears on its own one should understand that the Guru has imparted the right knowledge, the Guru's knowledge has had an impact.

सुरति गहौ संसै जिनि लागौ, पूंजी हांन न होई।
एक तत सूं एता निपजै, टार्‌या टरै न सोई ॥7॥

O seeker! Do not forget your own self. Seek the soul, do not fall in doubt. The soul is such a wealth that never diminishes , the soul principle is such that creates the wealth–the wealth of contentment that does not go away even by effort.

निहचा है तौ नेरा, निपजै, भया भरोसा नेरा।
परचा है तौ ततषिन, निपजै, नहीं तर सहज न बेरा ॥8॥

By relying on spirituality and by having faith in it this wealth appears quickly. And by self-realization it emerges immediately. If any of this does not happen, then know that you have been finished naturally, that is, that wealth cannot be achieved.

जे लूट्‌या जिनि षबरि न पाई, कसि करि यंद्री डांडी।
तन मन की कछु षवरि न पाई, सुरति बिगोया रांडी ॥9॥

The ones who have been looted by illusion and are not even aware of it, they give a heavy punishment to their sense organs. They are not aware of the body and the mind. Running after illusions, their spirituality gets destroyed.

बिंद और भग बाघणि औरैं, बिन दांतां जग षाया।
प्रांण पुरुष का मर्म न पाया, छोड़ि बिगूते माया ॥10॥

Bindu or sperm is one thing, beauty another. People think that lust is the success of the bindu and it' s complete usage or bliss but actually this is not so. Because the success of the sperm and its actual usage lies in making it go upward and thereby stable, so that it can be of help in achieving supreme bliss and bestow immortality. The tigress chews with her teeth while eating but beauty eats the world up without using any teeth whatsoever. Those who are swept by their physical desires destroy their self and they do not reach the secret of the supreme spirit. Leaving that, they fall in the trap of illusion and are destroyed by that.

सौंट्‌यौ लाकड़ि ज्यूं धुण लागै, लोहै लागै काई।
बिन परतीति कहा गुरु कीजै, काल ज ग्रास्यां जाई ॥11॥

Just like termites eat up the dry wood, just like iron gets rusted similarly if a seeker without faith becomes fodder for death then what can the Guru do.

रांडी तज्यां न षसिया जीवै, पुरुष तज्यां नहीं पनारी।
कहै नाथ ये दोनयूं बिनसे, धोषा की असवारी ॥12॥

A man cannot live without a woman (a man is being called a'khassi' because he is spiritually impotent) and a woman cannot live without a man. In this manner both are riding on false hopes and both meet their destruction (end).

वैसन्दर मुषि ब्रह्म जो होते, सुद्र पढाऊं बांनी।
असंमेद विधि ब्रह्म-जग निपजां, नै जुगति जमाया पांनी ॥13॥

The one who casts his doubts in the yogic fire of Vaishwanar. Even though he may be a Shudra but I also teach my precepts to such a one. In this manner (by dispelling doubts) that actual Ashwamedha Yagya (a very important fire ritual) is completed, the fire ritual of supreme consciousness has been completed and through clever deliberation the water got frozen, that is the sperm prone to flowing down and restless now is stable in the crown of the head.

तो जुग रांड्या जोगेसवर व्याह्या, सिव सक्ती सूं फेरा।
जा पद मिंदर पुरुष बिलंव्या, वहि मिंदर धर मेरा ॥14॥

When the God of yoga, Shiva is himself married, because Shiva the supreme spirit has taken vows of marriage with Shakti–supreme power, Uma, Sati then it is no surprise that the entire world is with women, but the temple in the form of a position, an elevation where supreme spirit is residing, that temple is my home, that is by escaping the clutches of the woman I have merged in the supreme consciousness.

या रहनी मैं घर घर बासा, जोग जुगति कर पाया।
सिध समाधि पंच घर मेला, गोरष तहां समाया ॥15॥

Thus I have through the path of yoga found a way of living devoid of a woman (illusion) and I reside in my actual house (the abode of supreme consciousness) and through profound meditation have brought the five sense organs into that home (supreme consciousness) meaning that I have made the sense organs inward looking, now no one can know where Gorakh has merged.

हाली भींतरि षेंत निदांणैं, बगु मैं ताल समाई।
बरषै मोर कहूकै सावण, नदी अपूठी आई ॥16॥

In a normal situation, the seeker tills his field (protects his soul intellect through discriminative intelligence, drives away from the soulless intellect) the mind in the form of a heron plays in the pond (external pleasures) but now all the external pleasures have become internalized. All his movements have become internalized and instead of finding bliss outside he has started finding it inside. In normal circumstances the is the rainfall of illusion and the mind in the form of a peacock used to happily sing but now the mind-peacock is raining and has given up all the outward focussed movements and the rainfall of illusion has also left its propensity to tie down and has turned into the knowledge that liberates and is instead of flowing towards the world has changed its course and has come back.

गऊ पद मांहीं पहौकर फकदै, दादर भर्र्य झिलारै।
चात्रिग मैं चौंमासौ बोलै, ऐसा समा हमारै ॥17॥

When the gross existence of the seeker merges in the subtle soulful life, in that subtle life the subtle mind is in bliss. That situation (chaumasa–the four months when it rains incessantly) when the soul (chaatak bird) is looking for its dear (cloud that is God) and faces him. When the soul or the chaatak bird is present inside, the seeker has such a beautiful season present in front of him.

आसा तृष्णा थिर है बैठी, पद परचै सुष पाया।
सूकै तरवर कूंपल मेल्ही, यहि बिधि निपजी काया ॥18॥

When hope and desires leave their restless self and sit in a stable manner that is, when hopes and desires get tired then one experiences the bliss of meeting supreme consciousness, in this manner the huge tree of illusion dries up and new saplings of spirituality sprout up. It's real form is successful.

पूरब देश पछांहीं घाटी, (जनम) लिष्या हमारा जोगं।
गुरू हमारा नांवगर कहीए, मेटै भरम बिरोगं ॥19॥

Prana or life breath is our country, the Sushumna energy channel is a valley. From birth our destiny has ordained that we do yoga. Our Guru is that the boatman, he dispels our doubts and other diseases.

नव ग्रह मारि अगनि मुखि झौंक्या, दुदरहि लग्या डोरी।
परम पुरुष पिंजरि बिलंब्या,भई अगम गति मोरी ॥20॥

I have killed and thrown into fire all the nine planets, by the rise of true knowledge I have overcome the good and bad effects of the planets. The supreme individual is a part of this body and merged within it , in this manner I have achieved liberation.

अकथ कथ्या अनअषिर बांच्या, अगम गवन करि लीया।
हंस बिलंब्या बूंद न ढ़लकै, वहि सरवर बंध दीया ॥21॥

I have bound the conversation with the supreme consciousness without any letters, it cannot go anywhere now, that is why I have reached the supreme consciousness. In that tale, the swan (soul) is so merged in the supreme consciousness that there is a dam over the lake of the semen which does not let even a drop slid away, therefore complete celibacy has been achieved.

बोलै नाथ गगन घर वासा, अंतरि बसीया जाई।
परम पुरस मेरै कागद मांड्या, दिन दिन कला सवाई ॥22॥

Nath says that in our abode in the sky that is the trikuti or the brahmarandhra. In this way we have now started staying within ourselves. Our paper which represents the supreme spirit is now ready and it's aspect is increasing day by day that is, the spiritual experience increases day by day.

ऐसे रमहुँ जैसे नष सिष भेदै, संक्या सरीर न लूटै।
चलत फिरत पद माहिं समावैं, जामण मरण भै छूटै ॥23॥

Drench yourself in this experience so much so that from the toe to the head, it spreads in the entire body and is not able to loot the doubt (the effect of illusion is not there) such a profound meditation should happen that not just while sitting to meditate but while walking, moving, that is, every moment one is deeply merged in the supreme consciousness so that the fear of life and death may disappear.

मरि मरि जाय सुसंसा माहीं, तन का मरम न पाया।
समझ्या होय तो पद पंथ औरैं, धोषै जनम गामाया ॥24॥

The ones who die in doubt have not understood the importance of the body. The ones who doubt lose their precious birth in doubt and betrayal.

या पद की कठिन है करनी, केवल-मता पुरुष की रहनी (सोई)
या रहनी तैं पारस निपजै, लोहा कंचन पद भेटूयां पद होई ॥25॥

The one who obtains a vision of the supreme consciousness has a difficult life to live. This kind of life leads to the emergence of the 'paras mani' which turns iron into gold, which is its actual form. Implying that leading such a life leads a normal human to reach supreme state, which is its actual reality.

नींझर नीर अगनि मुषि बरषै, सीचै बाग हमारा।
या रहनी तैं पैकंबर निपजै, तिसिया मरै सँसारा ॥26॥

The waterfall of ambrosia falls over the fire of supreme consciousness and our garden expands, that is, the experience of supreme consciousness increases. This kind of life leads to the birth of the ones who have the knowledge of spirituality and the world (of illusion) dies because of a lack of nourishment.

यंद्र मिल्यां तैं धरती निपजै, यंद्री बरषै देही।
गुरू हमारा बांनी बोली, मांणिक चुगि चुगि लेही ॥27॥

When the Lord of rain Indra is kind, the earth produces grains etc, similarly when the sense organs are within control, one gets to chew on the grains of knowledge. This is the speech of our Guru. This is what our Guru has taught us.

पाथर मैं पारस अबिनासी, ज्यूं असट धात मैं सोनां।
यूं सब जुग माँहि समझि अबिनासी, ता धटि पाप न पूनां ॥28॥

Just like the 'avinashwar mani' (a kind of precious metal) is situated inside a stone, just like gold is present in the eight metals, similarly consider the indestructible supreme consciousness spread across the entire world. The one who has reached the supreme state, his body is beyond merit and sin.

बहती नदी भाव भरि थांभी, सूरिज देषि पछांहीं।
दुर्लभ देवल मन अगोचह, ता बेल्यां फल षांही ॥29॥

By watching the sun set–that is, by watching the sun in the Muladhar chakra go through the path of Sushumna energy channel to the moon situated in the crown chakra, sahasrara, the lake of emotions (external looking) got stalled. This is how this body got the rare status, the body got perfected and the mind became the invisible supreme consciousness. That is how the yogis eat the fruit of truth that grows on the branch of illusion.

नव लख किरणि अपूठी प्रकटी, कोटि किरणि मुषि आगै।
कहै नाथ धरम का पेंडा, संसे बूंद न लागै ॥30॥

Doubt does not touch a seeker, all around he sees a vision of light. This is the meaning of behind the nine lakh rays and in front of the crore rays.

गिरही कै घरि जनम हमारा, संगति सुरति दिढांणी।
कहै नाथ जीव ब्रह्म एकै, जब सिव घरि सक्ति समांणी ॥31॥

I have taken birth in the home of a householder , have firmed my spiritual mindset in the company of saints and great souls. In this manner when the supreme spirit Shiva merges in his supreme power Shakti then the individual soul and the universal soul become one.

अनहद धुनि मैं रहनि हमारी, तत्त देखि मन लागा।
आपा माहीं आपा प्रकट्या, जब जाय धोषा भागा ॥32॥

Our abode is in the Anahata nada, the unstruck sound. We have witnessed the truth. Our mind is focused on that, in this manner when one saw the soul manifest in all existence, then all doubts came to a halt.

जे नर जोनि अजोनी सिंभू, सिध पुरष सूं मेला।
जा रहनी मैं थान हमारा, ता घटि पुरिष अकेला ॥33॥

The one who in his human self has witnessed the realized supreme individual Shiva and the one who lives such a life which is our condition, in his body the supreme being manifests.

उरधै भरै सो थिरि है पीवै, सूधै घटि संवारी।
अधै लोचन सब जग सूझे, सालिम सब अंधियारी ॥34॥

The one who stabilizes the Kundalini energy in the crown of the head he becomes stable and partakes of the nectar. The one who keeps the pitcher straight. The one who looks at it with worldly eyes cannot drink the nectar but the one who views it with the eyes of knowledge, the reality of the world is expressed in front of his eyes and the one whose outward looking eyes are complete, he cannot see spiritual effulgence anywhere.

तूंबी मैं तिरलोक समाणा, तिरबेणी रिव चंदा।
बूझौ हौ कोई ब्रह्म गियानी; अनहद नाव अभंगा ॥35॥

The three worlds are assimilated in this body and it also contains the universe. In the trikuti, the sun and the moon all are here. Someone who has true knowledge can only understand this.

आवा गवण भरम का मारग, पुरषां पंथ बताया।
सबद अतीत अनाहद बोलै, अंतरि गीत समाया ॥36॥

The continuous movement of coming and going is the path to delusion. The real path has been laid down by those realized beings who have activated the unstruck sound–the anahata nada–and have merged in that.

बिमल पंथ बीजल ज्यूं चमकै, घरहरती घन गाजै।
ता रहनी मैं जोगी का घर, अनहद बाजा बाजै ॥37॥

This pure path is flashes like the lightning, it roars like the clouds. By walking on that path one gets the vision of divine light and the unstruck sound is heard. This is the abode where the yogi resides.

जा पद मिंदर धजा फरहरै, मढी संवारे चेला।
कोटि कला जहां अनहद बांणी, गावै पूरिष अकेला ॥38॥

38. The state that is equal to the temple that has the flag of kaivalya- supreme liberation (meaning the king's palace and the temple) it is equal to these places, O yogi, make that state as your castle (live there). There only the supreme being stays with crores of his aspects and sings the Anahata nada constantly.

नौ नष पातरि आगैं नाचैं; पीछैं सहज अषाड़ा।
ऐसैं मन ले जोगी षेलै, तब अंतरि बसै भँडारा ॥39॥

The way of life, the abode of the yogi should be the middle path. He should maintain a balance between consumption and sacrifice. Despite all the objects of consumption in front of him, he should not be attached to them. That is why it is said that nine lakh dancers dance in front of him and the arena of the monastery is behind him. Thus his existence is between the two. In this kind of situation, if the yogi is still deeply meditating, then his inner world is said to be complete.

ग्यान कहै तौ त्रिस्ना हारै, सूरज देषि पछांही।
सतगुरु मिलै तो सांसा भागै, मूल बिचार्‍या मांहीं ॥40॥

The sun that is situated in the root chakra meets the moon in the crown chakra by passing the path of sushumna energy channel, through yoga practice knowledge is attained and desires are destroyed. If the right guru is found, then accepting the ultimate truth in one's heart, all doubts are vanquished.

अंजन माहि निरंजन भेट्या, तिल मुष भेट्या तेलं।
मूरति माहिं अमूरति परस्या, भरा निरंतरि षेलं ॥41॥

Just like oil is inherently present in the sesame seeds, that is how the pure one, that is, god is present in the kohl. Just like oil is extracted from the seeds similarly I have taken out the pure consciousness from the kohl that is, illusion and in the idol I have touched the one beyond touch and in this way I have received continuous spiritual bliss.

जहां नहीं तहां सब कछु देष्या कह्यां न को पतिआई।
दुबिधा भाव तवै ही गइया, बिरलां पदां समाई ॥42॥

Where there is a void I have seen everything. (the entire universe has emerged out of the supreme reality and that universe has the essence and principles, that is why supreme consciousness is everything). Nobody will believe if I say this. That time, while witnessing the supreme void, merging in the state of deepest meditation, my duality came to an end, I experienced the convergence of the supreme void with the supreme consciousness.

दिषणि हमारी डीबी पाकै, अगनि वलै मुलतानं।
ऐसे हम जोगेस्वर निपनां, प्रगट्या पद निर्वानं ॥43॥

In the south (root chakra) our food items is being prepared, the experimental ingredient Kundalini is being prepared and is burning. In Multan that is the northern region, in the brahmarandhra – the cranial apparatus in the crown of the head, in the supreme void. This way I became the God of yoga and the path to my liberation manifested.

बाफ न निकसै बूंद न ढलकै, सहजि अंगीठी भरि भरि रांधै।
सिध समाधि योग अभ्यासी, तब गुरु परचै सांधै ॥44॥

When someone cooks food in this natural stove where no steam escapes or no drop of water falls meaning the seeker becomes adept in this kind of meditation that the base emotions of anger, greed, lust, ego are not able to raise their head, then neither does sperm dissipate, then the yoga practitioner reaches the state of Samadhi or profound meditation and then the supreme consciousness introduces itself to him.

धीरजि थंम जडोरि धुनि समानां असमानं।
अटल दुलीचा अषै पद, जहां गोरष का दीवानं ॥45॥

The immortal state is supported by the pillar of patience and with the string of deep concentration stands firm in the sky (supreme void) without any support, this is the immovable seat. This is where Gorakh's court is. This is Gorakh's couch.

इति ग्यान तिलक

पंच मात्रा

The description of the traits of a Yogi–

बोउं अनादि बोलंत षरतर पंथ। जिभ्या इंद्री दीजै बंध ॥
जोग जुगति मैं रहै समाइ। सो जोगी सिर भद्र कराइ ॥1॥
द्वादस मंदिर सिव थांन। तेहूँ उत्तम ब्रह्म ग्यांन ॥
द्वादस निहचल एक मैं रहै। ते जोगी सिर टोपी बहै ॥2॥
देषै ये तत सून्य अकास। पंच तत्त मैं महा पुरिस का बास ॥
पंच तत्त लै उनमनिर है। अछूया होइ तौ जोग्रेंद्र कहै ॥3॥
पंच तत्त करोहु बिचार। बाहर भीतर येकंकार ॥
भिछया मांगै नग्री द्वार। माया मोहूँ तजै जँजार ॥4॥
अरध उरध बीची कंमली भोग। सुणौ हो अवधू अध्यातम जोग ॥
मनमूंडै तौ मस्तक मूंडी। नही तर पड़ी नरक की कूंडी ॥5॥
ये तो येक अवधू पंच तत्त मात्रा का बिचार। बंदत गोरष दसवै द्वारि॥
आदि संष अनिल उपाया। अनंत सिधां लै मस्तकि लाया ॥6॥
कान सुणाय गुरँ दीन्ही दीष्या नवखँड प्रथी मांगों भीष्या ॥
भिछया मांगि निरतरि रहै। ते जोगी कानां मुद्रयां बहै ॥7॥
अहुँठ हाथ गल कंथा पाई। चंद सूर दोउ थेगली लाई ॥
अहुँट कोटि दस धागा भरौ। गुरु परसादै दूतिर तिरौ ॥8॥

काया पड़ासण मन जोगौटा। पांचौं इन्द्री करौ कछौटा ॥
जत सत क्रीया संजम चलवौ। डंडा लाठी डीबी पाबौ ॥9॥
पछिम उत्तर दछिण पूरब। वै तो जोगी जोगौटा चलावौ ॥
माथे जटा दरसन बिकराल। तौ अबधू जोगी बंची काल ॥10॥
सींमी सेली अर जपमाला। बाई फेरो गगन मंझारा॥
नव बैहैतर पवनां मूल। षट्र चक्रं गंगा गौरी तिरसूल ॥11॥
अलष पुरिष तहां कू ध्याया। नग्र कोट उरध थी आया॥
चीत चक्र मैं जै पवनां गहै। ब्रह्म अगिनि प्रगट जल रहै ॥12॥
बीस्नं बीस्नं करै सब कोय। बिना निरंजन मुकति न होय ॥
मूल चक्र तहां सहस्र दल बाट। मन पवन लै षौलौ कपाट ॥13॥
गौरष बिस्न लागा बाद। गीरष लेर बजाया नाद ॥
बीस्न कीया मृध का रूप। मार्‌या मृघ ध्याया अवधूत ॥14॥
पूरब जाता पछीम हांस। मार्‌या मन मृघ भषीले मांस ॥
नाली चांपी सींगी नाद बजाय। यही सींगी नाद गगन कूं जाइ ॥15॥
गगन मडल मैं रहै समाइ। अनंत सिधां पाई जोग बाइ ॥
सींगी नाद गगन कूं जाइ। अह निसि चंदा (रहै) गगन समाइ ॥16॥
पांचूं इन्द्री पूरै स्वाद। ते अवधू बजावै सींगी नाद ॥
अनहद नांद उरध का मूल। चंद सूर सुषमन अस्थूल ॥17॥
वारि गंगा पारि गंगा, मंझी जोगोटा ध्यांन ॥
गंग जमन लै मेर चढ़ाई, तहां प्रगट्या ब्रह्म गियांन ॥18॥
सींगी सेली और षड़ासण, अंनत सीधां लीन्हा जाइ।
द्वादस डीबी उरध का मैला, अलेष मंढ़ी ताहां गगन समाइ ॥19॥
सोना रूपा ग्रही कूं दीन्हा। आदी पत्र ले ईश्वर कूं दीन्हा ॥
जोगारंभ तहां सीध समाइ। आदि धरंम सुरग उतपना आइ ॥20॥

बारा बरस का मूवा समांण, श्री गोरषनाथ जगाया।
चौसठि जोगणि भ्याष्या पूरै, अनंत सीधां आदि पत्र पाया ॥21॥
आदी पत्र आदी उत्यंम अनादि धरम संकर कूं पेस।
निगुरा कूं गड़बड़ बोलिये सुगरा कूं उपदेस ॥22॥
येता येक पंच मात्रा का ऊचार अंनत सीधां तहां सुण्या बिचार।
मच्छन्द्र प्रसादै जती गीरष कहै। तै अवधू पंच भू आत्मा लहै ॥23॥
जे जोगी जाणै पंच मात्रा का भेव। सो आपै करता आपै देव ॥
ये पंच मात्रा जोगी बूझै। ताकूं त्रिभुवन सूं सकल देवता पूजै ॥24॥

इति श्री पंच मात्रा गुणंत कथंते करंते पापेन लिपंते पुन्ये न हरन्ते आवागवण बिब्रजते अमरलोकी सगछते ॥ वो उं नमसिवाय। उन्मोस्यवाय। गुरु मछंद्रनाथ पादुका नमस्ते। इति श्री गोरषनाथ जी की पांच मात्रा ग्रंथ जोग सास्त्र संपूरण समाप्ता

गोरष गणेस गुष्टि

गणेस पूछै गोरष कहै।
तुम्हें स्वांमीं कहाँ थे आव्या, कहा तुम्हार नाम।
अम्हें निरंतरि थैं बर आव्या, जोगी अम्हारा नाम।
स्वांमीं जोगी तौ ते बोलिये जिन एता मेर मेषला रच्या।
तुम्हें कौण जोगी।
अम्हें निरंजन जोगी अतीत गुर चेला।
स्वांमीं ते क्यूं जाणिये।
रहति करि जाणिये, सबद करि प्रवांणिये।
स्वांमीं रहित ते क्या बोलिये, सब्द ते क्या बोलिये।
सब्द बोलिये सबथैं बिबरजित, रहति बोलिये तृगुण रहित।
स्वामी सबथैं निरंतर ते क्या बोलिये।
सरब थैं ब्यबरजित बोलिये अवधू सुछिम, त्रिगुण बोलिये सत रज तम।
तौ स्वामी सुछिम ते क्या बोलिये, सत रज तम ते क्या बोलिये।

सुछिम ते बोलिये अवधू दिष्टि न देषिये मुष्ट न आवै। सतगुन बोलिये पवन रजगुन बोलिये पानी। तृगुण बोलिये तामस रूपी। पंच तत्त पचीस परकीरती बोलिये आदम।

तौ स्वांमी पंचतत्त्व ते क्या बोलिये, पचीस परकीरती ते क्या बोलिये।

पंच तत्त बोलिये पृथ्वी आप तेज बाइ आकास, येक येक तत्त।

संजुगत पंच पंच परकीरती बोलिये। प्रथम पृथ्वी प्रकीरती बोलिये

अस्त 1 मास 2 तुचा 3 नाडी 4 रोम 5 एतो पृथ्वी को प्रकीरती बोलिये ॥1॥

दुतिये आप प्रकीरति बोलिये लाल 1 मूत्र 2 प्रसेद 3 सुकल 4 सुनीत 5 एती आप की प्रकीरति बोलिये ॥2॥

तृतीये तेज प्रकीरति बोलिये पुद्या 1 तृसा 2 न्यंद्रा 3 आलकस 4 क्रौध 5। एती तेज प्रकीरति बोलिये ॥3॥

चतुरथे बाई प्रकीरति बोलिये गांवण 1 धावण 2 बलगण 3 ग्यांन 4 अगोचरि 5। एती बाई प्रकीरति बोलिये ॥4॥

पंचमें आकास प्रकीरति बोलिये माया 1 मोह 2 लज्जा 3 राग 4 द्वेष 5। एती पंच तत्त पचीस परकीरति का भेद बोलिये ॥5॥

स्वांमी पृथ्वी का कौंण बरण, आप का कौंण बरण, तेज का कौंण बरण, बाई का कौंण बरण, आकास का कौंण बरण।

पृथ्वी का पीत बरण, आप का सेत बरण, तेज का रक्त बरण, बाई का नील बरण, आकास का काला बरण।

स्वांमीं पृथ्वी का कौंण स्वाद, आप का कौंण स्वाद, तेज का कौंण स्वाद, बाई का कौंण स्वाद, आकास का कौंण स्वाद।

पृथ्वी का मधुर स्वाद, आप का षारा स्वाद, तेज का तीषा, स्वाद, बाई का षाटा स्वाद, आकास का मलवंधा स्वाद।

तौ स्वांमीं पृथ्वी का कौंण सुभाव, आप का कौंण सुभाव, तेज का कौंण सुभाव बाई का कौण सुभाव, आकास का कौंण सुभाव।

पृथ्वी का बैठा सुभाव, आप का सीतल सुभाव, तेज का ताता सुभाव बाई का चंचल सूभाव, आकास का ऊभा सुभाव।

तौ स्वांमी आकास का कौंण घर कौंण द्वार कौंण आहार कौंण निहार कौंण ब्यौहार।

बाई का कौंण घर कौंण द्वार कौंण आहार कौंण निहार कौंण व्यौहार।

आप का कौंण घर कौंण द्वार कौंण आहार कौंण निहार कौंण

ब्याहौर।

तेज का कौंण घर कौंण द्वार कौंण आहार कौंण निहार कौंण ब्यौहार।

पृथ्वी का कौंण घर कौंण द्वार कौंण आहार कौंण निहार कौंण ब्यौहार।

आकास का ब्रह्मंड घर श्रवन द्वार सुनै सू आहार जिह्वा निहार दिम्भ पाषंड ब्यौहार।

बाई का घर नाभी नासिका द्वार बासना अहार निरबासीक निहार अहं क्रोध ब्यौहार।

तेज का पीता घर चछू द्वार द्रिष्ट देषै सु आहार हरष निहार प्रीती माह ब्यौहार।

आप का लिलाट घर यन्द्री द्वार स्त्री आहार बिंद निहार मैनुन ब्यौहार।

पृथ्बी का घर कलेजी गुदा द्वार षाइ सु आहार अमरी बजरी निहार लोभ लालच ब्यौहार।

तौ स्वांमी पृथ्बी का कौंण गुरू तेज का कौंण गुरू बाई का कौंण गुरू आकास का कौंण गुरू।

पृथ्वी का गुरू मन देवता, बाचा सरूपी, आपका गुरू चंद्र देवता बुधि सरूपी, तेज का गुरू सूरज देवता अनादि सरूपी आकास का गुरू श्री गोरष जती अविगति सरूपी।

स्वांमीं जी प्रिथी की कौंण भारिज्या। बाय की कौंण भारिज्या। अपकी कौण भारिज्या। तेज की कौंण भारिज्या। आकास की कौंण भारिज्या।

अवधू प्रिथी की भारिज्या आसा धनवंती। अप की भारिज्या मनसा चौरटी। तेज की भारिज्या कलपनां चंडाली। बायकी भारिज्या चिंता डाकणी। आकास की भारिज्या संक्या शीलवंती।

स्वांमी जी प्रिथी कौंण गुणीं। आप कौंण गुणां। तेज कौंण गुणां बाय कौंण गुणां। आकास कौंण गुणां।

अवधू प्रिथी मूल गुणी। अप बृध गुणां। तेज रूप गुणा। वाय प्रमल गुणां आकाश मैथन गुणां।

तौ स्वांमी पंच तत्त की कथं उतपती, कथं षपती। अवगित उतपनां ॐ। ॐ उतपदिते आकास। आकास उपतनी बाई। बाई उत्पन्यां तेज। तेज उत्पन्यां तोया। तोया उत्पनी मट्टी। मिट्टी ग्रासंत तोया। तोया ग्रासंत तेज। तेज ग्रासंत बाई। बाई ग्रासंत आकास। आकास ग्रासंत ॐ। ॐ ग्रासंतते अबिगत। अबिगत गति रहेत, आवते न जावते एवं पंच तत पचीस प्रकीरति का भेद बोलिये।

निरंजन देवता। पांणीं का जामन। अगनि का पुट। पवन का

थंभा। सुरति निरति सोध्या। सुनि मैं समाया। अविगत सरूपी एवं उचितम्।

पापे न लिप्यते पुन्ये न हारते जोगारम्भे भवे सिधा आवागवन निबर्तते ॐ नमो सिवाई ॐ नमो सिवाई श्री स्यंभुनाथ पादुका नमस्तुते।

ज्ञान द्वीप बोध

(गोरष दत्त गुष्टि)

गोरष– स्वांमीं कि तुम्हें ब्रह्मा कि ब्रह्मचारी,
कि तुम्हें बांभण पुस्तक कि डंडधारी।
कि तुम्हें जोगी कि जोग जुगता,
कौंण प्रसादैं रमो छछंद मुक्ता ॥1॥

दत्तात्रेय– अवधू न अम्हें ब्रह्मा न ब्रह्मचारी,
न अम्हें ब्राह्मण पुस्तक न डंडधारी।
न अम्हें जोगी न जोग जुगता,
आप प्रसादैं रमौं छछंद मुकता ॥2॥

गोरष– आपा मेटणा सतगुर थापणा,
अनपरचै जग षाया।
गोरष कहै सुणौ हो स्वामी,
तुम्हें कौंण कहां थैं आया ॥3॥

दत्तात्रेय– अवधू होता गुपत गुपत थैं प्रगट,
रहता पुरुष की छाया।
दत्त कहै सुणौ हो गोरष,
हम गैवी पुरस गैब थै आया ॥4॥

गोरष– स्वामी अजर व्यंद असाध बाई,
अप्रबल बिष्न की माया।
गोरष कहै सुणौं को दत्तातृये,
क्यधूं सीझंति जल व्यंदकी काया ॥5॥

दत्तात्रेय– अवधू कन्द्रप न बाई अप्रबल न माया,
आकार निराकार श्रूषिम निकाया।
जलो न जलबिंबो दरपनों न छाया,
दत्त न गोरष काया न माया ॥6॥

गोरष– कैंणस्य आवै कौणसि जाय,
जो बोलै सो कहां समाइ।
जो गंमि होइ स कहिये भेव,
गोरष कहै सुनो दतदेव ॥7॥

दत्तात्रेय– अवधू न कोइ आवै न कोइ जाई,
कांसा नाद मधि समाई।
येकै सुत्रैं प्रोया हार,
सांभलि हो गोरष कहूँ विचार ॥8॥

गोरष– स्वांमीं कौंणस्य माता कौंणस्य पिता,
कौंणस्य गुरू उपदेस स्थिता।
कौंणस्य आसण करौ विश्रांम,
कौण घर सो दाषौ ठांम ॥9॥

दत्तात्रेय– अवधू षमा मांता सत पिता,
ग्यांन गुरू परचाया स्थिता।
अलेष आसण तहां बिश्रांम,
सांभलि गोरष दाषूं ठांम ॥10॥

गोरष– स्वांमीं कौंण मुकत कौंण दुष सहै,
कौंण सि बिणसै कौंण अजरावर रहै।
जो गंमि होइ सु कहिये भेव,
गोरष कहै सुणौ दत देव ॥11॥

दत्तात्रेय– अवधू ब्रह्म मुकता प्रकीरति दुष सहै,
प्रकीरति बिनसै ब्रह्म अजरावर रहै।
गुहय ग्यांन कथिलै अपार,
सांभलि गोरष कहौं बिचार ॥12॥

गोरष— स्वांमी कौणसि सुषिम कौंण अस्थूल,
कौंणस्य डालां कौंणस्य मूल।
जो गंमि होइ सु कहिये भेव,
गोरष कहै सुणौ दतदेव ॥13॥

दत्तात्रेय— अवधू ब्रह्म सूषिम तत सथूल,
पवनस्य डाला मनस्य मूल।
गुरहि ग्यांन कथिले अपार,
सांभलि गोरष कहौं बिचार ॥14॥

गोरष— स्वांमी कौंणस्य गुर कौंण सि चेला,
किहि बिधि होय अनंत सिधाँ सौं मेला।
ब्रह्म कमल का कहिये भेव,
गोरष कहै सूणौ तददेव ॥15॥

दत्तात्रेय— अबधू परमात्मा सि गुर आतम चेला,
सहज सुनि होइगा अनंत सिधां सूं मेला।
ब्रह्म कमल उरध मुष षिला,
साँभलि गोरष उनमल कला ॥16॥

गोरष— स्वांमीं कौणस्य कला,
किस बिधि षूठै त्रिकुटी ताला।
नाद बिंद का कहियै भेव,
गोरष कहै सुणौ दतदेव ॥17॥

दत्तात्रेय— अवधू उनमनि ध्यांन पवन बिधि काया,
नाभ दम षूटै त्रिकुटी ताला।
दसवैं द्वारि ब्यंद का बास,
साँभलि गोरष नाद का प्रकास ॥18॥

गोरष— स्वांमीं कौणसि कंटक कौंण उचाट,
किहि विधि षूलै ब्रह्म कपाट।
अगम पंथ का कहियै भेव,
गोरष कहै सुणौ दतदेव ॥19॥

दत्तात्रेय– अवधू कंटक सोई जिहि अतिवंत क्रोध,
उचाट सोई आत्मा बिरोध।
गुरु गमि षूलै ब्रह्म कपाट,
सांभलि गोरष ऊजू बाट ॥20॥

गोरष– स्वामी कौनसि दया कौंन सि धन,
कौंण सि बूडण कौंन सि तिरण।
कौंन सि ग्यान करम का भेव,
गोरष कहैं सुणौ दतदेव ॥21॥

दत्तात्रेय– अवधू बूडण सोइ जा कंटक षुधि,
तिरण सोई जु निरमल बुधि।
ध्यांन सोइ जा दया धरम,
ग्यांन सोई बिबरजित करम ॥22॥

गोरष– स्वांमीं कौंण स्य बंधा कौंण स्य मुकता,
कौंण सि जोगी कौंण सि जुगता।
देव कला का कहियै भेव,
गोरष कहै सुणौ दतदेव ॥23॥

दत्तात्रेय– बंध्या सोई जु करमहि बंध,
मुकता सोई रहै निरदंद।
जोगी सोई जुगति मन रहै,
गोरष पूछै दत्तातृय कहै ॥24॥

गोरष– स्वांमी कौंण स्य जुगता कौंण स्य जोग,
कौण स्य काया व्यापै रोग।
इनका हम से कहियै भेव,
गोरष कहै सुणौ दतदेव ॥25॥

दत्तात्रेय– अवधू जुगती सोई जो जुगि जुगि ताला,
जुगति सोई जो बिषै निराला।
योगी सोई मन भ्रम न रहै,
गोरष पूछे दत्तातृय कहै ॥26॥

गोरष– स्वांमी कौंण सि भरम कौंण स्य धरम,
कौंण सि निसचल कौंण अधरम।
अगम ग्यांन का कहियै भेव,
गोरष कहै सुणौ दतदेव ॥27॥

दत्तात्रेय– अवधू भ्रम सोई जिहि ब्यापै संसा,
धरम सोई दरसण आदेसा।
निसचल सोई जो ल्यौ स्यूं रहै,
अधरम सोई जो मिथ्या कहै ॥28॥

गोरष– स्वांमीं कौंण सि मिथ्या कौंण सि साच,
कौंण सि षरा कौंण सि काच।
कौंण सि कहै सबद का भेव,
गोरष कहै सुणौ दत देव ॥29॥

दत्तात्रेय– अवधू माया मिथ्या ब्रह्म सु साचा,
सबद सु षरा प्यंड को काचा।
सबद बिचारी जहां मन रहै,
गरेरष पूछै दत्तातृय कहै ॥30॥

गोरष– स्वांमीं कौंण सि काया कौंण सि माया,
कौन सि भ्रम जग धंधै लाया।
अपार धंद का कहै भेव,
गोरष कहै सुणौ दतदेव ॥31॥

दत्तात्रेय– अवधू मन कलपत लागी माया,
करम आचरै तहां लूं काया।
ध्यान बिना जगु धंद अपार,
संभलि गोरष कहूँ बिचार ॥32॥

गोरष– स्वांमीं कौन सि ध्यांन कौन सि ग्यांन,
कौन सि मन कौन सि आसांन।
ग्यांन ध्यांन का कहियै भेव,
गोरष कहै सुणौ दतदेव ॥33॥

दत्तात्रेय– अवधू ध्यान सो ब्रह्म सू रहै,
ग्यांन सोई जो सब गमि कहै।
मन सोइ जहां मनहि समांन,
आपण जाणो सोई आसांन ॥34॥

गोरष– स्वांमीं कौन सि मानैं कौन सि जानैं,
ससिहर सूर कौन समि ठांनै।
प्रकास अगोचर कहियै भेव,
गोरष कहै सुणौ दतदेव ॥35॥

दत्तात्रेय– अवधू जानै सोइ परचै जग,
नांथ न जाणै सोइ बिषियारत।
ससिहर सूर अगोचर बासा,
सांभलि गोरष कहूं प्रकासा ॥36॥

गोरष– कौंन अगोचर कौंन प्रकास,
कौंन घरि षेलै निरास।
कौंन सिधा का कहियै भेव,
गोरष कहै सूणौ दतदेव ॥37॥

दत्तात्रेय– अवधू ब्रह्म अगोचर मन प्रकास,
परचै घरि षेलै निरास।
परम ज्योति यहां सिध गहि रहै,
गोरष पूछै दत्तातृय कहै ॥38॥

गोरष– स्वांमीं कौंणसि परचै कौंण प्रतीत,
कैसे थिर चंचल चीत।
न पवन की कहियै भेव,
गोरष कहै सुणौ दतदेव ॥39॥

दत्तात्रेय– अवधू गुर परिचय मन प्रतीत,
निसचल अस्थीर चंचल चीत।
पवन थिरंता मन थिर रहै,
गोरष पूछै दत्तातृय कहै ॥40॥

गोरष— कौनसि निसचल ले बंधे बंद,
जुरामरण अजराबर कंद।
गगन पद का कहियै भेव,
गोरष कह सुणौ दतदेव ॥41॥

दत्तात्रेय— अवधू निसचल सो जो न पड़ै काया,
तृगुण रहत सो गगन समाया।
सहज पद परम नृबानं,
सांभलि गोरष ए परवांन ॥42॥

गोरष— स्वांमीं कौंन सकति कौंन सीव,
कौंन तीनि भवन का जीव।
कौंण सि आसा पुरवई भेव,
गोरष कहै सुणौ दतदेव ॥43॥

दत्तात्रेय— अवधू सकति सोइ जो सबहीं सोषै,
सीव सोइ जो सबको पोषै।
जीव इक तीनि भुवन जगनाथ,
सोइ सङ्ग जो पूरइ आस ॥44॥

गोरष— स्वांमीं कौन कौन ले कथिबा ग्यांन,
कौंण तत्त ले धरिबा ध्यांन।
कौंण समाधी तुम्हें लागे भेव,
गोरष कहै सुणौ दतदेव ॥45॥

दत्तात्रेय— अवधू आत्मा चिनंति कहा कथिबा ग्यांन,
तत्त्व बिचारिबा कहा धरिबा ध्यांन।
दत कहै हम सहज समांन,
सांभलि गोरष पद निरबांन ॥46॥

गोरष— स्वांमीं कौंन तत तुम रहौ समाई,
कौंन तत तुम मधे आई।
कौंन परचै तुम्हें कहियै भेव,
गोरष कहै सुणौ दतदेव ॥47॥

दत्तात्रेय– अवधू दत्त जु लागा तत्त सों,
तत्त दत्त ही मांहि।
दत्त तत्त परचा भया,
तब दूजा कहणां नाहिं ॥49॥

गोरष– स्वांमीं त्वमेव दत्तं, त्वमेव देवं,
आद मधी तुम्हें जान्या भेवं।
तुम्हें नारायण तुम्ह कृपाल,
तुम्ह हो सकल बिस्व के पाल ॥50॥

दत्तात्रेय– स्वांमीं तुमेव गोरष तुमेव रछिपाल,
अंनत सिधां माहीं तुम्हें भोपाल।
तुम हो स्यंभू नाथ नृबांण,
प्रणवे दत्त गोरष प्रणांम ॥51॥

गोरष– स्वांमीं दरसण तुम्हारा देव,
आदि अंति मधि पाया भेव।
गोरष भणई दत्त प्रणांम,
भोग जोग परम निधांन ॥52॥

ज्ञान दीप बोध ग्रंथ, जोगब सास्त्रं पढ़ते हरंते पापं, श्रुत्वा मोषि।
लभ्यते जोगारम्भे भवेसिधा आवागवन निवरतते। येवं
ग्यांन दीप बोध संबादे जोग सास्त्रं सपूरण
समाप्त। ॐ नमो सिवाये ॐ नमो सिवाये
गुरु मछिंद्र पादुका नमस्तते।

महादेव गोरष गुष्टि

ईश्वरोवाच ॐ अविगत उतपते इच्छा। इच्छा उतपते आकास, आकास उतपते वाय। वाय उतपते तेज। तेज उतपते तोयं। तोयं उतपते मही।

अविगत ते इच्छा। इच्छा तै आकास। आकास नाम, स्याम बरण दसवैं द्वार वासा, दाहिणे पैसार, वामं श्रवण निकास ,नाद सुनै सो आहार दंभ बड़ाई ब्यौहार। राग दोष हर्ष शोक मोहादिक ये पांच प्रकृति आकास की बोलिये। इन आकास मारग जीव अनुसरै तौ सेतरज षानि भोगवै।

आकास से वायु नाम, नील वरण, नाभि वासा, इला पैसार, पिंगुला निसार, गंध वासना आहार, क्रोध व्यवहार। गावण, धावण, बलगन, संकोचन, पसारण, ये पांच प्रकृति वायु की बोलिये। इन वायु मारग जीव अनुसरै तौ अंडरज षानि भोंगवै :

वायु ते तेज नाम, रक्त वरण, त्रिकुटी वासा दाहिणे नेत्र पैसार, बामें निसार, दृष्टि देषै सो आहार, मोह ब्यौहार। क्षुधा, त्रिया, निद्रा, आलस, क्रांति ये पांच प्रकृति तेज की बोलिये। इन तेज मारग जीव अनुसरै तौ रज (?) षानि भोगवै।

तेज से आप नाम, स्वेत वरण, ललाट वासा, जिभ्या पैसार, इन्द्री निकास, स्त्री आहार, काम ब्यौहार। लाल, मूत्र, प्रस्वेद, रूधिर मज्जा ये पांच प्रकृति आपकी बोलिये। इन आप मारग जीव अनुसरै तौ

उदबीरज षानि भोगवै।

आप ते पृथ्वी नाम, पीत वरण, कलेजे वासा, मुषा पैसार, मूल-द्वार निकास, षावे पीवे सो अहार, लोभ लालच ब्यौहार। अस्थि, मास, त्वचा, नाड़ी, रोम ये पांच प्रकृति पृथ्वी की बोलिये। इन पृथ्वी मारग जीव अनुसरै तौ पिंडरज षानि भोगवै।

इति पंच प्रकृति, पंच घर, दस द्वार, पंच अहार, पंच ब्यौहार, पंच वरण, पंच षानि चौरासी लाष जीव जोनि भ्रमते। तथा ये पंच कर्मानि बोलिये सुनो गोरष अवधूत। ईश्वरो कथंति। महा ग्यांन कर्म पटल प्रथमो अध्याय।

ईश्वरोवाच पंच तत्त्वभेद कथितं। पृथ्वी ग्रासंति तोया। तोया ग्रासंति तेज। तेज ग्रासंति वायु। वायु ग्रासंति आकास। आकास ग्रासंति इच्छा। इच्छा ग्रासंति अविगत। अविगत रहंत, आवते न जाते। जैसा है तैसा हो रहते। असंष मनि नाम। अवरण वरण। हिरदै वासा।

भाव घर, अदृष्टि द्वार, सहज पैसार, समाधि निकास, अभी अहार, अर्थ ब्यौहार इन मन मारग जीव अनुसरै तो साजोज्य मुकति भोगवै।

असंष बुद्धि नाम। अवरण वरण, निर्मलू बासा, बिचार घर, अनाहद द्वार, निहशब्द पैसार, अनभै निकास, रसा अहार, अगह ब्यौहार इन बुद्धि मार्ग अनुसरै तौ सामीप मुकति भोगवै।

सहज सून्य चिंता नाम अवरण वरण त्रिकुटी बासा विवेक घर, अजपा द्वार, निहकाम पैसार, संतोष निसार, कमरंद अहार, अगम व्यौहार। इन चित मारग जीव अनुसरै तौ स्वरूप मुक्त भोगवै।

परम ध्यानं च अहंकार नाम, अवरण वरण, विषमी, वासा, विवेक लय घर, नृवासीक द्वार, अगम पैसार, अगोचर, निसार, अजर अहार, अगाध व्यौहार इन अहंकार मारग चित्त अनुसरै तौ सालोक मुक्ति भोगवै।

प्रांण अंतहकरण नाम, अवरण वरण, अस्थिति वासा, धीर घर

अकिल द्वार, ग्यांन पैसार, विग्यांन निसार, अमरा अहार, अबंध व्यौहार। इन अंतहकरण मारग जीव अनुसरे तौ महा मुक्ति (भोगवै) आत्मा परमात्मा भवति। जोगेस्वर जीव एकं भवति। परम सून्य भावे स्थिति। पारब्रह्म भवे लीनं। सत्यं सत्यं च वदाम्यहं। तत्त्वग्यांन श्री शंभूनाथ अकथ कथितं सुनो हो गोरष अवधूतं परम जोग संप्राप्रितं जोगी। ईश्वरी कथंत महाग्यांन इति ग्यांन इन्द्रादि बोलिये। इति ग्यांन पटल द्वितीयो अध्याय।

इति गोरष महादेव सम्वाद।

सिस्ट पुराण

ॐ एक उपरांति लेष नाहीं। दोय पाषै सिस्टि नाहीं। आपा पाषै परचा नाहीं। काया उपरांति क्षेत्र नाहीं। सील उपरांति व्रत नाहीं। चक्षु उपरांति दृष्टि नाहीं। श्रवण ऊपरि सुरति नाहीं, निर्भय उपरांति अभय नाही। संजम उपरांति सुचि नाहीं। संतोष उपरांति सुख नाहीं। अमर उपरांति सिद्धि नाहीं। अभय उपरांति करामति नाहीं। माता उपरांति जन्म नाहीं। गर्भ उपरांति नरक नाहीं। षलंत उपरांति हरिण नाहीं। चित चंचल उपरांति रोग नाहीं। ब्रिध उपरांति मृत्यु नाहीं। काल उपरांति बैरी नाहीं। नासिका उपरांति रूप नाहीं। दया उपरांति धर्म नाहीं। ध्यान उपरांति ग्रंथ नाहीं। चंदन उपरांति काष्ट नाहीं। बिंद उपरांति उत्पति नाहीं। समुद्र उपरांति गंभीर नाहीं। पाताल उपरांति अर्थ नाहीं। सूरज उपरांति तप्त नाहीं। काया उपरांति रतन नाहीं। संच उपरांति शास्त्र नाहीं। अजप उपरांति जाप नाहीं। अघोर उपरांति मंत्र नाहीं। नारायण उपरांति इष्ट नाहीं। निरंजन उपरांति ध्यान नाहीं।

?या बोध

आओ सिद्धौ षोज बताऊँ। आदिनाथ का पूत कहाऊँ ॥
जोगारंभ की याही बांणी। सब घटि नाथ एकै करि जांणी ॥1॥
जोगारंभ हिरदा मै मांड़ौ। दया उपावो जूती छाड़ौ ॥
नांगां पांवां जे नर मूवां। ताका कारज पहली हूवा ॥2॥
आप सवारथ घालौ धूंई। ता मैं चींटी केती मूई ॥
तजो कहरि नजरि भभूत, बटबा फाउड़ि जिनि लेउ हाथ ॥
एता आरंभ परिहरौ सिद्धौ; यों कथंत जती गोरष नाथ ॥3॥
माष चंलता धरणि दिष्टि लागै। ताकै कांटा कदै न लागै ॥
पहली आरंभ हम भी करते। जीवजंतु बहौतेरे हतते ॥4॥
आंरभ तजौ गूदड़ी चलावौ। निरति सुरति अविनासी सूं लावौ ॥
अबिनासी पुरुष का लागा रंग। रिद्धि सिद्धि ताही के संग ॥5॥
रिधि छाड़या सिधि पाइए, सिधि संकर कै हाथि ॥
छांड़ौ सकल अकल कूं ध्यावौ, यों कथंत जती गोरष नाथ ॥6॥
आसन तजि अनत जिनि जावौ। अकलप भिछ्या बैठा खावौ ॥
कनक न पकड़ै मोरौ न झेलै। आई रिद्धि कौ जोगी ठेलै ॥
हरया तिणांका न सतावै जीव। सो जोगी कहिये प्रतकि सीव ॥
चकमक कफ नावं न धरौ। पर आत्मा का परला जिनि करौ ॥
अगनि न बालौ धुंआ न घोटौ। भिछ्या कर पात्र ले वोटौ ॥
ग्वाँडा बिच आसण जिनि मांडौ। मोह लगाय आप जिनि भांड़ौ ॥
बाई बावड़ी कौ मन नहिं दीजै। देषत दिष्टि काया तन छीजै ॥
पंडित पढ़ि गुणि करै न आसा। देषि एकंत जु रहौ निराशा ॥

काहै कौ पढ़ि गुणि भला कहावै। जब लगि हिरदै दया न आवै ॥
जब लगि हिरदै दया न आई। जब लगि कहिये सुद्ध कसाई ॥
कनक न पकड़े सबद न बाहै। जोगी कागद कहां ते लावै ॥
तन मेरै पोथी मन मेरै लेषनि एती निज तत निसपती।
यो कथंत गोरष जती ॥
वहां चलिबे का करौ विचार। अगम अगोचर सुलप आकार ॥
घड़ा देवरा औधड़ देव। तहां जोगेश्वर लाग्या सेव ॥
पंच चेला मिलि पूरया नाद। धरणि गगन बिच भई अवाज ॥
दीपक एक अषंडित बिन बाती। तहां जोगेस्वर थापनां थापी ॥
अगम अगोचर सकल ब्रह्मंड। ता दीपग कै चरण न प्यंड।
सिषा न नैन सीस नहिं हाथ। सो दीपग देख्या जती गोरखनाथ ॥
ता दीपक कै डाल न मूल। ता दीपक कै कली न फूल ॥
ता दीपक कै रंग न रूप। ता दीपक कै छांह न धूप ॥
ता दीपक के सबद न स्वादं। सा दीपक के बिद्या न बादं ॥
ता दीपक कै मोह न माया। सो दीपक सूनैं सून समाया ॥

इति दया बोध संपूर्ण।

कुछ पद

आदि नाथादि पार ब्रह्म ॐ शिव सकती। नाद बिंद ले काया उतपती।
नाद-बिंद रूपी बोलिए ॐकार।
बिद रूपी बोलिए काया। प्रथम आदि उतपती माया॥
उदै भईला सूर अस्त भईला चंदा। दुहु बिच कल्पना काल का फंदा ॥
उदै ग्रह अस्त एक करि बास। तब जानबा जोगींद्र जीवन आसा ॥
बारह कला रवि सोलह कला ससी। चारि कला गुरुदेव निरंतर बसी ॥
हीण पद सु-राया लागा डंसा। तन का तेज ले उड़िया हंसा ॥
हंस का तेज ले थिर रहै काया। काल का भेद कहौ गुर राया ॥
द्वै पष छेदि एक ह्वै रहणां। चंद्र सूर दोउ सम करि गहणां ॥
ऊंच भै उपरै, मध्य निरंतरै (आई) ता तलि भाठि जराई ॥
सीजि अमीरस कंचन हुआ। यहि बिधि पिंजरै बनावै सुआ ॥
उपजंत दीसंत निपजंत नाहीं। आबरण नास्ति संसार माहीं ॥
बूझिले सतगुर बुद्धि भेद सिद्ध संकेत। परचा जाणि लगावो हेत ॥
ऊरम धूरम जोतो झाला। नौ कोटि षिड़की पूरले ताला॥
ताला न टूटै षिड़की न भाजै। पिंड पड़ै तौ सतगुर लाजै ॥
मरे सागर धुनि धुसर कूंची। तहां सकल बिध है सोइ सूची ॥
इहि बिधि जोगी अतीत होई। अमर पद ध्यावत बिरला कोई ॥
सहज मरे अष्ट पग धरणां। ग्यांन खड़ग लै काल संहरणां ॥
अमर कोट काया एक ब्रह्म मध्ये। जीत ले जमपुरी राषि ले कंधे ॥
आतमा झूझ जती गोरषनाथ किया। संसार बिणास्या आपण जिया ॥1॥

झूझंति सूरा बूझंति पूरा अमर पद ध्यावंत गुरु ग्यान बंका।
दल को मारि जंजाल को जीति ले, निर्भय होइ मेटि ले मन की संका।
अझूझि झूझिलै पैस दरिया। मूल बिन बृष अमीरस भरिया ॥
तन मन लैकरि शिवपुर मेला। ग्यांन गुरु जोगी संसार चेला।
मन राइ चंचल थांन थिति नाहीं। बांधि ले पंच भूत आत्मां माहीं ॥
अलष अकथ चछु बिन सूझिया। सिद्ध का मारग साधकै बूझिया।
उलटि यंत्र धरै सिषर आसण करे, कोटि सर छूटतां धाव नाहीं ॥
सिलहट मध्ये कांवरू जीतले, निर्मल धुनि गगन मांही।
मन की भ्रमना तब छूटंत होइ जोगींद्र जब बिचारंत निहसब्द की बाणी ॥
नैण के दांता सार धरि पीसिबा, तब योग पद दुर्लभ सत्य करि जाणी।
उलटि गंगा चलै धरणि ऊपर मिलै, नीर में पैसि करि अग्नि जालै ॥
घटहिं में पैसि कर कूप पानी भरै, तद पाइ परि पुरुषा आप उजाले।
ग्यान के प्रगटे श्रीस्यंभूनाथ पाया। अकल अकथ जती गोरषनाथ ध्याया ॥2॥
भूल्या सो भूल्या बहुरि चेतना। संसा के लोहे आपा न रेतना।
भेष तजि भ्रम तजि राषि सत्य सोई। तत बिचारतां देवता होई ॥
आपा सोधौ ब्रह्म निरोधौ सहज पलटौ जोती।
काया के भीतर मणि माणिक निपजै, तहां धुनि धुनि बरषै मोती ॥
अरध उरध संपुष्टि करीजै। संषणि नाल अमीं रस पीजै ॥
अषंड मंडल तहं नाद मेरीलै। हरि आसण तहं भगति करीलै ॥
अलेष मंदिर तहं शिव शक्ति निवासा। सहज सुन्न भया प्रकासा।
तहां चंद बिना चांदण अगिन उजाला। एतन भेदंत बृद्ध से बाला ॥
करतार तजिहूँ साकत हूँ न जाई। मन मृग राषिले बाड़ी न पाई।
आकास बाड़ी पाताल कूंआ। भरि भरि सींचता जो सिद्ध हुआ ॥
अवधू अमर कोट काया अलेष दरवाजा।
ग्यान गढ़ आसण प्राण भयो राजा ॥
अवधू फेरि ले तौ तत सार बुद्धि सांच।
नहीं तौ लोहा गढ़ि ले तौ कंचन नहीं तौ कांच ॥
अवधू सिद्धा पाया साधक पाया, ते उतरिया पारं।
अथंत जती गोरषनाथ जेते न जानंत बिचारं, ते जलि भये अंगारं ॥3॥

सप्त बार-नवग्रह

गोरष जोगी कथै बिचारं। ये तत जीतै सातौ वारं ॥टेक॥
आदित वार ब्यौरि ले आपा आप ब्यौरत पुंनि न पाप ॥
दुहुं पंषां सों आरंभ करै। अनभै करि जमपुर परहरै ॥
सोमवार ससि षटण भरौ। सतुगरु षोजौ दूतरि तिरौ ॥
दसवैं द्वारि दीजै बंध। तौ अजरावर थिर ह्वै कंध ॥
मंगलवार अम्हें पाया भेव। आतमां अछै निरंजन देव ॥
पंच पुहुप लै पूजा करौ। मति बुधि लै सिव पुरी संचरौ ॥
बुधिवार मति बुधि प्रकास। अहि निसि रहिबा जोग अभ्यास ॥
दिढ करि लोचन आसा पास। सिधि साधौ अमरापुरि बास ॥
ब्रहसपतिं वार विषम मन लिया। ग्यान षड़न लिया विग्रह किया ॥
अहुठ कोटि दल दीया पयाणां। जम मस्तकि बाजै नीसाणां ॥
सुक्रवार सूषिम जल साधि। लहरि न पसरै सहज सामधि ॥
माया मारि मरि थिर जु होइ। आत्मा परचै मरै न कोइ ॥
थिरि थावर जु सनीचर बार। काया मध्ये सातौं बार ॥
सतगुरु षोजौ उतरौ पार। सुसमवेद सुषमना विचार ॥
वेद पुरान पढ़ै चित लाइ। विद्या ब्रह्म थिरि थाइ।
मछिंद्र प्रसादैं जती गोरष कहै। सप्त वार कोई बिरला लहै ॥
आदित आंष्मां सोम श्रवण, मंगल मुष परवांण।
बुध हिरदै बृस्पति नाभी, सुक्र ते इंद्री जांण ॥
शनि गुदा वाय राह ते मंन, केत ते नासिका रहै।
सप्त वार नवग्रह देवता काया भींतरि श्री गोरष कहै ॥

ब्रत

एक बरत गुरु मुषि लहै भेवा। दूजा ब्रत संतोष सेवा।
तीजा ब्रत दया चित रहै। चौथा ब्रत ब्रह्म कौ लहै ॥1॥
एक ब्रत जो इंद्री गहै। दूजा ब्रत राम मुष कहै।
तीजा ब्रत मिथ्या नहि भाषै। चौथा ब्रत दया मनि राषै ॥2॥
सांचों ब्रत कहै ये चारी। जिस भाव सो लेहु बिचारी।
और सकल जग का ब्यौहारा। तासौ कदे न पावै पारा ॥3॥
सील संतोष सुमिरण ब्रत करै। ताकै भूषी कौंण कहि मरे।
मन इंद्रियन कौं अस्थिर राषै। राम रसाइन रसनां चाषै ॥4॥
इन ब्रत समि ब्रम नहीं कोई। बेद अरु नाद कहै मत दोई।
ता थै ए ब्रत हिरदय घारौ। गुरु साधौं की साष बिचारौं ॥5॥
सील ब्रत संतोष ब्रत, छिमा दया ब्रत दांन।
ये पांचों ब्रत जो गहै, सोई साध सुजांन ॥6॥
इन ब्रतां का जांणै भेव। आपै करता आपै देव।
मन पवनां लै उनमन रहै। एते ब्रत गोरषनाथ जी कहै ॥7॥

पंच अग्नि

ॐ मूल अगनि का रेचक नांव। सोषि लेह रक्त पीत अर आंव।
पेट पूठ दोऊ सम रहै। तौ मूल अगनि जती गोरष कहै।
भुयंगम अगनि का भुयंगम नांम। तजिबा भिछ्या भोजन ग्रांम।
मूल की मूस अमीरस थीर। तिसकूं कहिए हो सिधो पवन का सरीर।
ब्रह्म अगनि ब्रह्म नाली धरि लेउ जांण।
उलटंत पवनां रवि ससि गिगन समांन।
ब्रह्म अगिन मधे सीझिबा कपूरं। तिस कूं देषि मन जायबा दूरं।
सिव धरि सकति अहैनिस रहै। ब्रह्म अगनि जती गोरष कहै।
काल अगनि तीनि भवन प्रवांनी। उलटंत पवनां मोषंत पांनी।
षाया पीया षाष होय रहै। काल अगनि जती गीरष कहै।
रुद्र अगनि का त्राटिका नांम। साषि लेव होठ कंठ पेठ पूठि नव ठांम ॥
उलटत कसे पलटंत चांम। तिसकूं कहियै हो सिधो त्राटिका नांम ॥
रुद्र रेवंती संजमे षिवंती। जोग जुगति करि साधंत जोगी।
पंच अगनि भरि पूर रहै। सिध संकेत श्री गोरष कहै।
पूरिको पीवत वायु कुंभको काया सोधनं।
रेचकी तजंत विकार त्राटिको आवागवण बिबरजतं।
सिध का मारग कोई साधू जांण। पंच अगनि श्री गीरषनाथ बषांणै।
पांचौं अगनि संपूरण भई। अनंत सिंधा मधे जती गोरष कही।
इति श्री पंच अगनि पठंते सुणंते कथंते करंते पापे नह लिपंते
पुंने न हांरते। ॐ नमो सिवाय ॐ नमो सिवाय।
गुरु मछंद्रनाथ के पादुका नमस्तुते।

अष्ट मुद्रा

स्वामी जी अष्ट मुद्रा बोलिए षट भींतरि, ते कौंण कौंण।
अवधू यंद्री मध्ये मूलनी मुद्रा, कांम त्रिष्णा ले उतपनी कांम।
कांम त्रिष्णा समो कृतवा, मुद्रा तौ भई मूलनी ॥
नाभी मधे जलश्री मुद्रा, काल क्रोध ले उतपनी ॥
काल क्रोध समो कृतवा, मुद्रा तौ भई जलश्री ॥
ह्रदा मधे षीरनी मुद्रा, ग्यान दीप ले उतपनी।
ग्यांन दीप समो कृतवा, मुद्रा तौ भई षीरनी॥
मुष मध्ये षेचरी मुद्रा, स्वाद विस्वाद ले उतपनी।
स्वाद विस्वाद समो कृतवा, मुद्रा तो भई षेचरी ॥
नासिका मध्ये भूचरी मुद्रा, गंध निबंध ले उतपनी।
गन्ध बिगन्ध समो, कृतवा, मुद्रा तौ भई भूचरी ॥
चषि मध्ये चाचरी मुद्रा, दिष्टि विदिष्ट ले उतपनी।
दिष्टि बिदिष्ट समो कृतवा, मुद्रा तौ भई चाचरी ॥
करण मध्ये अगोचरी मुद्रा, सबद कुसबद ले उतपनी।
सबद कुसबद समो कृतवा, मुद्रा तौ भई अगोचरी ॥
ब्रह्मंड असथांनि उनमनी-मुद्रा, परम जोति लै उतपनी।
परम जोति समो कृतवा, मुद्रा तौ भई उनमनी ॥
यती अष्ट मुद्रा का जाणै भेव। सो आपै करता आपै देब ॥

इतौ अष्ट मुद्रा कथंत श्री गोरषनाथ जती संपूर्ण समापत सिवाय।

चौबीस सिद्धि

चौबीस सिद्धि बोलिये, प्रिथी कै विषै ते कौंण कौंण।

प्रथम अनूमां सिधि ताकौं लछिन, माया सुनि सूझै। महिमां सिधि ताकौ लछिन लघु दीरघ होय दिखावै। गरीमां सिधि ताकौ लछिन, ब्रह्म को रूप दिषावै। लघुमां सिधि ताकौ लछिन, अनेक रूप धरै। प्रापति सिधि ताकौ लछिन, यंछै सो करै। प्रकासक सिधि ताको लछिन। सरब सूझै। असत्या सिधि ताकौं लछिन, उपावै षपावै। आवस्था। सिधि ताकौं लछिन, ब्रह्मादिक अग्या में रहै। एती अष्ट भूतांन सिद्धि मनोजा सिधि ताकौं लछिन, सरब कांमनां का जांण। छुछुमुक्ता सिधि ताकौ लछिन, मन मानै वहां सरीर छाडै। अनूरा सिधि ताकौ लछिन, सीत उसन तैं रहित होय। परकाया प्रवेश सिधि ताकौ लछिन और काया प्रवेस करै। सूरज बसि सिधि ताकौ लछिन, सूरज आग्या में रहै जल बसि सिधि ताकौ लछिन, जल आग्या मैं रहै। दूरि श्रवण सिधि ताकौ लछिन, दूरि की सुणैं। दूरि दरसण सिधि ताकौ लछिन। दूर की दरसै। कांस कांमोद सिधि ताकौ लछिन, कांमनां यंछै सो करै। अप्रहता सिधि ताकौ लछिन, मन मांनैं तहां जाय। देवता सैल सिधि ताकौ लछिन, सर्व देवतां सूं केला करि आवै। रूपसेल देवता सिधि ताकौ लछिन, सरब देवता का रूप धरै। हारै नाहीं सिधि ताकौ लछिन, कहूँ प्रकार हारै नाहीं। त्रिकाल सिधि ताकौ लछिन, छमास की आगली कहै छमास की पाछिली सूझै। अगनि बसि सिधि ताकौ लछिन अगनि मै जलै नही। सबद बसि सिधि ताकौ लछिन, सबद फरै। यती चौबीस सिधि ब्रह्म ग्यांनी कै आड़ी आवै। यती चौबीस सिचि सिचि आई होय तौ सतगमु प्रसादी तै त्यागैः सोई जोगेश्वर सोई ब्रह्म ग्यांनी। बल अपार जती गोरषनाथ समझावै। यती चौबीस सिधि त्यागै। सोई परम ज्योति कूं पावै।

बतीस लछन

ग्यांन पारछ्या-निरलोभी, निहचल, निरबासीक, निहिसबद।
विचार पारछ्या-निरमोही, निरबंध, निसंक, निरबानं।
बमेक पारछ्या-सरबंगी, सावधांन, सति सारग्राही।
संतोष पारछ्या-अजाचीक, अबांछीक, अमांननीक, अस्थिर।
निरबल पारछ्या-निहितरंग, निहपरपंच, निरदुंदी, निरलोप।
सहज पारछ्या-सुमती, हुह्दी, सोतल, सुषदाई।
सील पारछ्या-सुचि, संजम, सति, श्रोता।
सुंनि पारछ्या-ल्यौ, लषि ध्यांन, समाधि।
एती अष्टांग जोग पारछ्या, भगति का लछिन।
सिधां पाई साधिका पाई, जे जन उतरै पारं ॥

अष्ट चक्र

ॐ गोरष देव अष्ट चक्र बोलिये घट भीतर। ते कौंण कौंण बोलिए। अवधू प्रथमें आधार चक्र बोलिए गुदा अस्थांने, चक्र दल कंवल, षटसै सांस। तिस चक्र ऊपरि द्रिष्टचक्र, लिंग अस्थांने षट दल कंवल षटसै सांस। तसि चक्र ऊपरि मणिपुर चक्र, नामि अस्थांने, दस दल कंवल, षट सै सास। तिस चक्र ऊपर अनहद चक्र, हिरदा सथांने द्वादस कंवल, षटसै सास। तिस चक्र ऊपर विसुध चक्र; कंठ सथांने षोड़स कंवल, एक संहसर सास, अजपा गायत्री पारब्रह्म ध्यांन। तिस चक्र ऊपरि अगनि चक्र नेत्र सथांने षोड़स दल कमल एक संहस्र सास अजपा गावत्री पारब्रह्म ध्यांन तिस चक्र ऊपर गिनांन चक्र, ब्रह्मंड सथांने एक सहंस्त्र दल कमल एक सहंस्त्र सास। अजपा गावत्री पारब्रह्म ध्यांन। तिस चक्र ऊपरि सुछिम चक्र, बिग्यांन सथांने एक बीस सहंस्त्र दल कमल। ए अष्ट कमल का जांणौं=भेव। आपै करता आपै देव।

इती अष्ट चक्र कथंत जती गोरषनाथ सम्पूर्ण।

रह रासि

ॐ आदेस आदेस अलष अतीतं। तदा न होती धरती न आकासं ॥
तदा काले सिंभू भई उतपन्य।
माता न लेबी दस मास भारं। पिता न करिबा आचार बिचारे ॥
जोनी न आयबा, नाभि न कटाइबा। पुस्तग पोथी ब्रह्मा न बचायबा।
तहां अलेष पुर पटणि अनोपम सिला तहां बैठे गोरषराई।
तुम दमड़ी चमड़ी का संग्रह करौ। गुर का सबद ले ले दोजिग भरौ ॥
गुप्ती चक्र चलावौ हथियार। षंडित बुधि बहोत अहंकार ॥
ऊभा ते सिध बैठा पाषांण। श्री गोरष वाचा परवांण।
अनंत सिधां मैं रहरासि कही। गोदावरी कै मेलै ऐसी भाई ॥

(घ) प्रति के परिशेष में गोरखनाथ के 27 पदों का अपने ढंग का एक सुंदर तिलक दिया हुआ है, जो आगे दिया जाता है। वह किसी निरंजनी साधु का किया जान पड़ता है। क्योंकि उन्हीं के संप्रदाय के ग्रंथों की (घ) प्रति में अधिकता है। कर्ता का नाम दिया नहीं है। प्रति में पहले पूरे पद दिये गये हैं, फिर तिलक। मैंने पदों की प्रथम पंक्ति ही दी है। सारे पद को दुहराना व्यर्थ होता। पदक्रम भी मैंने प्रति का नहीं रक्खा है, बल्कि प्रतीकों के प्रथम अक्षरों को लेकर अचारानुक्रम से रक्खा है। इससे पदों को ढूँढ़ने से सुबीता होगा।

अवधु जाप जपौ बनमाबी चीन्हौ।

जाप समझौ तिहि करि अगम जपीए।टेक। बदन प्रांन सुसम भजतां। काया कंचनी बसि होवै। तौज होय चवै कहै। एक अक्षर यड़ाकार कुंभक सुनि नाभि बांणी बसि हुई जो पिंड-ब्रह्मड में समतत है। द्वै अक्षरी दूजी नाड़ी। दोय पष पांन अपांन। तिहि करि भौ पारि उतरे। त्रे अक्षरी सुषमन त्रे मंत्र जपी।

ब्रह्मकुंड ब्रह्मद्वार। चौ अक्षरी परा चारि षांणी चारि बांणी बसि हुई ॥1॥

अवधू बोल्या तत्त्व बिचारी।

अवधू बोल्या तत्त्व बिचारी। तत्त्व ईस्वर विचार। पृथी काया बंक। सुरित। बली समाई। अष्टकुली हरवत काया। जल माया। टेक। मन पवन परैं अगम ईश्वर। रवि ससि पार गियाई। रबि ससि मन पवन तार तिमिर गियाई (गिघाय-यथा दृष्ट) गया। तीन गुण त्रिवधि संसार नहीं। चारि जुग मैं बाई। सिधि करतां आया। पंच सहस मैं षट अपूठा पंच संहस सुर कंवल, बाय षट प्रांण कंवल सपत धात आठई बाय। मनी मनारी। द्वादस बाय कला त्रिकुट कै बिषै। चवदै तबक ऊपरैं चित मेल्यौ। षोड़स कवल बसीत पंषुड़ी समझ्या जुरा गई। दसवै उनमनी। सम तति हूवा सबद ॥2॥

आंबिलियौ थलि मौरियौ।

आंबलीयौ आत्मा। थल ब्रह्म। नींब बपु। बिजौरा बिअचारा। टेक। ऊंट सिचांणै जग ग्रह्यौं। ऊंट आपौ। सिचांणौ सबद। कैरूं करम। बांझ आत्मां। बेटौ ग्यांन। पुरिष न दीठौं। पुरिष परमेश्वर बिना और पुरिष। लाकड़ बूड़ै सिला तिरै। लाकड़ कठोर सिला सुध। ऊंट आपौ। प्रनालौ प्रीति सुसलौ सांसौं। मछ मन। डूंगर ब्रह्म। जल संसार। ससौ सांसौ। पांणी बूंद। ब्रह्म अगनि। रहट रटणि। सूल बिरह। कांटा क्रम। गया आत्मां नौ नाड़ि पंच भू। फूल कंवल। करंडीया कली। पग करम बिनां चोरी। गाय मनसा धर्‌या मैं व्यावै नहीं ॥3॥

आवौ नै जोसी जोवौ बिचारी।

बाय नहीं थेकर बादल घट। तारा गुण। तेज त्रिगुण। थंभौ सबद बाप बप। भाया भाया। पीव प्रांण मांहि डोलै। द्वै कर माया गंगा जमुन सास उसास। बिचि षाट षट। पांच यंद्री छठौ मन। हंस प्राण बिछाय। दोष गुण तलै ऊपरि। चावल चोषौ ॥4॥

आवौ माई धरि धरि जावौ।

धरि धरि धर्‌या की तासीर जाई ॥टेक॥ पारा बिंद नाद सबद, ससि सूर ताता सीला। पवन गोटिका। आकास ब्रह्म। गगन कँवल। डीबी मनसा। सुनि समाधि ॥5॥

गेसा रे उपदेस दाषै श्री गुर राया।

स्वास सुसमवेद। बिधि हदि। अजपा जाप। बिषमी संधी नाभि। बिषनाड़ी सुषमन ॥6॥

ॐ नमो निवाय स्वामी ॐ सिवाय।

अह निस राति दिन बाई ईश्वर बिनां बहै है। कौणं मंत्र कौंण उपाय बसि होय। ताका रे मैं चेला। टेक। गुरू कहै ऊँकार जो छै सूं मूल मंत्र छै। ताहि करि संसार पंडित छै। नाभि हृदा बिचि बहै तौ देवगुरू बतावा। सो ते साधे बिना सिधि नाहीं। ऊंकार करि नरहरि ब्रह्मा महादेव प्रसिधि है। नाद सब कौ निधांन। षट चक्रां बेधिवे कूं बाई ही संम्रथ है। बाई ही सोहं द्वैं बित रष नहीं पिंड़, बिषै असधि बहै। बिंद कूं बाई जीतै। मनकूं मन मारै। मनकं मन तारै। त्रिभवन मैं मन मन दैषै। आदि मनहीं समाइसी (समडिसी–यथा दृष्ट)। अति सुधि मनह समझ्या काम। मन ही सूं बिषै छूटै अनि करणी नाहीं। बिंद रज की भांड है। बारा कला सूरज, सोला कला ससि। रज रेत सम जे है तब परम गति होय। यती समि कीयां आपै आप है। पंच तत्त्व की समझि है ॥7॥

गुरु कीजै गहला निगुरा न रहिला।

कोयला मन। दूध तीरथ। काग मंन। पहुप पुरांन। आभा काया। काग काल। उतर सबद में। पछिम पाछिली बुधि। दूजा अरथ। उतर मताया। पाछिल परमेश्वर। चींटी मनसा। गजिद्रं मंन। गाया आत्मां। बाघ ग्यांन ॥8॥

गोरष् बालूड़ौ बोलै सतगुर बांणी।

गोरष बालूड़ा जीवन परण्या नहीं। अगनि ब्रह्म। पांणी राम रस ॥टेक॥ षीलौ मन। भींसि काया। बिरौले बिचार। सासू सुरति। बहू बुधि। कोयल बांणी। आंब आत्मां गगन ब्रह्म। मछली मनसा। बुगलौ काल। करसंण कांम पाकौ। रषवालौ काल। मृधला मनोरथ। पारधी मन। सींगी सुरति। नाद सबद ॥9॥

गोरष कहै सुणौ मछिंद्र।

चिंतामणि सरीषौ चित। द्वादस नै षोड़ि। षट नैं षोड़ि। नौ द्वारै नै षोड़ि। चबदै ब्रह्मंड का मोल एक दम। पवन हीं जल। अंबर आत्मां। बीज ब्रह्म। बटक प्रांण ॥10॥

गोरष गोपालं लो।

गोष्ट थी पाली। गगन की गाय मनसा। मही मन। अनभै ईश्वर। टेक। ममित मिट्यो। तब माया मुंई। बाप बपु। छोरू यंद्री। लाल गवाल प्रांन। गाय मनसा। अनहद ईश्वर सबद। संष असत काया। गगन कंवल। सुनि असथांन गगन। गाय मनसा। परवार मन पवन। सुरति निरंतरि प्रांण घरि। बरण रहत मनसा गाय ॥11॥

गोरष जोगी तोला तोलै।

तोला मन तोलैं पवन। ग्यांन सूं बांधै। तब अमोल। टेक। जे बिंद छै तौ कद आत्मां न पड़ैं बिंद पड्यां कोटि मोल जाय। जैसी उपजै भली बुरी तैसा करम करै। गगन ब्रह्म। अमर रांमरस। पून्यं चंद बिषै रत षीजै। बिंद तोला तोलि लै ॥12॥

च्यारि पहर आलिंगन निंद्रा।

आलिगन कांमनींद। टेक। अमावस अग्यांन करि मन सूंनो। घट ही सूंनौ। मंगल झूठा। दस दोष की काया। पड़िवा उजालौ ग्यांन तौ अनंद। पंच बसिवौ ही ठांम। ससि पहली पहरौ। बीचि कौ पहरौ त्रिगुणी माया। तीन पहरा गया। धांम देह। दूजा घट परमेस्वर बांमौं अंग माया। जम भै भागौ ॥13॥

तत वणिजीलो तत बणिजीलो।

तत नाम पंचभूतोर गाय। मन बछौ। नौ द्वार बाषर बरह बरत।

उडियांन अडिग। सिरा कौ हाट सुनि। अभ्यास बनिज। कूड़ा लैन दैन ॥14॥

तत बेली लो तत बेली लो।

तत बेलि आत्मां। डाल करम। मूल मन प्रकृत, छाया नहीं। माया जल बिनां बधै। टेक। कुंजर मंन। काया बाड़ी। बेलि आत्मा सुबधि। धरती रोपी पुरष प्रांन। मूल एद्धा। ससि चंद्र। पांन भांण। सूरिज पवन। फल पूंनिम। चंद ग्यांन। गगन ब्रह्म। झाल बिरह। दाया लहै काटत कूंपल मेल्है। स्वाद सींच्य कुमलावै ॥15॥

नाथ बोलै अमृत बाणी।

कांमलि काया। पांणी प्राण। टेक। पडरवा परकीरति। षूंटा मन। दमांमा दम, ऊंट काया। कऊवा काल, डारी बसु भली। पीपल पारब्रह्म। मूंसा मंन। बिलाई कुबधि। बटाऊ प्रांण। चलै ब्रह्म पंथ। चौरासी बाट थाकी डोकरी आत्मां। षाट षट। कूकर मन। चोर संसार। धणी इस्वर काढ़ै। ढोर संसार। ऊजड़ गुण नहीं। बली ब्रह्म, गागरि गुण। पणिहारी आत्मां॥ कामानि कामना। अंगीठी आत्मां। बैसंदर बिकार। मगरी माया। चूल्हौ चित। रोटी रटणि। पोवै कुमति रंडीया आत्मां। बहु वुधि। सासू सुरति। मगरी काया। प्रांणी प्रांण। कूई कँचल ॥16॥

पूछौ पंडित ब्रह्म गिमांन।

बीज कांम। निसपती ग्यांन। मूल माया बिनां पांण तरवर। पांन परकीरति। फूल कांमनां। बांझ का पूत ग्यांन। लिंग प्रांण। बाड़ी काया रहत ईश्वर। कँवल काया। भृंग मन। स्वास वेद। सोहं बाणी। गंग जमनां स्वास उसास। बिचि गोरष षेलै ॥17॥

बंदंत गौरषनाथ दसवै द्वारै।

स्वरग रंध्र के पुरष चढ्या। यकीस ब्रह्मंड ऊपरि ससमवेद। टेक। द्वादस अंगुल की बाई। रज बीरज की सकति बस हुई। ससिम षोडसु सरकंवल। सिव थांन सहंस पंषुड़ी। थांन जीव सीव धरि। अनहद सबद। पछिम ऊचैं भांण ग्यांन। डीबी मनसा। पाताल गुणां परै। चंद सूर ताता सीता। धर्‍या का गुण भस्म कीया। नादी बिंदी नाद बिद सींगी। आकास आत्मां। थेगली काया। छसै सहंस स्वास। बहतरि नाड़ी। सूइ सुरति। बावन बीर मन। यड़ा पिंगुला सुषमनी। आसमानं ब्रह्मद्वार ॥18॥

बदंत गोरषनाथ परसिलं केदारं।

केदार ब्रह्मद्वार। पांणी राम रस। टेक। ऊंचा परबत। राग दोष। ता आगैं बाट। यला पिंगुला किलिमिलि पवन। कांवरू काया। पूरण बिगरि दसवौ द्वार ॥9॥

बांधै बछरिया पीवौ पीवौ पीरं।

बछरी यंद्री। षीर यंम्रतरस। अजरांवर मारै न। टेक। आकास ऊंची दसा। धेनि आत्मां। त्रिभवन त्रिगुणी काया। राजा जीव पूछ परकीरति नाहीं। बारह बछरा सौ बारह कला सूरज की सो बांधौ। सोलह कला चंद्रमा की सो यंम्रत सरवै। धेनि आत्मां। रैणिं चेतन आरबल। अचर ब्रह्म। कचरा माया। विषै रस। पाच ग्वालिया पांच यंद्री। आत्मां धेनि। अमृत रस। गगन ब्रह्म ॥20॥

बोल्या गोरष धर जोई।

धर हिरदा। तत आत्मां ॥ टेक ॥ त्रियाली त्रिगुणी माया। आसण मन यंद्री। मन मैं तन बसि कीया। मब मै कुंभ काया बसी। कलस कंवल। पैर षोज। पुरषै पुरष निपाया। जिहि तटि ताता सीला न ऊगै। तौ ग्यान न उदै होय। तहां आसण करै। मन मांहिला हीरा साध। सोधि लीणां तत ग्यांनी। बिमल नृमल ॥21॥

मनसा देबी ब्यौपार बांधौ।

मनसा ब्यौपार ब्रह्म सूं कीयौ। पवन करि पुरुष। मन बिनसतौ उपज्यौ। मनसा कहै रे जोगी मन अध्यात्म लागौ काया पटण मैं ॥टेक॥ यकीस हजार छसै दम आदि का पूरष मन कै हाथि। जपमाला दीनी। यड़ा मन पिंगुला पवन। सुषमनां सुरति। अहनिस राति दिन। प्रनाली नाड़ि उलटि बहै। षट छह सासूं षोड़ि काया। कँवल मैं दहे करि परिसिध। परब्रह्मचारी प्रांन। हंस ही पवन। जल ब्रह्मा नौसै नाड़ि नदी सोई। पणिहारी आत्मां। गंगा तीर तहि कै तटि। बणिज ब्रह्म सूं। चंदसूर मन पवन। गगन ब्रह्म-द्वार घोर अंधार गुणां हौ हूवौ। पंच यंद्री पौढ़ी। सुनि प्रगट्या दसवें द्वार। काया हो कन्था। मन मन जगोटा ॥22॥

मेरा गुर तीन छंद गावै।

त्रिगुणी माया ॥टेक॥ कुंभार काया कै बसि। हांड़ी ही माया। अहीर (महीर-यथादृष्ट) कै महकी माया। ब्राहमण कै ब्राहमणी लाया। राजा कै सेल माया। बांणीयां कै हींग माया। तेली कै तेल माया। जंगलि बेलि माया। एक ऊँकार नांनां प्रांण पोया ॥23॥

म्हारा रे वैरागी जोगी।

जोगणि मनसा। मन जोगी। मन सरोवर ईश्वर। गगन ब्रह्म। मठ आसन। टेक। सासू सुरति। ससुरौ सबद। जोगणि मनसा। नाभि बसै ब्रह्म अस्थांन के बास ॥24॥

रमिरे रमिता सूँ चौगांन।

अहरणि नाद-बिंद की काया। ताती सीली नाड़ी ए पवन। मूलं द्वार पांचौ आसन करि। टेक। सहज ही पलांण। पवन की धोड़ा। ल्यौ लगामं। चित चाबक। चेतन असवार। ग्यांन गुरू। तिल ब्रह्मद्वार हीरौ पांन। अहीर अपांन ॥25॥

सरवा रे सरवा त्रिभवन थे गरवा।

मन त्रिभवन सारिषौ। टेक। जगत मन कौ पसारौ। मन काया गहै। उलटि फिरि षीर होय। निसपती जोगी काल भषै। गरुड़ मन, भुवंगम। पांन अषांन नांन्हौ कीयौ ॥26॥

सोनां ल्यौ रस सोनां ल्यौं।

सुनारी कुनारी नहीं। सास उसास धमणि। गगन अंतह करण। टेक। मूल नाभि नाद अहराणि। बिद काया। गगन ब्रह्म। अषै गगन आसाण। बिषै कोयला। ताता सीला गुण न लीया। चंद सूर मन पवन सम। काम रती कौ स्वाद। मासौ मत उनमन मैं रहै। अरध उरध मन। तीन सुनि ब्रह्म मैं। उनमनी डोरी। मन तराजू। पवन गदियांनां। तोल्यौ ब्रह्म बराबरि ॥27॥

■■